The sociology of religion

A clear and comprehensive introduction to the sociology of religion, this book combines a discussion of the ideas of the main theorists with a wide range of comparative material illustrating the diversity of religion. It demonstrates the significance of the theoretical issues in the context of specific religious beliefs and practices. This unique approach shows how theories relate to and illuminate specific areas of religion in both primitive societies and in world religions such as Buddhism and Christianity.

Malcolm Hamilton takes a broad comparative view which draws on the insights of history and anthropology as well as sociology. He surveys the range of classic and contemporary theory, discussing the work of Marx, Durkheim, Malinowski, Radcliffe-Brown, Freud, Weber, and brings the story up to date by setting out the most influential recent theoretical perspectives. Each chapter on a theoretical topic is followed by a chapter on particular beliefs and practices, thus providing a sense of the multiplicity of religious beliefs and experiences and enabling readers to place their own assumptions in a wider perspective.

The Sociology of Religion will be essential reading for students of the sociology of religion, comparative religion and religious studies, and will also be of great interest to sociologists and anthropologists generally.

Malcolm B. Hamilton is Senior Lecturer in Sociology at the University of Reading.

The sociology of religion

Theoretical and comparative perspectives

Malcolm B. Hamilton

London and New York

First published 1995
by Routledge
11 New Fetter Lane, London EC4P 4EE

Simultaneously published in the USA and Canada
by Routledge
29 West 35th Street, New York, NY 10001

© 1995 Malcolm B. Hamilton

The publisher and the author wish to state that every effort
was made prior to publication to secure permission for the
illustration on p. x.

Typeset in Times by LaserScript, Mitcham, Surrey
Printed and bound in Great Britain by
Mackays of Chatham PLC, Chatham, Kent

British Library Cataloguing in Publication Data
A catalogue record for this book is available from the British Library

Library of Congress Cataloging in Publication Data
A catalogue record for this book has been requested

ISBN 0–415–02187–1 (hbk)
ISBN 0–415–10659–1 (pbk)

Contents

Preface

No form of social activity or set of social institutions comes in quite the bewilderingly diverse variety that is characteristic of religion. Religious conceptions and beliefs seem limited in their diversity and strangeness only by the limitations, whatever they might be, that the human mind is subject to. The human capacity for belief seems almost boundless. In no other sphere, consequently, are sociologists, anthropologists, psychologists, and other social scientists presented with such seemingly intractable and puzzling problems of understanding. True, anthropologists have shown us how remarkably variable are such things as kinship systems and family patterns. These aspects of social life are such that the particular forms of them with which we happen to be familiar are usually so taken for granted as absolutely normal that deviations from them in other societies appear almost incredible. But anthropologists assure us of their sheer normality in their own context. Kinship systems and family structures, however, can only come in a limited variety of forms. Not so religious beliefs and activities, the profusion of which defies the capacity of any single scholar to comprehend and new ones continue to germinate while both old and new continuously change and evolve.

Strange, then, that the sociology of religion has been open to the accusation by some of being the sociology of Christianity (Turner, 1991) or even of sects and secularisation when such a wealth of subject matter presents itself for analysis. Perhaps the sheer variability of the subject matter is so daunting that it has compelled or, at least, tended to promote a rather narrow specialisation in the areas mentioned. This preoccupation with limited themes is, however, a rather recent one. Earlier theorists cast their nets much more widely and for this reason retain, as this book among other things seeks to demonstrate, a fair measure of relevance today. Spencer, Tylor and especially Frazer drew upon as diverse a range of material as they could lay their hands upon. Durkheim based his entire theoretical treatise on religion on ethnographic data pertaining to the aborigines of Australia. Freud relied for ethnographic detail in his studies on the subject to a considerable extent on the work of Frazer. The early functionalists such as Malinowski and Radcliffe-Brown were anthropologists who had first-hand fieldwork experience of societies very different from their own. Max Weber's scholarship in the area of the world religions is proverbial.

This book seeks to recapture the theoretical legacy of these scholars, based as it was upon a comparative perspective taken for granted in their day as essential for the successful objective study of human social systems but which today is all too rare. Theorising at the level of generality of the classic writers in the field has never, however, completely died out and a further purpose of this volume is to bring the story up to date in setting out the most influential recent theoretical perspectives as well as classical approaches, thereby showing their linkages and the extent to which the latter have attempted to synthesise and build upon the insights of the former. It has to be acknowledged, however, that in this field, as in so many in what is still a relatively novel subject like sociology, we remain at a rudimentary state of knowledge and understanding, especially with regard to religion which has tended to be treated as rather a peripheral area failing to attract many to specialise in it. This is not to say that progress has not been made. This book, hopefully, in surveying the range of classic and contemporary theory makes this, if nothing else, clear.

Theoretical discussion and debate alone and without reference to substantive issues are, of course, sterile. The purpose of theory is to promote understanding of the substantive. Here, then, the various theoretical approaches in the sociology of religion are each treated in conjunction with substantive questions. Each chapter devoted to a theoretical perspective is followed by a chapter on a substantive issue. The themes which follow in this way have been chosen with their particular appropriateness in mind. They are intended to illustrate the application of the theories and ways in which they have been used to throw light upon a specific and concrete area. The range of substantive issues chosen also serves to provide a series of topics illustrating the diversity of religious conceptions and actions. They include anthropological literature pertaining to primitive societies, a major non-Western world religion, namely Buddhism, as well as various aspects of the Christian traditions.

Arrangement of the material in this way should facilitate understanding of theory but some readers may well prefer to read all of the chapters dealing with theories first, that is, Chapter one and all the even numbered chapters, returning to the substantive chapters, namely the odd numbered ones, later when a full picture of the variety and scope of theoretical perspectives has been obtained.

This book has grown out of almost twenty years teaching the sociology of religion at the University of Reading during which time I have incurred many debts to my colleagues there. I am particulary grateful to those of my colleagues who read the manuscript at various stages in its evolution, namely Christie Davies and Peter Waddington. I must also express my thanks to Bryan Wilson, Jim Beckford and Michael Hornsby-Smith all of whom read the (at that time very much longer) manuscript with impressive care. All of them in making so many helpful suggestions and in pointing out numerous errors have helped to make this a better book. Such errors and faults that remain, and there are undoubtedly many, I must acknowledge as entirely my own responsibility.

1 Introduction

WHAT IS THE SOCIOLOGY OF RELIGION?

The human capacity for belief is virtually limitless. It is this capacity, and the striking diversity, indeed strangeness, of the beliefs and associated practices it has generated in human society and history which have captured the attention and stimulated the curiosity of many writers on religion including sociologists. There are those, some sociologists among them, who might agree with Lucy in the Peanuts cartoon reproduced opposite, at least as far as certain fundamentals are concerned, but even if they were correct, Charlie Brown's answer, despite the dubious authenticity of the reference to Melanesian frog worship, makes it plain that if they are all alike they are also very different. Even if frogs are not worshipped anywhere, there are many other beliefs which seem equally odd, even bizarre, to the outsider.

The sociologist, however, is not simply puzzled by this diversity but by the fact that such beliefs and practices exist at all. The sociology of religion can be said to consist of two main themes or central questions, namely, why have religious beliefs and practices been so central a feature of culture and society and why have they taken such diverse forms? The sociology of religion poses the question of the role and significance of religion in general, in human society, as well as that of understanding the particular beliefs and practices of particular groups and societies.

In one respect both of these central questions have been stimulated by the same puzzlement. Although things have changed dramatically since, the sociological approach to the study of religion had among its roots a nineteenth-century rationalism or positivism which questioned and rejected religious notions as illusory, irrational and otiose in a modern society in which science as a mode of understanding of reality would predominate and in which religious ideas would atrophy and die in the face of the superior conceptions and explanations of science. These thinkers saw religion as a natural phenomenon to be objectively and scientifically studied and explained like any other natural phenomenon. To explain it in such a way was largely to explain it away. Indeed, the very centrality and universality of what were seen as irrational notions and actions, and which were in many cases undeniably odd and puzzling, seemed to cry out for explanation. It seemed all the more urgent for the understanding of the evolution of human society and culture and indeed for the understanding of human nature itself, because in past societies religious ideas and beliefs constituted, to a large extent, the entire world view and value system and were not a special realm coexisting alongside mundane conceptions as had come to be the case in the contemporary society. As Max Weber put it, past societies had lived in a 'magic garden' whereas modern society had witnessed a thoroughgoing 'disenchantment' of the world. How was it possible, then, for past societies to have lived and prospered in an enchanted world and how was it possible that such notions could have been so central and significant? Hence the major task of the sociology of religion was to account for the very presence of religious beliefs and practices in human society. As Berger has pointed out, this was an even more fundamental challenge for religion than the discoveries of the natural sciences since it not only threatened to undermine acceptance of religious claims but purported to be able to explain why such claims were made and accepted at all and why they appeared to have credibility (Berger, 1971, p. 47). By some it was also seen as having the task of dispelling such residual irrationality from the contemporary society and of quickening its replacement by science, and by others of creating a substitute for it which would preserve the essential benefits that, in their view, it provided for past societies but without the supernaturalism and irrationality which characterised it – a substitute founded upon sound and objective principles established by the discipline of sociology itself.

This attitude has given way, during the course of the twentieth century, to one which is less imperious and which is less dismissive of and often agnostic towards the veracity of religious statements and claims. Today sociologists of religion need not be disbelievers and may themselves be committed to one or other form of faith, although others maintain an atheistic or agnostic position. The fundamental concern of most of them, however, as sociologists of religion, remains much the same, namely to further the understanding of the role of religion in society, to analyse its significance in and impact upon human history, and to understand its diversity and the social forces and influences that shape it.

Despite the emergence of more tolerant attitudes, however, very different views can still be found on the question of the stance that the sociologist of religion should or can adopt towards the evaluation of the truth, rationality, coherence or sense of beliefs and consequently the nature of the sociological enterprise in this area.[1] One such view holds, in complete contrast to those who would reject all religious belief and treat it entirely as a natural phenomenon, that religion is not amenable to sociological analysis at all. In this view religion is not just another social institution or human product like any other. Religion is not something that can be subjected to rational explanation or at least is alleged to spring from some fundamental source of a non-naturalistic or spiritual character which cannot be understood in any other way than in religious or spiritual terms.

An extreme form of this view is that belief can be explained in no other way than that it is the truth and has been revealed as such. This is a very weak argument. It would place only one set of religious beliefs out of court as far as sociological understanding is concerned, namely those of the believer. Every other system of belief would be legitimate territory for the sociologist to explore. From the perspective of the discipline of the sociology of religion, however, this is an incoherent position. If the sociologist were to pay heed to this argument when put forward by a Christian then it would also have to be heeded when put forward by a Buddhist, a Muslim, or a devotee of Melanesian frog worship. The sociologist would then be in the position of accepting what neither a Christian, a Buddhist, nor a Muslim would be inclined to accept, namely that all three were based upon truth. Furthermore, sociology as a discipline would find itself in the absurd position of simultaneously holding that a particular belief system was and was not a legitimate object of analysis, since individual sociologists of different faiths would each wish to exempt their own from sociological analysis. Christian sociologists could present sociological analyses of Buddhism and Buddhists of Christianity, each unacceptable to the other. Clearly, those who would question the sociology of religion as a viable field of enquiry cannot be selective about which religious systems can be placed outside its scope.

There are, of course, those who, along with Lucy, would claim that all religions do share some common fundamental basis – appreciation of the divine, the spiritual, the sacred, the transcendental, perhaps – but their view is rarely well substantiated as Charlie Brown's reply would suggest. Attempts to state what this fundamental essence is are generally vague, unsatisfactory and unconvincing. In any case, even if there were some common factor impervious to sociological, psychological or other explanatory analysis, this would leave a great deal, indeed the greater part of the substantive content of systems of belief, open to socio-logical treatment. The sociologist or psychologist could, at least, search for the reasons for the differences between belief systems. Whatever the nature of the underlying essence, the specific and concrete forms that this appreciation of the spiritual takes could be related to varying social or psychological conditions.

Some of those who believe that religion entails the inexplicably tran-scendental would be quite content to allow sociology and psychology this broad scope (Garrett, 1974). Why the enquiry has to be limited in this way and not allowed to attempt to investigate the nature, source and causes of what believers experience and interpret as sacred or transcendental, is generally not stated.

Others, even some sociologists, would limit the scope of the subject to the sympathetic description and interpretation of different belief systems ruling out causal generalisations (Eliade, 1969; Towler, 1974). Comparison would be allowed only in so far as it did not seek to go beyond the understandings of believers themselves. Religion is seen as understandable only in its own terms, as a phenomenon which is *sui generis*. This approach has a long tradition in Europe and in particular Germany and Holland and is generally known as the phenomenological or hermeneutic approach (Morris, 1987, p. 176; Kehrer and Hardin, 1984).[2]

Eliade, for example, argues that we cannot understand religious phenomena by attempting to reduce them to social or psychological facts. They must be understood in their own terms as stemming from the human experience of the sacred. Each is an expression of this experience and the sacred is something which is irreducible to any kind of explanation.

Against such views some have reacted by offering thoroughgoing defences of reductionist approaches (Cavanaugh, 1982; Segal, 1980, 1983, 1989). Others have criticised the anti-reductionists for asserting the autonomy or *sui generis* nature of their subject matter without sound justification and for attributing to religion an ontological reality that they do not demonstrate that it has. Such claims, according to these critics, simply constitute an attempt to rather arbitrarily rule certain questions out of court, motivated by the anxiety that to ask them carries a threat to the religious convictions of those who make them and to religious belief in general. It is illegitimate, such critics argue, to attempt to preclude a reductionist account of religion on *a priori* grounds (Wiebe, 1990). On the other hand, Wiebe (1978, 1983, 1984, 1990) has sought a middle way between reductionism and radical non-reductionism, arguing that reductionists are wrong in claiming, in so far as they do, that an understanding of religion *necessarily* requires a reductionist account. Others who have sought a middle way include Dawson (1986, 1987, 1988, 1990) and Pals (1986, 1987, 1990) although they do not agree on what this middle way should be nor do their critics believe they have found it (Segal and Wiebe, 1989).

Clearly, these debates will probably continue unabated and the issues cannot be resolved here. Neither can or will the sociological study of religion wait upon their resolution. Perhaps they are ultimately irresolvable. Perhaps they can only be resolved by actually attempting to understand and to explain religious belief, behaviour and experience sociologically and psychologically, the success or otherwise of this enterprise providing the test of the various points of view. In the face of such disagreements the approach of the social sciences to religion must be accepted as a viable one, at least as viable as the hermeneutic approach.

In any case, even if there were some irreducible element in religious experience, the concrete forms it takes may well be mediated by psychological and sociological processes. The extent to which religious beliefs and practices can be understood in terms of such processes is an empirical question and it must be left to the disciplines concerned to attempt to discover relationships and patterns, or social and psychological influences. This means, of course, that the sociology of religion is not necessarily incompatible with phenomenological and hermeneutic approaches.

Perhaps the most prevalent and currently respectable stance which is taken towards religion by contemporary sociologists is that which in one of its versions has been called 'methodological atheism' (Berger, 1973, pp. 106 and 182). This holds that it is necessary to 'bracket' aside the question of the status of religious claims reserving judgement on whether they are ultimately founded upon some irreducible and inexplicable basis. This approach would take the sociological analysis of religion as far as is possible on the assumption that it is a human product (or projection, as Berger puts it) and amenable to the same sort of explanations as other forms of social and individual behaviour using whatever methods are deemed appropriate for the social sciences.

The neutrality of this methodological agnosticism[3] with regard to the claims of religious beliefs clearly has considerable advantages. It protects the sensibilities of those who would otherwise feel uncomfortable with the idea of treating religious belief empirically. More importantly, it is not necessary for the sociologist to adjudicate on the matter of the truth or falsity of any given set of beliefs under investigation. In fact, in many cases it would be impossible to do so. If, for example, it were observed that in a given society certain 'medicines' claimed to have magical curative powers were utilised, the sociologist could hardly set about carrying out all the various tests to determine whether there was any evidence for the substances used having definite medical properties before going on to analyse the beliefs and practices sociologically. Even more importantly, there would be little point in doing so since what matters in attempting to understand and explain the given pattern of belief and behaviour or assessing its social effects is the tests that the believers and the practitioners have undertaken and the evidence that is available to *them* as they see it. The existence of evidence in the eyes of the sociologist is neither here nor there in accounting for what the people themselves believe or what they do.

On the other hand, methodological agnosticism also suffers from a major weakness if it is applied too rigidly – if it is taken to imply that the question of truth or falsity of beliefs need never arise for the sociologist as an important matter to decide upon and which might play a central role in accounting for belief – if, in short, it is used to defend a relativist position. This would place too great a constraint upon the discipline. One of the conclusions that a sociological investigation of a system of beliefs might come to is precisely that it contains much that is false, incoherent, etc. In the example used above of medicines with magical curative powers it might be that extensive tests of the substances used have been carried out by medical science which finds no evidence for the claims of those who use them. Clearly, then, if the sociologist accepts the findings and conclusions of medical science, there is a discrepancy between what the practitioners regard as good evidence and what the sociologist does. The crucial sociological question is thus moved on a stage to become not 'why do the believers believe what they believe?' but 'why do the believers consider that they have good evidence for believing what they believe?'. Now it might be that the sociologist observes that the practitioners count only positive instances in establishing the evidence in support of their belief. It is a very common error in all cultures and societies to notice only positive instances and to discount negative ones. Every time someone recovers after the medicine is administered it is noted upon and remembered and the recovery attributed to the use of the medicine. Most failures, however, are not particularly commented on and soon forgotten. It is very easy for a firm commitment to a belief to become established in this way from only a few apparently positive instances while, in fact, most instances are negative. Careful observation may establish that this all too human tendency is what occurs.

Of course, one could remain within the constraints of methodological agnosticism and decline to make any unfavourable comparison with the practitioners' conception of what counts as good evidence. The account would simply be that they believe what they believe because by these means of establishing the truth of something there is, for them, good evidence for it. Yet to stop here would seem to leave something vital out of the account. We cannot help but think that their methods involve making a mistake – not because we just have a different set of beliefs about the appropriate procedures for establishing the truth of propositions but because such procedures are universally those by which truth must be established. And it is because they are universally valid that those who have not followed them can come to see for themselves that they have made a mistake, just as anyone might come to this conclusion.

A sociological account, then, of why the practitioners believe what they believe might make reference to mistaken or faulty procedures for establishing truth and cannot help but imply, or conclude thereby, that the belief is false. This is not to say, of course, that it might not equally be concluded that what at first sight appeared to be ill-founded is not so because there does seem to be good evidence for it or because the belief might turn out to be other than what it was originally thought to be. But it seems unduly restrictive to say that we should never entertain the possibility or conclude that any beliefs are false or mistaken or that we should never allow this to enter into our understanding of them.

From a broader perspective, there is again good reason to retain the possibility that sociology might conclude certain beliefs to be false. They may, for example, conflict with sociological accounts of the world. The religious account of a particular social institution, for example, may directly confront the sociological account of it. There is no choice here but to deny the validity of the religious account. Sociology, like any objective discipline, offers an alternative view of the world and may need to take a stance on the propositions of other views including religious ones. It might, for example, challenge the view that there are supernatural powers, such as witchcraft, which have real, concrete, material effects in the world and the attribution of material events to the action of such powers (Segal, 1980).

Whether the content of religious beliefs is considered to be true or false, valid or invalid, depends, of course, on an assessment of the nature of such beliefs. If religious statements are of the same kind as ordinary empirical statements, if in postulating the existence of various spiritual entities they are making statements of the same kind as those that state, for example that black swans, unicorns and yetis exist, then they may be judged to be true or false and this judgement may play an essential role in the sociological analyses of them.

But things are often not quite as straightforward as this. Let us take an example from a well-known study of the witchcraft and related ideas of an East African people, the Azande (Evans-Pritchard, 1937). The Azande attribute most deaths to witchcraft. If one confronts the Azande with the 'facts' of the case, for example, that the deceased was bitten by a poisonous snake and that this is the reason for the death, the Azande will persist in their attribution of the death to witchcraft. Even if one explains the action of certain toxins in the body and the manner in which snake poison brings about death in certain cases, the Azande are likely to remain unimpressed and will not relinquish their belief that the death was caused by witchcraft. They might reply that they know very well that the deceased was bitten by a poisonous snake and may accept the account of how snake poison can cause death but will still attribute the death to witchcraft. Why was the man bitten by the snake at all, they will ask? Why was the snake in just that place at just that time? Why the deceased and not someone else? All this is due to witchcraft according to the Azande. It is because of the malevolent intentions of someone with witchcraft powers that the man stepped on the snake. It is because of witchcraft that the snake was there in the grass just at the time he put his foot down in that place.

Whereas we would attribute these things to chance, the Azande refuse to accept that pure chance or coincidence explains the event. Also, where normal empirical explanations stop, the Azande will go on to ask the further question of why the events happen as they do. Religious beliefs are often of this nature. The kinds of question posed by religion are often beyond the province of science. Science cannot give us the answer to such questions, cannot tell us why things are as they are and happen as they do. Whether or not one accepts the answers that religion gives to such questions, or even that such questions make any sense or are capable of being answered, the fact may be that they are not questions of the kind that science asks and the answers to them are not, therefore, the same kind of claims about the world that science makes. This observation will clearly have implications for the way we seek to understand and explain it. It is probably no accident that claims like those of the Azande in relation to witchcraft are made when serious illness or death is involved – circumstances that are difficult to accept. It may well be that there are social or psychological reasons which are associated with such ideas. Also, accusations of witchcraft, as we shall see, take a very definite pattern in terms of the nature of the social relationships between accuser and accused. These, and many other observations, would suggest that witchcraft beliefs are closely related to social and psychological processes which are very important in understanding them. This does not necessarily mean that they can be wholly accounted for in terms of such processes but we should remain open to the idea that it might be possible to do so.

Azande witchcraft beliefs, while they are not simple causal explanations of events like those that science gives, still postulate the existence of powers which have real, concrete, material effects. Other religious beliefs may be quite different again. The claim, for example, that a member of an Australian aboriginal tribe might make that he is a white cockatoo, may, on coming to appreciate it in its wider religious and social context, be seen as not an empirical claim at all and not amenable to judgements of truth or falsity. Seen in its wider context it may appear to be of a nature which makes it misleading or illegitimate to evaluate it as valid or invalid.

This point has been cogently argued by the philosopher D. Z. Phillips in a critique of reductionist approaches to religion which usually misconstrue, according to Phillips, the nature of religion in assuming that its propositions are mistaken hypotheses about the facts. While not denying that they might be such and that, if they are, a reductionist approach would be applicable, he nevertheless believes that religious propositions are often not of this kind at all. In fact, in so far as they are truly religious propositions and not mere superstitions and the like, they are to be understood rather as ways of looking at and coming to terms with such things as good fortune and misfortune. Religious statements have an internal sense and meaning and therefore an autonomy which cannot be assailed by reductionist approaches. Even when a religious statement appears to be a hypothesis about the facts and which might appear, therefore, to be a mistaken one, it might nevertheless embody an expression of feelings and attitudes which give it its real force and significance in people's lives. It may even be the case that the person making a religious statement construes it as a hypothesis about the facts; the underlying meaning of it may, however, be quite different.

> When a man tells us that the misfortune which has befallen him is due to the ghosts of slain warriors, or that God cares for him all the time, it is difficult, as we have seen, to disprove this in the way one could disprove a similar statement about a human being. The issue is complicated in that it is clear both that the person believes in some queer kind of causal connection between the slain warriors and his present misfortune, or between God and events in his life, and that the conditions needed to establish such a causal connection are manifestly absent. It is not surprising that any attempt to give a coherent account of his beliefs ends in confusion. He seems to be believing in the causal efficacy of some kind of agency although no sense can be made of his belief. Can a man believe what does not make sense? It is important here to resist the temptation to answer in the negative, just as it is important not to deny that the metaphysician means what he says. It is not that these people do not mean what they say. They do. The point to emphasise is that what they want to say cannot be said. Further, the reason why they want to say these things cannot be explained by revealing an error. One does the metaphysician an injustice if one thinks he is blind to facts because he half-perceives and misconstrues features of the language we share with him. Similarly, we may well do the believer in magic or religion an injustice if we think, as some of the early anthropologists tended to do, that he is blind to, or has an elementary understanding of, the causal connections the rest of us appreciate. The source of the trouble lies deeper – in his hopes and fears. His beliefs about magic and religion are the product of his emotions.
>
> (Phillips, 1976, pp. 108–9)

A very similar perspective to that of Phillips is that espoused by Robert Bellah (1970a) who sees religion as essentially to do with symbols which are non-objective and which express the feelings, values, and hopes of subjects, or which organise and regulate the flow of interaction between subjects and objects, or which attempt to sum up the whole subject–object complex, or even to point to the context or ground of that whole. These symbols also express reality and are not reducible to empirical propositions (Bellah, 1970a, p. 93). This position Bellah terms 'symbolic realism'. It treats religion as a reality *sui generis*. 'To put it bluntly', Bellah states, 'religion is true' (1970a, p. 93).

Critics of reductionism such as Phillips and Bellah, then, rightly caution us against misconstruing the nature of many religious beliefs. However, just as we should not prejudge the issue of the nature of any particular system of belief, as the critics of the extreme positivist position correctly say, neither should we deny ourselves the capacity to make judgements after extensive examination of beliefs. Just as we should not assume that religion is nothing other than a human product which can be fully explained wholly in the same way as any other social institution, neither should we assume that there is always some irreducible element in it and thereby preclude the possibility that it might some day be accounted for in this way. Also, it is somewhat contentious to relegate those beliefs which do make claims about the world to the sphere of mere superstition as Phillips does. To do so is to relegate, very probably, by far the greater part of the totality of religious beliefs and conceptions, or interpretations and understandings of them, to the sphere of superstition. That spiritual entities and forces can materially affect the course of events and thereby human fate and well-being, for example, is a central aspect of most systems of belief which we normally think of as religious. Phillips' conception of the 'truly religious' is very much a specific interpretation of what constitutes the essence of religion; an interpretation probably not shared by many believers themselves. In any case, even if Phillips be conceded the licence to reserve the term 'religion' for this particular type of conception, he leaves the vastly greater part of what is conventionally thought of as being religion to the very reductionist type of analysis of which he is so critical. Whether a reductionist analysis is or is not appropriate for the whole of this field would, however, remain an open question. Even in the case of beliefs which do make empirical claims about the world it may not be possible, legitimate, or significant for the sociological understanding and explanation of them to reject them as false or accept them as true.

Also, even if there are aspects of religion which cannot be construed as empirical propositions, we can still ask and perhaps answer the question why people think in this way and why they make sense of their experience in the particular way they do. Phillips seems to think that such questions have no meaning and that once one understands what is being said by someone who makes a religious statement, one has understood all that there is to understand. It is difficult to see why understanding should be limited in this way. Surely one can ask under what conditions people come to think or not to think in religious terms and what conditions are associated with particular forms of religious expression. Those who would rule out sociological explanations of religion tend to confuse the necessity of identifying an experience as a religious one with the attempt to explain that experience (Proudfoot, 1985). While it is necessary to give a *description* of religious belief and experience in terms which do not violate the understandings of the believer or the person who has the experience, we are not thereby precluded from *explaining* it in terms of concepts, categories and relationships which are not necessarily shared by that person; just as we must describe the experience of a person who takes an hallucinogenic drug in his or her own terms, we need not explain it in terms that he or she uses such as, for example, that the experience was a manifestation of a powerful supernatural entity. Thus, according to Proudfoot, we may distinguish between descriptive and explanatory reduction. The former is the failure to identify a belief, experience or practice in terms which the subject can agree with and is an illegitimate misidentification. The latter consists in explaining the belief, experience or practice in terms which the subject does not necessarily share or approve of. This is a perfectly legitimate and normal procedure. What writers like Phillips do is to extend a perfectly justified embargo on descriptive reduction to explanation in order to build a 'protective strategy' which seeks to place everything construed to be religious out of bounds in terms of reductionist explanations.[4] Phillips, according to Proudfoot, gives us examples of descriptive reduction and then proceeds to criticise those who have offered reductive explanations. The strategy is such that religious statements and understandings of the believer cannot be contested. Also, in claiming that truly religious beliefs should never be understood to be really factual hypotheses about the world, and that, if they are, they are not truly religious but mere superstition, Phillips further protects religious statements from any possibility of falsification or conflict with other perspectives including sociological and psychological theory.

One of the important points to emerge from this discussion is that the sociology of religion must have an impact upon our attitudes towards religion whether we start from a position which is favourable or unfavourable to it. The empirical study of religion in its social context is challenging both for the believer and the unbeliever. Our attitudes to religious statements are bound to be affected by the discovery that there are definite relationships between religious beliefs and social and psychological factors but they may be affected in several different ways.

First, it may leave our initial position of neutrality untouched. We may feel unable to say anything about the validity of religious claims. If, for example, it were to be shown that certain forms of belief were more common among the materially deprived, that in itself might not warrant any conclusion that such beliefs were nothing more than delusions brought about by material deprivation as some kind of compensatory mechanism. It might be the case that the materially deprived are simply more attuned to the spiritual than those whose prosperity blinds them to its importance. If it were shown that the dominant stratum in a given society supported conservative and traditional denominations while the poor and oppressed espoused sectarian forms of religion, this does not in itself mean that the beliefs of these respective groups are merely the expression of the material or status interests of the groups in question. They may be thus and at the same time express certain truths which the various groups genuinely espouse. It is an important principle that a statement or claim must be judged independently of the interests an individual might have for believing it. It is not automatically suspect or to be explained solely in terms of the self-interest of the believer.

On the other hand, the existence of sectional interests associated with different beliefs, or an association between them and material conditions, may bring us to alter our attitude to them because we come to see them in a new light or as something other than what we thought they were. The second way sociological studies may affect our attitudes to religious beliefs, then, might be to bring us to doubt them when we had previously accepted them.

Third, the fact that we come to see them as other than what we thought they were may lead us to see them as not so nonsensical and more meaningful than we had thought. We may come to acknowledge, perhaps, that they do express a kind of truth.

It is important to note, then, that the sociology of religion does not depend upon any resolution of the question of the truth or validity of religious claims, nor is its essential concern with such questions. Neither does it need to adopt any particular position on this matter, either sympathetic, oppositional or neutral. It all depends on what the beliefs are and the circumstances of each case. It does, however, require a readiness to change one's attitudes and an acceptance of the possibility that one will be changed as a consequence of pursuing it.

WHAT IS RELIGION?

So far in the discussion reference has been made to 'systems of belief' as well as to religion and the example of witchcraft beliefs has been used to illustrate points. Some may consider witchcraft beliefs to be something quite different from religion and more closely related to superstition. This raises the whole question of the scope of the sociology of religion and comes down to the question of defining 'religion'. This is not an easy matter and there are many definitions offered by authorities on the subject which disagree markedly with one another.

For this reason some sociologists have argued that it is better not to attempt to define the subject of investigation at the outset and that it is only after extensive investigation that one is in a position to do this. Max Weber, for example, one of the greatest scholars in the field, declines in the opening sentence of his major general treatise on the subject to give a definition of religion. This could only be done, he argues, at the conclusion of our studies (Weber, 1965, p. 1). The anthropologist, S. F. Nadel, in his study of the religious beliefs and practices of a West African people, comments that however the sphere of 'things religious' is defined, there will always remain an area or border zone of uncertainty and it will be difficult to determine just where the dividing line between religion and non-religion is. He proposes describing, therefore, everything that has a bearing upon religion so as to be sure not to leave anything out and suggests that it will be necessary to feel one's way towards the meaning of the term (Nadel, 1954, pp. 7–8).

Weber, however, it would seem, did not advance sufficiently in his own studies to come to a clear view on the question since he did not leave us with a definition. How advanced do we have to be before we can be clear on the matter? More significantly, how can we be sure that we are including in our investigations all that we should in order to become sufficiently advanced if we do not attempt to demarcate the limits of our subject at the outset? Nadel is probably correct in arguing that any definition will entail an area of uncertainty but how can he know what has a bearing on religion when he does not know where the boundaries are in the first place? Goody points out this procedure carries the danger of leaving the investigators' criteria implicit rather than opening them to general scrutiny (Goody, 1961, p. 142). Clearly, no investigation can proceed without some conception of what the limits of the subject matter are and to avoid confusion it is better to make this explicit at the outset even if such conceptions are imperfect and have to be altered in the light of deeper understanding.

In considering attempts to define religion one point always to be borne in mind is that they are not always free from the influence of theoretical predilections and purposes. That is to say, what theorists think religion is often depends upon the explanation of it they favour. They do not always seek to simply demarcate the sphere of investigation but also to state or imply things within the definition which support their theoretical interpretation of it. Their definitions are couched in terms that exclude phenomena which would otherwise be thought to belong but to which their theories do not apply, or which include phenomena which would not otherwise be thought to belong because their theories necessitate their inclusion.

The debates that occurred during the nineteenth century among anthropologists and sociologists on the question will serve to highlight many of the central issues involved in the problem of defining religion. An early contribution was that of Edward Tylor who proposed what he called a minimum definition, namely 'belief in spiritual beings' (Tylor, 1903, p. 424). This definition was bound up with Tylor's account of the origins of religion in a system of thought which he referred to as animism – the belief that all things, organic and inorganic, contain a soul or spirit which gives them their particular nature and characteristics. The definition was soon subjected to criticism from those who objected to the emphasis of Tylor and others upon intellect and reason in explaining the origins of religion and who thought that emotions lay at the root of religion. Marett objected to the emphasis upon 'beings' since he believed that the essence of religion lay in an experience of a mysterious and occult power or force which was associated with deep and ambivalent emotions of awe, fear and respect. Experience of this power or force predated conceptualisations of spirits, deities and so on (Marett, 1914). Others were unhappy with the other aspect of Tylor's definition, namely its focus on beliefs, pointing out that this ignored practices, which they considered to be more important than beliefs and the real essence of religion (Smith, 1889; Durkheim, 1915). Durkheim, for example, pointed out that belief in spiritual beings implied belief in supernatural entities but some systems of belief generally acknowledged to be religions, such as Theravada Buddhism, were not founded upon such conceptions. Central to Durkheim's own definition was a distinction between the sacred and the profane. Religion, he said, is:

> a unified system of beliefs and practices relative to sacred things, that is to say, things set apart and forbidden – beliefs and practices which unite into one single moral community called a Church all those who adhere to them.
>
> (1915, p. 47)

In its inclusion of practices as well as beliefs and its emphasis upon the group this definition shows the influence of Robertson Smith who had argued that rituals are prior to beliefs which are little more than rationalisations of practices and who had emphasised the social and collective nature of such ritual. It was this 'eminently social' (1915, p. 10) character of religion which in Durkheim's view differentiated it from magic. Magic has no Church, he argued. The magician has only his clientele with whom he individually deals. Religion is an affair of the community and entails a congregation or Church.

This brief summary of early debates and definitions shows that the crucial problems centred on the question of beliefs versus practices and that of the nature or character of religious entities or forces and of the spiritual or supernatural realm. The first problem is easily dealt with by simply including reference to both in the definition without necessarily implying that one is more important than or prior to the other. The second problem remains a matter of difficulty and contention. Terms such as 'sacred' and 'supernatural' come from a Western context and are not always readily applicable to the beliefs of non-Western societies since they carry various culture-bound connotations. Durkheim's claim that religion has to do with the sacred and that this is a universal conception in human society has been challenged by anthropologists. Goody, for example, found that no distinction between sacred and profane is made by a West African people he studied (Goody, 1961). Similarly, Evans-Pritchard found the distinction was not meaningful among the Azande (Evans-Pritchard, 1937). It is often the case that distinctions made in one culture and thought to be basic and obvious are not made in other cultures (see Worsley, 1969). This is a valuable lesson that anthropology has taught us.

The idea of the sacred or supernatural, then, is one which exists in the mind of the observer and not necessarily of the believer or actor. The distinction might, nevertheless, be a useful analytical one which the anthropologist and sociologist can use to describe and classify their data. There are, however, problems with it even as an analytical distinction which centre on the criteria by which the sacred is distinguished from the profane. Durkheim spoke of 'things set apart and forbidden'. Anthropologists have claimed that this does not aid them in distinguishing a sacred from a profane sphere in the societies they have studied. While many peoples do have a category of things set apart and forbidden, these things are not always those that figure in religious belief and ritual and, on the other hand, things which do figure prominently in religious belief and ritual may not be set apart and forbidden.

Durkheim also speaks of the sacred as commanding an attitude of respect. Unfortunately neither does this provide a reliable criterion since, in many religious systems, religious objects and entities do not always receive respect. Idols, and the gods and spirits they represent, may be punished if they do not produce the benefits they are expected to. Even in a Catholic context, in Southern Italy for example, a saint who does not respond in the desired manner after long and repeated prayers may be severely admonished, the statue turned upside down, even whipped or discarded and replaced with that of another saint. In any case, this criterion is hardly sufficient to distinguish the sacred from the profane since many things and persons who have nothing to do with religious activities may command respect.

Problems such as these led Goody to reject the attempt to define religion in terms of the sacred.

> it is no sounder for the observer to found his categorization of religious activity upon the universal perception by humanity of a sacred world any more than upon the actor's division of the universe into natural and super-natural spheres, a contention which Durkheim had himself dismissed.
>
> (Goody, 1961, p. 155)

It certainly seems to offer no advantage over terms like 'supernatural' and 'spiritual'. Others have tried to overcome the difficulties that these entail by using terms which appear to be less culturally specific. Spiro defines religion as 'an institution consisting of culturally patterned interaction with culturally postulated superhuman beings' (Spiro, 1966, p. 96).

This does not answer the point made by Marett and others in criticism of Tylor that some religious systems may not be concerned with 'beings'. Also, while it includes action as well as belief, in referring to interaction, this might be considered a rather restrictive way of doing so in that it might exclude Buddhism in certain of its interpretations and certain mystical forms of Hinduism which do not involve 'interaction' as such with the Buddha or any deity. More problematic, however, is its use of the term 'superhuman' rather than 'supernatural' or 'spiritual'. Superhuman beings, Spiro tells us, are beings believed to possess power greater than man, able to work good or ill for man, and which can be influenced by man. Theravada Buddhism is safely included in such a definition since the Buddha can be regarded as superhuman if not supernatural. In any case, the fact that, according to strictly canonical interpretation, the Buddha, having achieved enlightenment, ceased to exist as a distinct entity or ego, need not be a problem since most Buddhists do not think of him that way in practice. If that small minority who are strictly atheistic in their understanding of the nature of the Buddha have to be excluded as not followers of a religion, then so be it. The final point Spiro makes is that most Buddhists believe, in any case, in a whole variety of gods, spirits and demons, the existence of which Buddhism does not repudiate.

While there is no compelling reason to include a major world belief system such as Buddhism as expressed in 'official' doctrines and teachings, it would be odd to exclude it by a definition such as Spiro's. The justification of this procedure in terms of the claim that most Theravada Buddhists misunderstand the nature of the doctrines they ostensibly espouse, or act in ways that imply beliefs other than those they are assenting to in calling themselves Buddhists, is less than satisfactory on two counts. First, to misunderstand a doctrine or to act in ways that imply assent to a different belief, even one which is contradictory, is not the same as rejecting it. If the majority of those who call themselves Theravada Buddhists were to openly repudiate the official teachings, there would be grounds for saying that there are two distinct forms of Theravada Buddhism, only one of which might then qualify for inclusion in the category of 'religion'. There is no evidence, however, that this is so, only that many Buddhists have an imperfect understanding of doctrine while simultaneously holding beliefs which seem to contradict it; not an uncommon situation in many religious traditions.

Second, there seems little justification in giving priority to the interpretations or understandings of the majority above canonical interpretations in order to ensure that 'Buddhism' is included as a religion. Is there any more reason to conclude that canonical Theravada Buddhism is not a religion while popular Theravada Buddhism is than that those who espouse popular Theravada Buddhism are not really Buddhists, or imperfect ones? The latter would seem the more reasonable conclusion, in which case Spiro's strategy for getting Theravada Buddhism into the net fails. Also, the fact that he resorts to the strategy of claiming that most Buddhists believe in all manner of beings other than the Buddha and are, therefore, followers of a religion betrays a certain lack of confidence in his definition. It is precisely because these other beings are, in fact, supernatural that the danger of excluding Buddhism is averted.[5]

The term 'superhuman' is, in any case, not entirely clear. Would it include other very exceptional human beings as well as the Buddha; Napoleon or Hitler, for example? How powerful or extraordinary does a human being have to be to be considered superhuman? Furthermore, as Herbrechtsmeier (1993) points out, the notion of superhuman is culturally specific and to impose it upon the belief systems of others is to introduce a cultural bias and distortion. Ideas about what it is to be human vary widely across cultures and we cannot take it for granted that being 'greater than human' will mean the same thing in different contexts. The unreflective use of the term by Spiro disguises the cultural meaning derived from the Western context that it carries.

Another attempt to avoid the pitfalls of terms such as 'supernatural' and 'spiritual' is that of Robertson (1970), who uses the term 'super-empirical'. His definition is as follows:

> Religious culture is that set of beliefs and symbols (and values deriving directly therefrom) pertaining to a distinction between an empirical and a super-empirical, transcendent reality; the affairs of the empirical being sub-ordinated in significance to the non-empirical. Secondly, we define religious action simply as: action shaped by an acknowledgement of the empirical/super-empirical distinction.
>
> (Robertson, 1970, p. 47)

It is doubtful if 'super-empirical' is much of an improvement on 'sacred' or 'supernatural'. It is probably more widely applicable than ideas of sacredness or the supernatural but it is questionable whether it is as universally applicable as Robertson believes. Whether or not other cultures acknowledge any distinction between a sacred and profane sphere or between the natural and supernatural, Robertson argues, their beliefs imply the existence of a super-empirical realm by which he means conceptions which go beyond the readily observable and accessible, which are brought to bear on and relate to the empirical and, to distinguish religion from science and theoretical analyses, which attribute to the non-empirical an 'otherness' which gives it its religious character. This is rather vague and it is very doubtful if this 'otherness', whatever it might be, is implied in all systems of belief one feels should be included in the notion of religion.

Difficulties of the kind that Spiro's and Robertson's definitions run into are inevitable according to another anthropologist, Robin Horton, since they are attempting to do what cannot be done, namely to imply something about the nature and mode of existence of religious entities whilst simultaneously being universally applicable (Horton, 1960). The diversity of conceptions pertaining to religious entities is so great, he argues, that any attempt to say anything at all about their nature and mode of existence is bound to render the definition inapplicable to some conceptions; 'we can point to no single ontological or epistemological category which accommodates all religious entities. Secondly, we find that every major ontological and epistemological category we can devise contains religious as well as secular entities' (Horton, 1960, p. 205).

Horton, consequently, proposes a definition that avoids any intimation of the nature or mode of existence of religious entities but which is expressed in terms of religious action. He says:

> in every situation commonly labelled religious we are dealing with action directed towards objects which are believed to respond in terms of certain categories – in our own culture those of purpose, intelligence and emotion – which are also the distinctive categories for the description of human action .
> . . . The relationships between human beings and religious objects can be further defined as governed by certain ideas of patterning such as categorize relationships among human beings . . . . In short religion can be looked upon as an extension of the field of people's social relationships beyond the confines of purely human society. And for completeness' sake, we should add the rider that this extension must be one in which human beings involved see themselves in a dependent position '*vis-à-vis*' their non-human alters – a qualification necessary to exclude pets from the pantheon of gods.
>
> (Horton, 1960, p. 211)

This definition represents the fullest development of a trend which we have seen exemplified in the other definitions we have considered, namely to reduce that element which specifies the nature of religious entities to as general a statement as possible and to move towards specification of the kind of relationship that believers have with the realm of the religious. Spiro's emphasis on interaction testifies to this as does the definition offered by Goody, namely, that 'religious beliefs are present when non-human agencies are propitiated *on the human model*' (Goody, 1961, p. 157 italics added). It is significant that it is anthropologists who have moved in this direction. They, more than anyone, are aware of the difficulties of definitions based upon culturally specific terms and of the dangers of ethnocentricism entailed by them. It is important to avoid imposing concepts and categories derived from one culture upon the data pertaining to another which do not fit or which are inappropriate. This is not to say that the sociologist cannot use concepts of his or her own and which are not part of the conceptual universe being analysed provided that they do not do violence to, distort or misrepresent the beliefs in question (see Runciman, 1970).

This type of definition, however, is not the only approach to the problem that has been adopted. Definitions so far discussed have mostly been of the type known as substantive. They state what kind of thing religion is. The alternative is a functional definition which states what religion does. Durkheim's definition contains a functional element in referring to religion uniting followers into a single moral community, the church. Functionalist definitions are what is often termed 'inclusive', that is to say they include a broad range of phenomena within the concept. In fact, by implication, anything which performs the said function or operates in the said way counts as religion even if not conventionally thought of as such. If religion is defined as that which promotes unity or social cohesion, then anything which does this is religion. This inclusiveness is often deliberate. Functionalist definitions are usually linked to a theoretical perspective which seeks to explain religion in terms of an alleged and essential integrative role. Often such theorists claim that systems of values and beliefs such as communism, fascism and nationalism function in this way and include them in the category of religion. An example of an inclusive definition is that of Yinger: 'religion is a system of beliefs and practices by means of which a group of people struggles with the ultimate problems of human life' (1970, p. 7).

The trouble with such definitions is that they are too broad. It seems odd to include belief systems and ideologies which, like communism, are specifically anti-religious. And as Scharf says of Yinger's definition, 'it is cast in wide terms which allow almost any kind of enthusiastic purpose or strong loyalty, provided it is shared by a group, to count as religion' (Scharf, 1970, p. 33). For example, fanatical supporters of a football team might, under this definition, be counted as followers of a religion. Members of the fan club of a pop singer might also be considered to be struggling with the ultimate problems of human life which for them might be the pursuit of something which the music and personality of the star seem to provide.

The difficulty, of course, lies in the term 'ultimate problems of human life'. What are they? Who is to say what they are – the sociologist or the believer? Yinger provides a list of examples. Other sociologists tend to provide a rather different list (Campbell, 1971). The ultimate problem of human life might be, for many people, simply how to enjoy it as much as possible, how to avoid pain and ensure pleasure. Campbell points out that what are presented as 'problems' or the 'ultimate problems' in any given society or sub-culture is a cultural variable. We learn to identify what constitutes a problem and since religion is usually an important part of the culture in which this learning takes place, religious considerations enter into what is and is not defined as a problem. The second difficulty with this type of definition is that it tends to be circular. Penner and Yonan (1972) agree for a closely related reason. The term 'ultimate' in the definition can generally only be defined in terms of religion. Also, they point out, an important criterion for a coherent definition is violated, namely that the definiens (the defining statement) must not be broader than the definiendum (the term to be defined). Clearly, the term 'ultimate' is broader than 'religion' since it connotes what is incapable of further specification.

The third difficulty with such definitions is that they prejudge the important empirical question of the role or effects that religion does have in society by stating in the very definition of it what ought to be demonstrated empirically. This allows defence, for example, of a functionalist theory which claims that religion is a universal factor in social life because it is essential for the integration of society and the promotion of social stability, against any evidence that could be cited in refutation of it. If a society were to be described in which there did not appear to be any system of religion, the functionalist could reply that absence of something which looked like religion in the conventional sense does not invalidate the theory because any set of values and beliefs which promote integration and stability is, for such a theorist, religion. By defining religion at the outset as that which promotes stability the theory cannot be wrong and no evidence can count against it. It becomes a non-empirical statement which would be true not as a matter of fact but by definition. The possibility of it being false is ruled out of consideration with the consequence that it becomes immune to the test of evidence and loses its explanatory value. It becomes itself a statement of faith and blind to other possibilities such as that religion can be a cause of conflict and instability as much as an integrative force.

Functional definitions should be avoided, therefore, since they prejudge empirical questions which must be resolved by actual enquiry and investigation. If ideologies and belief systems such as communism and nationalism do share characteristics with religions or are found to play a similar social role they might better be described, as Robertson (1970, p. 39) suggests, by the term surrogate religiosity.

It would seem, then, that a substantive definition is preferable and one which implies as little as possible about the nature of religious entities. Horton's appears to be about the closest one can get although even this is not without areas of uncertainty. It would seem to exclude the more mystical and contemplative forms of belief and practice which are often considered to be religious, unless one sees them as involving communication with the divine, the totality of being, or whatever, since communication is a form of interaction. It hardly takes, in these practices however, the pattern of human interaction. Horton's definition might also be considered to exclude magical practices. This would not be a dis-advantage in the view of many theorists who believe religion and magic are different and should be distinguished. Others see them as inextricably inter-woven, however, and would wish to define religion in such a way as to include magic. We shall return to the question of the distinction between magic and religion in a later section. There it will be argued that while magic and religion are best defined separately they are, nevertheless, closely related and have to be understood in terms of the same general approach.

This discussion of the definition of religion has not entirely resolved what is a very difficult question. Its point is not so much, however, to arrive at a final or even very satisfactory definition but rather to highlight a number of important issues: the close and often problematic relationship between definitions and theoretical predilections; the dangers of prejudging empirical issues by definitional fiat; the dangers of ethnocentrism in the use of concepts; the dangers of leaving definitional criteria implicit. A possible reason for the difficulty encountered by sociology and other disciplines in defining religion might, of course, be the consequence of the fact that it is not possible to capture by the use of a single concept the diversity of what we call in everyday speech religion, probably in inconsistent and contradictory ways. What this points to, perhaps, is the need to define a series of concepts which would collectively cover the range, extending the idea that magic and religion should be so differentiated. In dealing with 'religion' we may be dealing, in fact, with many different things – philosophical systems, cosmologies, systems of morality, even forms of drama, literature and other symbolic representations. Robertson has pointed out that there has been a trend towards breaking up the unitary concept of religion into various dimensions or aspects which may vary independently of one another (Robertson, 1970, pp. 27 and 51). And William James in *The Varieties of Religious Experience* remarked, in speaking of the great variety of definitions of religion, that 'the very fact that they are so many and so different from one another is enough to prove that the word "religion" cannot stand for any single principle or essence, but is rather a collective name' (James, 1961, p. 39).

One possible preliminary division is represented in Figure 1.

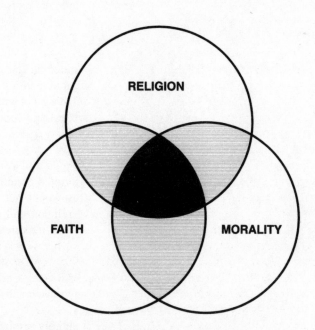

Figure 1 The relationship between religion, faith and morality

Religion would essentially be as defined by Horton. Faiths would include those systems of belief and associated practices, philosophies of life, mystical doctrines, etc, which do not involve interaction on the human pattern with the non-human. Third, we might distinguish moral systems from religions and faiths as being concerned solely with principles and ideals of behaviour. Traditional 'world' religions such as Christianity and Islam are simultaneously religions, faiths and moral systems and fall, consequently, in the centre of the diagram where all three categories overlap. Other systems of belief might be simultaneously faiths and moral systems but lack the religious element as defined here. Still others might conceivably fall in the area religion/moral system and faith/religion but this is less likely. Many primitive belief systems would fall into the category of pure religion having no real concern with morality and not being faiths. Some systems of belief might be pure faiths with no element of religion or concern for morality; for example, certain contemporary self-realisation groups and Human Potential movements. Finally, there are moral systems which embody no element of religion and which cannot be described as faiths, for example, humanism.

2 Religion and reason

It is convenient to divide types of explanation of religion into psychological and sociological theories and the former again into intellectualist and emotionalist theories. Such a division is utilised by Evans-Pritchard (1965) who points out, however, that it is only a crude classification since some theorists do not fall neatly into a single type, but it will serve to organise the material of this chapter. It also reflects, if very approximately, the historical succession of theoretical approaches. In this chapter we shall examine psychological theories of the intellectualist variety. Psychological theories hold that religion is an affair of the individual and springs from sources within the individual, whereas sociological theories hold that religion is an affair of the group or society and that individual religiosity stems from social sources. Intellectualist psychological theories interpret religion as stemming essentially from human reason while emotionalist theories trace the roots of religion to the emotional side of human nature.

Intellectualist psychological theories see religion as the product of the human tendency to seek to understand the world and of human reason and capacity to deduce, generalise and draw conclusions from observation and experience. The intellectualist approach was one of the earliest to be formulated and took a strongly evolutionary character in accordance with the intellectual trends of the time, that is, the nineteenth century, although its roots go back further, to the Enlightenment of the previous century. The most important intellectualist thinkers were August Comte, Herbert Spencer, Sir Edward Tylor and Sir James Frazer.

Comte's evolutionary scheme of the development of human thought, which he thought was the key to the development of society, was set out in his *Cours de Philosophie Positive (The Positive Philosophy)* published between the years 1830-42. In this he set out his 'law of the three stages' which states that in the intellectual development of humanity there are three distinct stages, namely, theological, metaphysical and positive.

In the first stage, the theological, thoughts and ideas about reality are essentially religious in nature. The metaphysical stage is a transitional stage between the theological and positive stages, the latter representing modern scientific thought. In the theological stage natural phenomena are believed to have a life and personality of their own and similar to that of human beings. Natural phenomena are explained and understood by likening them to human behaviour and are seen as having a will and as acting intentionally.

Comte further divides the theological stage into three sub-stages. In the first, fetichism, all things, even inanimate objects, are believed to be animated by a life or soul like that of human beings. This, Comte argued, underlies all religious thought and was perfectly understandable when seen in the context of early human development. It was quite reasonable and logical to generalise from human nature and experience to the rest of reality, to see all things as having the same essential nature, and to conclude, in the absence of any better knowledge, that this nature would be much like that with which they were most familiar, namely their own.

In the second sub-stage, polytheism, material things are no longer seen as animated by an indwelling life or soul. Matter itself is seen as inert in itself but subject to the external will of a supernatural agent. Belief in supernatural or divine agencies arose as a consequence of the human capacity and tendency to generalise. Supernatural agencies were progressively attributed with more general spheres of jurisdiction. They were increasingly seen as not attached to specific objects but manifest in all objects of a particular kind or belonging to a given category. The process goes something like this. At first it is believed that in every single oak tree there is an indwelling spirit. But because all oak trees are alike it comes to be believed that there is a general spirit governing all oak trees. Then, because all trees are similar, it is concluded that there must be a spirit which governs all trees. In this way a conception of a god of the forest grows up and also conceptions of other gods. This is the stage of polytheism in which a pantheon of gods and deities with power to affect the world and human beings is worshipped and propitiated. At this stage a priesthood emerges whose task it is to mediate between the human realm and the gods. This priesthood constitutes a new class freed from normal toil and able to spend time in thought, contemplation and speculation. With the emergence of the priesthood we see the emergence of learning.

Taken a step further, the process which led from fetichism to polytheism leads logically on to the final sub-stage of the theological phase, namely monotheism. This is characterised by the development of the great world religions and the emergence of distinct religious organisations such as the church.

From this monotheistic stage human thought passes through the transitional metaphysical stage in which spirits and deities give way to more abstract conceptions of general principles or forces which govern reality. This, in turn, gives way to the scientific thought of the positive stage which seeks to explain reality in terms of causal laws and generalisations.

Comte, however, did not think that with the arrival of science religion would disappear entirely. Religion, he thought, was not only an attempt to explain and understand reality but also the unifying principle of human society. In effect Comte, as Preus (1987) has pointed out, produced two theories of religion each rooted in one side of his paradoxical sense of his times. On the one hand, he believed in the inexorable progress of knowledge and mastery of nature but on the other he feared a social crisis and breakdown. The first produced his evolutionary theory in which religion was the first stage in the advance of human thought; the second led him to see society as requiring an ordering, regulating and unifying authority or power and the name of religion being attached to whatever fulfilled this function.

If, then, traditional religion must vanish with the growth of science then it would have to be replaced with a new form of religion based upon sound scientific principles. Since the science which is concerned with understanding the principles of social unity and cohesion is sociology, then the new religion would be a kind of applied sociology and the sociologist would be the high priest of this new secular creed. So seriously did Comte hold this view that he even devised the robes and vestments that the sociological priesthood would wear, the rituals they would perform and actually founded a Church of Positivism of which one or two branches still survive.

In this Comte differs from most of those who followed him who, for the most part, believed religion would disappear entirely in a modern rational society. For them, reason alone would govern conduct and they would have thought Comte's sociological religion with its priesthood, robes and rituals absurd. But like Comte they too believed religion to be a product of reason and of the human capacity to generalise in an attempt to understand and explain the world. Like Comte they too took an evolutionary approach and were concerned to reconstruct the manner in which our early ancestors perceived and understood their world. They were interested in characterising the most primitive and simple or earliest forms of religious conception from which they believed all later and more complex forms developed. In this way they believed it would be possible to uncover the roots which have nourished and still nourish the religious mentality. Writers like Spencer, Tylor and Frazer turned to primitive societies to find these roots since such societies, they thought, represent survivals from the early periods of human and social development.

Herbert Spencer's ideas on the origins and roots of religion were set out in his monumental *Principles of Sociology* published between 1876 and 1896. Spencer posed the question of why primitive peoples believed in things such as spirits, magic and so on, ideas which were clearly false and mistaken. Spencer did not conclude that primitive people were irrational but that since they had to operate on a basis of very limited knowledge, the, albeit mistaken, inferences they made about the world were understandable and reasonable.

A very important yet common experience that our primitive ancestors would have had, from which certain inferences would have been made, Spencer argued, was that of dreaming. For our primitive ancestors dreaming must have been like living in a separate reality not governed by the same limiting forces and laws of everyday existence. In dreams great distances could be traversed in a moment, one could go back in time, and meet those long dead. This would have suggested that we have a dual nature, that there is another aspect to the self – a dream self or soul. It would have further been inferred that if human beings have such a dual nature then all things would also have one. All things in the world, both animate and inanimate, would, in primitive thought, be believed to have a soul or spirit. In the same way as Comte characterised early thought as fetichistic, Spencer postulates the existence of a primal stage of human thought in which indwelling souls govern and determine the nature and behaviour of all reality. But for Spencer, the roots of religious thought lay in the more specific idea of ghosts. In meeting and speaking with the dead in dreams, it was suggested to the primitive mind that the spirit or soul in some way survives death. The first supernatural beings who were worshipped, according to Spencer, were the souls or ghosts of the dead. The idea of the ghost developed into the idea of divinities who were dead ancestors and in particular remote and mythologised ancestors who had founded distinct social groupings, such as clans and tribes. These ancestors were conceived as important, powerful and remarkable individuals who, after death, became gods who had to be recognised, respected and propitiated. Ancestor worship then, Spencer thought, was the earliest form of religion and lies at the root of all religion. From it developed all the world's great religions. Terms and conceptions used in such systems of belief reflect this origin. In Christianity, for example, is there not a belief in the Holy Ghost?

Correspondingly, the earliest rituals would have been those performed at death when the spirit passes on to the world of the ancestors, namely funerary rites. In discussing these, Spencer's account takes a markedly less intellectualist psychological tenor and a rather more sociological, indeed functionalist, turn. Funerary rites were a source of cohesion in society and the religious institutions which developed later became the bearers of tradition and the upholders of social stability.

Despite this functionalist element Spencer constructed a picture of the origins of religion which placed in the central position the capacity and tendency of the human mind to reason and draw inferences from observation and experience, and the desire to understand and explain the world. In constructing this picture, Spencer utilised, as Evans-Pritchard (1965) has pointed out, a process of introspection by which he attempted to place himself mentally in the position of a human being living during the early period of the evolution of the species and to imagine how it would have been and how one would have thought. Herein lies the weakness of the approach but before examining its deficiencies let us look at the rather similar ideas of Edmund Tylor.

Tylor's theories of the origins of religion appeared in his general study of primitive society, *Primitive Culture* published in 1871, of which they form a considerable part. It was Tylor who coined the term 'animism' which was, he argued, the earliest and most fundamental form of religion from which all others have evolved and he defined religion, as we have seen, as 'belief in spiritual beings'. The earliest conception of spiritual beings, he thought, was the animistic one of indwelling souls. Reality could be controlled and manipulated by controlling and affecting these spiritual entities. Animism was the theoretical aspect of the first belief system while magic was its practical technology.

Tylor agreed with Spencer in that he speculated that the source of such notions lay in the experience of dreams and visions. He agreed also that it was the human capacity for and tendency to generalise that led to the attribution of souls to all things, or, in other words, to animism. Tylor drew also upon the views of the philosopher David Hume who had, in his *Natural History of Religion*, first published in 1757, made the following observation: 'It is a universal tendency among mankind to conceive all beings like themselves and to transfer to every object those qualities with which they are familiarly acquainted and of which they are intimately conscious' (Hume, 1976, p. 33). This is, of course, the same claim that Comte made about the fetichistic stage of intellectual development.

Since the spiritual beings with which early humans populated the world derived from a human model, Tylor reasoned that they would be attributed with human characteristics such as intention, purpose, will, and so on. But certain of them, those governing major aspects of nature, were believed to be vastly superior to humans and much more powerful and therefore able to control their fate. They had to be propitiated, persuaded, cajoled in much the same way that other human beings are treated – by appeal, entreaty, giving gifts, the religious counterparts of which are prayer and sacrifice.

Tylor distinguished between religion and magic which he saw as based not upon the belief in spiritual beings but in impersonal powers and forces. Magic operates, he argued, on the principle of likeness and association. Things which resemble one another, in magical thought, are believed to be causally connected with one another. By operating upon or using something in certain ways the magician thinks it is possible to affect those things it resembles. Magic is, therefore, rather like science but based upon false reasoning. He did not see it as irrational but as understandable in the circumstances of ignorance and lack of sound knowledge of the real connections between things.

Tylor's ideas on primitive magic influenced the work of Sir James Frazer who achieved a certain fame for his enormous study *The Golden Bough* published in 1890 and which consisted of twelve large volumes. Frazer adopted an evolutionary scheme similar to that of Comte and which reflected the conceptual distinction between magic, religion and science that Tylor espoused. There have been three main stages of intellectual development, Frazer argued, namely the magical, the religious and the scientific.

Frazer, like Tylor, characterised magical beliefs and practices as being a kind of primitive science and technology, but one based upon mistaken reasoning which was the consequence of ignorance rather than irrationality and was reasonable given the conditions under which our primitive ancestors had to operate. Also, like Tylor, he thought that magical thought involved association of ideas in which certain types of perceived connection or association were taken to indicate real causal connections between things.

Frazer distinguished between two kinds of magic, homeopathic or imitative and contagious. In the former because two things are perceived to be similar, it is concluded that they must be connected such that, for example, what is done to one will take effect upon the other. Thus if a wax effigy of someone is made and a pin is thrust through it, then harm will be caused to the individual it resembles. Contagious magic is based upon the belief that if two things have been in intimate contact then action performed upon one will affect the other. For example, the hair or nail clippings of someone could be used to harm them by burning them whilst casting the appropriate spell.

Since such techniques do not actually produce the desired effects, Frazer went on to argue, in the course of time resort was made to other beliefs and practices, namely those of religion. Religion is based upon the analogy of human conduct, according to Frazer. The manipulative techniques of magic give way to supplication and propitiation of spirits. By a process of projection the faculties and powers of human beings are attributed to postulated supernatural beings who can be induced to aid humans in their purposes by various means.

Finally, as more and more is discovered of the real nature of the material world, religion itself begins to decline and to be replaced by solid scientific knowledge. This evolutionary development is, for Frazer, then, not simply one of progressive development since magic, though mistaken, is more akin in its logic to science than to religion which is, so to speak, a side-track in evolutionary development. Nor are these stages seen by Frazer as being marked by clear lines of division in time. Religion and even magic survive into the scientific age and are only progressively replaced. The prevalence of magic diminished during the stage of religious thought but it is not entirely extinguished, vestiges remaining even in the scientific age. Religion lives on but progressively loses its hold upon the human mind until eventually it will fade away as we find we have no further use for it.

One of the major objections that may be made to these nineteenth-century intellectualist, evolutionary theorists is that their claims were not based upon sound evidence but were largely conjectural. As we have seen in discussing Spencer, one of the methods used was that of introspection, an unreliable way, to say the least, of acquiring knowledge of the mentality of early man. Evans-Pritchard refers to such a procedure as the 'if I were a horse fallacy'. 'A logical construction of the scholar's mind is posited on primitive man, and put forward as the explanation of his beliefs' (Evans-Pritchard, 1965, p. 25). Certainly, there seems no reason to suppose that our primitive ancestors would have interpreted their dreams in the way Spencer and Tylor claimed they must have. Why should they not have dismissed them simply as dreams as we do?

The fact is that there is no evidence that early man was animistic in mentality, or that there were three stages of mental development in which religion replaced magic before giving way to science. Unfortunately we have little or no evidence at all relating to the beliefs and mentality of early human society, there being very few material remains pertaining to such things and those artifacts which have survived are of uncertain meaning and significance. The evidence from contemporary 'primitive' societies used by these writers is illegitimately taken to indicate the kinds of belief and practices that would have characterised early human beings. We simply do not know whether they have developed through time and cannot assume that they represent survivals of the primitive past. In any case, the ethnographic detail upon which these writers relied was fragmentary, unreliable and wrenched out of context. Such a method entails grave dangers of misunderstanding and misinterpretation. A criticism that can be made of them, for example, is that they all too easily assume that reported practices were nothing other than attempts to produce desired results. We know from more recent and more reliable fieldwork done since their day that many of the beliefs and practices of tribal peoples are of this kind but equally it would be wrong to see them all as being of this nature or to see them as solely of this nature. They may, for example have an expressive dimension (see Phillips, 1976).

The possibility that there might be a lot more to such beliefs and practices than the view which sees them as mere mistakes is suggested by the fact that magic is not relied upon by tribal peoples to produce desired results. If it were they would never have survived. For the most part they use ordinary everyday empirical techniques. They do not expect crops to grow by magical means without planting seeds, watering, weeding, protecting from parasites, and so on. They do not, in short, mistake connections which exist in the mind for real causal connections all the time or in the course of everyday activity. Magic is either reserved for special circumstances or is an adjunct to ordinary techniques.

Finally, the ethnographic evidence does not support Tylor or Frazer. The simplest societies, the hunter-gatherers, are not especially animistic, as Tylor's theories would lead us to expect. If anything, they are less animistic than many horticultural and agricultural societies. Neither do they manifest a preponderance of magic over religion as Frazer's theories would suggest.

Despite their deficiencies, however, these pioneering studies of the intellectualist theorists have made a lasting contribution to our understanding of magical and religious thought. Although their ideas were very much out of favour during the 1950s and 1960s, many anthropologists have returned to them. They continue to find their characterisation of magic and religion as concerned with explanation, understanding and desire to control the world to contain more than a grain of truth, even if the more specific claims of the intellectualists concerning the manner of origination of such ideas and their evolutionary schemes are rejected as unacceptable. We shall examine this 'neo-Tyloreanism' in the next chapter.

3   Magic

Magical beliefs and behaviour, while by no means confined to 'primitive' or tribal societies, have been studied in most detail largely by anthropologists working in this type of society. The neo-Tyloreans and their critics have tended to be anthropologists with direct and first-hand experience of such societies and their understanding has been based upon such experience.

In Western eyes the magical practices of tribal peoples appeared, when they were first observed and described, to be highly irrational. The initial reaction to the intriguing, puzzling and even seemingly bizarre beliefs and practices of tribal peoples reported by travellers, missionaries, or colonial administrators, was perhaps to dismiss them as the product of sheer backwardness and savagery. Even when more serious studies of them began to be made, they tended to be seen as representative of a primitive stage of human thought, the product of a primitive mentality and pre-logical in character, as, for example by Lévy-Bruhl (1922, 1926, [1960]) or, as we have seen, as pre-scientific by Tylor and Frazer.

Later, the more detailed and careful work of anthropologists who conducted intensive fieldwork among tribal peoples showed that these ideas were inadequate to aid understanding of their magical belief and practice. These peoples were observed to be as logical as ourselves and their reasoning processes to be of the same character as our own. Their practical knowledge of their environment and how to survive in it was shown to be very extensive, detailed and sophisticated. Also, the anthropologists reminded us that there were many beliefs and practices common in the 'civilised' societies which were not in essence any different from those found in 'primitive' societies and which would appear to the inhabitants of many an African tribe to be as strange, irrational and bizarre as some of their beliefs appeared to us. While Christianity had tended to reduce the element of magic in religious thought, it had by no means eradicated it and had its own mysteries such as the idea of the virgin birth. Outside the realm of religion as such, superstitions of all kinds abounded in allegedly rational, scientific, technically advanced cultures. If there was a difference between the more advanced civilised societies and tribal societies it was merely a quantitative rather than a qualitative one. The evolutionary approaches of nineteenth-century thinkers, who had for the most part done little or no fieldwork and had no direct experience of tribal societies, fell into disfavour and gave way to the functionalism of Radcliffe-Brown, Malinowski and their followers. Tribal peoples could not be treated as museum exhibits representative of some ancient past, this new generation of fieldworkers argued. Their beliefs and customs were not survivals from a distant past but an integral part of living and flourishing cultures. They had to be understood in terms of the role they played in such living systems.

If tribal peoples, then, were not to be characterised by a special and mystical mode of thought, if they were well aware of the causal links between things and could operate perfectly rationally and effectively in technical matters, in producing the requirements of life, in mastering the elements and materials of their environment, how could sense be made of their magical and other 'strange' beliefs and practices? There seemed to be a tremendous gap between their everyday activity on the one hand, and the prominence of magical thought and practice on the other.

Contemporary anthropology attempted to solve this problem by treating magical and related practices as essentially symbolic behaviour and as having functional significance. While it was clear that most practitioners of magic in tribal societies genuinely believed in the efficacy of their techniques and practised them to bring about concrete, material results, anthropologists nevertheless emphasised their symbolic character and the social functions of the behaviour as the real rationale behind them.

More recently the difficulties involved in the functionalist and symbolic approach (see Chapter ten) have led a number of anthropologists to reconsider the approach of Tylor and Frazer. These neo-Tyloreans, while rejecting the evolutionism and speculative character of the nineteenth-century writers, have revived the view that magical beliefs and practices must be interpreted as attempts to explain, understand and control reality. In other words, they are a set of ideas and practices akin to science and technology in many respects, and not essentially symbolic and expressive. These opposing points of view have stimulated a lively debate in anthropological and philosophical circles. Before examining this debate some general points about the character of magic as opposed to religion must be made.

The functionalist/symbolic approach applies equally well to both magic and religion whereas the neo-Tyloreans are mainly concerned with magic. However, magical practices are often closely related to religious beliefs and are frequently a part of religious rituals. It is not always possible, in any given instance, to distinguish between magic and religion.

Malinowski's distinction is probably the most useful. Magic is always related to some concrete purpose or definite outcome which the practitioner wishes to achieve. Religion, on the other hand, aims at no particular purpose or end result. 'While in the magical act the underlying idea and aim are always clear, straightforward, and definite, in the religious ceremony there is no purpose directed toward a subsequent event' (1974, p. 38). The rituals involved in religion are not designed to bring about or cause some effect. Religious rituals are performed for their own sake. Malinowski says, 'The ceremony and its purpose are one' and 'the end is realised in the very consummation of the act' (1974, p. 40). Magic is a 'practical art consisting of acts which are only means to a definite end expected to follow later on' while religion is 'a body of self-contained acts being themselves the fulfilment of their purpose' (1974, p. 88). A rite designed to prevent death during childbirth differs from a rite which celebrates the birth of a child in that the former aims at a definite end result while the latter has no further aim apart from the expression of sentiments in and through the rite itself.

In reality, Malinowski's categories are rarely found in pure form but are very much intermingled. Practices often embody elements of each although usually they lean more in one direction than the other. A more elaborate attempt to define magic as distinct from religion which uses the technique of separating out the magical from the religious aspects of a practice is that of William J. Goode (1951). While recognising that there is no sharp dividing line between them, Goode lists eleven criteria by which the magical aspect can be distinguished from the religious. They are as follows:

1 Magic is more instrumental, aiming at end results of a concrete and material kind.
2 Its goals are specific and limited.
3 It is more manipulative in its techniques.
4 It is directed at individual rather than at group goals.
5 It is more a matter of private practice than a group activity.
6 It is more susceptible to substitution of techniques – if one does not work, another is tried.
7 It involves less emotion.
8 Its practice is less obligatory.
9 It is less tied to specific times and occasions.
10 It is potentially more anti-social.
11 It is used only instrumentally and is not an end in itself.

A second general point to note about magic is that the concept is, of course, one which belongs to a particular cultural tradition – our own which other cultures may or may not share. Other societies do not always possess such a concept and have no notion of a distinct category of magic with its connotations of special and mysterious forces. In many societies, practices which we would be inclined to categorise as magical on the grounds that they have no sound empirical foundation are regarded as perfectly ordinary empirical techniques involving no extra-mundane forces. Firth (1939), for example, reports that Malay fishermen burn incense on the prows of their boats to attract fish to their nets. This is not seen in any way as a magical act. Although Malays do have a concept rather like our own concept of magic, this particular practice does not belong to it but is in their eyes an ordinary mundane technique that just happens to work. We, on the other hand, are inclined to believe that it does not work but we would be quite wrong to treat it as an instance of magic since this would be to impose categories and therefore meanings upon the practice quite alien to those it has for its practitioners. It would imply that it is an action which makes use of extraordinary and mysterious powers and techniques beyond the everyday world and modes of operation in it. If we were then to seek an explanation of the practice we would not get very far for we would be seeking an answer to an unreal question. The result could only be a distorted understanding of the belief and the practice.

Similarly, Nadel pointed out in his study of the religious beliefs and practices of the Nupe of West Africa (1954) that we might at first sight be tempted to classify many of their 'medicines' and curative practices as magical since, in our view, they are obviously ineffective and in some cases probably harmful. However, many of them are not thought of by the Nupe themselves as being in any sense extraordinary or magical. Again, Hsu (1983) has pointed out in his study of reactions to a cholera outbreak in South China that most of the residents of the town he studied did not distinguish clearly or at all between magical and mundane means of avoiding the disease. Many techniques were used which to Western eyes might appear magical but all the participants were concerned about was whether they worked or not. Often methods that we would be inclined to consider magical were seen by them as mundane, and conversely methods we would categorise as mundane were sometimes perceived by them as being magical. To take a more Western example, Vogt (1952) has argued that water dowsing or 'witching' as it is called in parts of the rural United States is not, despite this name, seen as a form of magic but is viewed as a rational, technical process and can be best described as a kind of folk-science or 'pseudo science'.

It is, consequently, very important to distinguish between the actor's and the observer's account of what is happening. The actor may consider he or she is performing an ordinary empirical act involving nothing mystical. The observer, on the other hand, may see the action as odd and in need of special explanation because there appears to be no connection between the means and ends of the activity.

There are, then, two criteria which we can apply to a 'magical' practice: it might be potentially 'magical' in the terms of the observer's categories and/or in terms of the actor's categories; and it might, as a matter of fact, be a sound practice empirically or it may not. Nadel points out that this creates four possibilities. He uses the term 'rational' to refer to practices which are not considered to be in any way out of the ordinary, and 'mystical' for practices which are considered to involve something extraordinary.

The four possibilities are:

1   Both actor and observer perceive the practice as ordinary empirical technique.
2   The actor considers that the practice is rational but the observer is convinced it is not empirically sound.
3   The actor conceives of the practice as clearly mystical but the observer is convinced that there is, in fact, a sound empirical basis for it.
4   The actor considers the practice to be mystical and, as far as the observer is concerned, there is no sound empirical basis for it.

The first possibility, where both actor and observer perceive the practice as an ordinary empirical technique – as rational – includes a great many practices and they, clearly, are not the concern of the sociology of religion. Some medicines used in primitive societies, for example, are indeed effective. Quinine and cocaine were first used in tribal societies before becoming part of the Western pharmacopoeia. The lesson of this is that we should not be too ready to label the traditional medicines used in non-Western societies as either quackery or magic but reserve judgement until careful investigations have been carried out. Many useful substances derived from plants are being discovered today by researchers investigating the properties of folk medicines.

The second possibility is that the actor considers that the practice is rational but the observer is convinced it is not empirically sound. Again, a large number of practices fall into this category. The practice of the Malay fishermen and the Nupe medicines are examples of this. One might also include such things as 'old wives tales' and superstitions such as the belief that to break a mirror brings seven years of bad luck or that turning one's money over under a full moon increases prosperity. It is difficult to see why we should refer to this type of practice as magic for the reason stated above. The question we wish to ask about this sort of thing is – why do people do such things in the absence of any supporting evidence that they work? We do not have to look into any beliefs about mystical forces and their nature for an answer since the practices do not involve any such beliefs. Neither is there any point in seeking the symbolic nature of conceptions of mystical forces since no such conceptions are involved.

The third possibility is that the actor conceives of the practice as clearly mystical but the observer is convinced that there is, in fact, a sound empirical basis for it. Quite a number of instances can be included in this category since it is not unusual in many societies to attribute the effectiveness of all sorts of substances and techniques to extraordinary powers or forces. An example would be the use of hallucinogenic substances, the properties of which are attributed by the users to spiritual powers operating in or through the substances as in the case of the peyote cult of Indian peoples of Central America.

Much more mundane things, however, may be considered to embody a mystical power which is the source of their effectiveness. A favourite knife, a particularly well-balanced spear may be thought to possess such extraordinary qualities. In fact, in so far as tribal peoples can be said to be animists, all objects contain certain spiritual powers which give them their particular qualities and capacities. Perhaps such ideas, also, were the origin of elements of legends such as the Sword of Excalibur.

The frequent attribution of what we consider to be mundane capacities of things to extraordinary powers need not imply that primitive peoples always see such powers as supernatural. The supernatural is a concept which belongs to the Western conceptual system. Other peoples may or may not possess such a concept. The extraordinary, the extra-mundane, does not necessarily belong to a separate realm of reality beyond this world. It may be conceived, as may various non-material entities – 'spirits', 'demons', 'powers', and so on – to be very much part of this everyday world but nevertheless special and out of the ordinary. In short, our conceptual categories may be quite inadequate to express the ideas and conceptions of other cultures, which may have considerable complexity and subtlety which are difficult to convey except in terms of their own languages and conceptual systems.

These considerations should alert us to a potential problem in giving an account of the beliefs of cultures very different from our own, often termed the problem of translation. How can the distinctive conceptions found in other cultures be conveyed without distortion in terms which may carry quite the wrong connotations or simply fail to convey the correct connotations? One way of coping with this problem which a number of anthropologists have used is to provide and to use terms from the languages of the peoples they have studied indicating the way those terms are used by native speakers in their own languages. Such a practice goes a long way towards avoiding misunderstandings but cannot, of course, completely remove the difficulty since it can only be used up to a point. Too extensive a use of the method would so pepper an ethnographic monograph with unfamiliar terms that it may become too difficult to follow. Taken to extremes the reader would practically have to learn the unfamiliar language.

A second danger involved in finding out about the beliefs of other peoples is that the fieldworker who asks questions may be forcing the respondents to think in unfamiliar terms and to confront issues and possibilities they have never had to consider before. This might be particularly true if they are asked, for example, about what appear to be, from the point of view of the investigator, ambiguities and contradictions but which have never been perceived to be so on the part of the respondents. There is a real danger that the answers they give will be unreliable, misleading, ill-considered or even invented for the purpose of the moment, namely to satisfy the inquisitive stranger.

The obvious way to avoid the problem is never to ask questions but simply to watch and listen in the hope that things will become clear in time. It is not usually clear from ethnographic studies whether anthropological fieldworkers always observe this ideal methodological rule. In practice it would clearly be very difficult to do so perfectly, since circumstances and conversations which would reveal what the anthropologist needs to know but which are taken as understood in the culture, will occur only infrequently and perhaps never at all, at least during the necessarily limited time in the field. In practice the best that can be achieved is simply to limit questions to those which the fieldworker feels would be ones which do not challenge assumptions, which do not, in the very asking, stretch the understandings of the actors or the limits of the conceptual systems under investigation.

The lesson to be drawn from the above observations is that learning about, understanding and even giving an account of the beliefs and practices of other cultures is not necessarily or usually straightforward and simple. There are many potential pitfalls and great care must be taken not to distort beliefs by forcing them into the framework of a conceptual system which is alien to them and which is incapable of expressing them. It has to be remembered that to describe the beliefs of other cultures is potentially to discover alternative ways of looking at the world.

The fourth and final possibility we need to examine stemming from the discrepancy between the actor's and observer's viewpoints is that where the actor considers the practice to be mystical and where, as far as the observer is concerned, there is no sound empirical basis for it. This category is straightforward and can clearly be labelled magic in the strongest sense since both actor and observer are agreed that there is something beyond ordinary empirical action involved even if they disagree about whether it achieves the intended effects. With such practices, what we have to account for is not simply the fact of the practice in the absence of, as far as we are concerned, evidence that it is effective, but also the belief that it involves something special and extraordinary. In taking account of the mystical element it is likely that the absence of evidence that the technique does actually work is highly relevant.

These various categories of 'magical' practice may well admit of rather different theoretical and explanatory approaches. There is no sense in looking for the symbolism in practices which are considered mundane by the practitioner. In the case of practices which clearly do work but which are considered mystical by the practitioner, the fact that they do actually work would seem to make an analysis in terms of symbolism less likely to be productive. A neo-Tylorean approach may prove more enlightening in this case. Where both actor and observer regard the practices as mystical, a neo-Tylorean approach could also apply but there would seem to be more scope for a symbolic approach than in the case of empirically sound mystical action.

With these preliminary observations made we can now proceed to examine the symbolic/functionalist and the neo-Tylorean approaches. The former is most explicitly set out and discussed in the work of John Beattie (1964, 1966, 1970). Beattie argues that magical beliefs and rituals must be interpreted as essentially symbolic in nature – as expressive acts and sentiments. Magic is not fundamentally, in his view, the application of empirical techniques which the actors believe will work but which in fact do not, although he acknowledges that the actors do believe they work and do carry them out in order to produce the desired results. It is fundamentally expressive, according to Beattie, the instrumental aspect being only a surface and superficial one. Magic is more like art than science and requires a different type of analysis from that of instrumental behaviour if we are to understand it. It requires an analysis in terms of the meaning of the behaviour.

What is being symbolised in rites and rituals, Beattie argues, are desires and sentiments of importance for society and for the individual. Some anthropologists who adopt this approach go even further than Beattie and claim that rites are really nothing more than symbolic statements and dramatic expressions about the structure of relationships which exist in groups and in the society (see, for example, Leach, 1954).

Clearly, the denial that the expressed purposes of rites on the part of their practitioners are what the rites are fundamentally concerned with raises the question of why the practitioners believe them to be instrumentally effective at all. If the expressed purposes of the rites are irrelevant to the way we must interpret and understand them, how are we to account for the fact that they are understood by the practitioner to be aimed at producing a concrete result? Beattie's answer is that it is the act of symbolising itself which generates the conviction of their effectiveness. The acting out of desires and the expression of sentiments create the conviction in their power to affect the world.

For Beattie, then, the question of whether magical rites are rational or irrational simply does not arise. It is not the sort of behaviour to which criteria of rationality can meaningfully be applied. Since it is not essentially instrumental, means–ends activity, despite its practitioners' own account of what they are doing, but symbolic in nature, the way to understand it is to uncover the meanings embodied in it.

The weakness of this symbolic interpretation of magic and ritual lies in its dismissal of the actor's own understanding and account of his or her own actions. There are serious dangers in taking such a position. The first difficulty it presents is that it is necessary to explain why the actor has this understanding of the behaviour. Beattie's answer that the act of symbolising something creates a conviction that the real world is thereby affected is not at all satisfactory. He does not, in the first place, show that this is so but only asserts that it is. It is not even a very plausible assertion. Why should the act of symbolising create such a conviction? Symbolic behaviour is common in all societies but does not for the most part lead to those who practise it believing that it is effective in acting upon the material world. The connection between the allegedly symbolic behaviour and the belief in its effectiveness, therefore, remains obscure and somewhat mysterious in Beattie's account.

This 'solution' to the problem of the discrepancy between the observer's and the actor's account of what is going on in magical ritual brings Beattie, in any case, to a position which is not far removed from that of Tylor and Frazer whose evolutionary, intellectualist theories Beattie, a functionalist, would repudiate. To say that because some action symbolises some desire it induces a conviction that the desire will be fulfilled is not very different from saying that magical thought substitutes ideal associations for real causal connections. It seems that Beattie believes that for practitioners of magic to symbolise an end deceives them into thinking that they are bringing about the end; the similarity, the ideal connection, is taken to be a real causal connection – precisely the position of Tylor and Frazer which Beattie rejects.

A second difficulty with Beattie's approach is that not all magical rituals act out the desired end or are in any way symbolic of it. They are clearly instrumental in form but do not symbolically recreate the desired event or outcome. Examples are the use of medicines, ordering or commanding a spirit to do something, and so on. This poses serious problems for Beattie's claim that conviction of the rites' effectiveness derives from the symbolic acting out of the aim.

Whether or not magical rites act out the desired end, equally serious a problem in Beattie's approach is the fact that he gives no explanation of why symbolic actions expressive of sentiments important for society should take an instrumental form at all. If the belief in the efficacy of the rites is the consequence of symbolising that which is of social value, why do they take an instrumental form in the first place? Why do they not simply symbolise in appropriate ways what is of social importance rather than looking as if they are intended to achieve a desired result? Instrumental behaviour is normally motivated by the prior desire and intention to achieve something concrete but Beattie argues that the belief that something concrete is being achieved derives from the action – action which is really directed at doing something quite different, namely expessing sentiments which are socially important.

The neo-Tylorean approach avoids these problems since it does not disregard the actor's own understanding of his or her own behaviour. A leading exponent of this approach is Robin Horton (1967, 1968, 1982). Horton argues that magical and religious beliefs are attempted explanations of phenomena and techniques for manipulating the world. In short they are like science and technology – like, but not exactly the same, not simply a sort of inferior science. They deal with the same kinds of questions and problems, they have similar aims, but their methods are different.

Horton points to a whole range of similarities between magico-religious beliefs and practices on the one hand and science on the other. For example, both search for unity underlying apparent diversity, for simplicity underlying apparent complexity, for order underlying apparent disorder, for regularity underlying apparent anomaly. Both science and magico-religious belief and practice construct a scheme of entities or forces which operate behind or within the world of common-sense observation. Also, both science and magico-religion transcend the limitations of common-sense views of causality and interconnection. Science will connect, for example, malaria with mosquitos whereas magical belief will connect it with malevolent individuals who have witchcraft powers. Science and primitive belief both tend to break up the world of common sense into various aspects and then reassemble them in a different way. They both abstract from reality, analyse and then reintegrate that reality.

The key difference between science and magico-religion concerns the absence of alternative perceptions in the latter.

> in traditional cultures there is no developed awareness of alternatives to the established body of theoretical tenets; whereas in scientifically oriented cultures, such an awareness is highly developed. It is this difference we refer to when we say that traditional cultures are 'closed' and scientifically oriented cultures 'open.'
>
> (1970, p. 152)

It is the 'closed' nature of traditional thought which gives it its compelling and unchallengeable character; it becomes sacred and any threat to it is the threat of chaos and disorder.

Horton lists a number of more specific differences between science and magico-religion. For example, words and language in a closed system of thought take on a special and often magical significance because words are the means of making contact with reality and in a closed system it is impossible to escape the tendency to see a unique and intimate link between words and things. More broadly, the differences between science and magico-religion can be divided into two groups – those connected with the presence or absence of alternative views of reality and those connected with the presence or absence of threats to the established body of theory. Again, Horton lists a great many instances.

For Horton, the whole basis upon which anthropologists have approached primitive beliefs is somewhat shaky. An important aspect of this basis has been the desire to find sense and value in magical belief systems, to claim coherence and comprehensibility for them by the claim that they are not really about explaining the world or achieving concrete results, whatever appearances and the understandings of the practitioners themselves might suggest, but are really symbolic. This attitude is one which is thought and intended to be tolerant and approving, rather than critical, of the cultures of tribal peoples. What Horton's approach implies is that, on reflection, it is actually a somewhat patronising attitude since it acknowledges the beliefs of such peoples to be false but kindly claims that they nevertheless have social value which the anthropologist can see but which the people themselves cannot (see also Horton, 1973 for an extended discussion of this point).

The desire to be generous in the description of other cultures on the part of anthropologists and to avoid interpretations that imply inferiority in comparison with Western culture is one which Gellner also believes has produced unfortunate unintended consequences (Gellner, 1970). He argues that in trying to make sense of apparently nonsensical primitive beliefs and practices anthropologists have found that they are able to do so if they place these beliefs and practices in their social context. They have tended to take into account just that amount of social context that is necessary to give the beliefs and practices the appearance of sense and reasonableness. This Gellner calls the 'tolerance-engendering' contextual interpretation of primitive magic and religion. It has a definite social function: 'The "Social" theory of religion appears to have, in our society, the following function: it enables us to attribute meaning to assertions which might otherwise be found to lack it' (Gellner, 1970, p. 41).

In Gellner's view there are serious dangers in this approach. It may lead to the misdescription and misinterpretation of other cultures. It may blind us to the possibilities for change in a system of ideas because change often does come about through criticism and questioning of prevailing ideas that come to be seen as inconsistent, inadequate or contradictory. It blinds us also to the possible uses of incoherence and ambiguity. Vagueness in concepts, ideas and beliefs is often very useful. It can allow a certain flexibility and subtlety. In short, Gellner is arguing that we can very often only make sense of other cultures by recognising the *non-sense* in their beliefs and practices.

In case this sounds rather functionalist – that he is claiming that everything is for the best in the best of all possible worlds such that even incoherence exists because it is good and necessary – Gellner points out that he is by no means denying that for the most part incoherence and contradictoriness in a system of ideas are highly dysfunctional. His point is that they can, however, be useful in some circumstances. They can also lead to change rather than the stabilisation of a social system. Every system of ideas embodies a degree of incoherence and inconsistency; there is no perfectly coherent, unassailable system of ideas. To think otherwise would entail a denial of the possibility of change or progress and would raise the problem of how we could ever explain change or progress.

Another advantage mentioned by Gellner that lack of clarity and ambiguity may have is that it can often be put to manipulative uses. It can be useful to groups and individuals involved in struggles for resources, power and advantage in furthering their interests and in controlling others. It is useful, for example, to be able to damn an opponent by utilising the slipperiness of meaning that words and concepts often have.

The advantage of Horton's approach, then, is that it does recognise the beliefs for what they are without having to assume that those who espouse them are in any way inferior, since being wrong about the world is not a prerogative of tribal cultures. Science is constantly having to revise its picture of the world and many scientific theories have turned out to be false. Recognition of this allows us to treat all beliefs from a sociological point of view as being on the same level. It is a common fault of symbolist interpretations that they assume that what does not appear to be founded upon a firm empirical basis must therefore be explained and understood as essentially symbolic behaviour. But as Peel (1968) has pointed out, what the symbolists actually mean in taking this position is that the practices they consider to require an explanation in terms of symbolic behaviour are not empirically well founded in their perception. They might well be so in the perception of the practitioners, however. The point is not whether the observing anthropologist or sociologist thinks the techniques work or not but whether the practitioners do. It is not legitimate to say that because we know that the techniques do not work that the practitioner must be symbolising something, when in the mind of the practitioner the techniques *are* thought to work.

It is not, however, only the symbolists who assume that an action requires special explanation only if it is one which does not seem to be founded upon a sound empirical basis. Intellectualist approaches have often made exactly the same assumptions, ignoring the fact that the practices are indeed thought to be empirically sound in the culture in which they occur. As Peel (1968) points out, both true and false beliefs should sociologically receive the same treatment since false beliefs are not false to those who believe them. A writer who takes this approach considerably further is Barnes (1974). He argues that none of the criteria used to distinguish science from non-science actually does so. He argues that a kind of dual standard has governed the usual approach to beliefs. Science is seen to be rational and unproblematic – it is not necessary to explain why scientific beliefs are accepted. A process of 'natural' reason underlies such beliefs. Magical and religious belief is seen as a deviation from this 'natural' reason requiring explanation.

Barnes discusses the various attempts to characterise science as a mode of thought and to determine what makes it distinctive. For example, science is said to be empirical and to deal with observed facts. In fact, Barnes argues, there are many unobserved theoretical entities in science. What counts as a fact is to some extent determined by theory. Science does not merely describe the world in factual terms. Again, if one says, as Popper (1963) does, that such criteria as falsifiability, simplicity, and so on are the distinguishing criteria of rational thought, there are problems, according to Barnes. It is not possible to review his detailed arguments here but, in short, his conclusion is that there is no baseline of natural reason against which one can judge some ideas as unproblematic and others as needing explanation. We have to treat all ideas, scientific and non-scientific in the same way. Consequently, magic and religion do not require special explanation. Any attempt to give to the ideas of modern Western industrial society a special status does less than justice to the ideas of others. Ideas, Barnes claims, only need a special explanation if they are not the normal and standard beliefs found in the society. Most beliefs are held because they are part of a culture and acquired through the process of socialisation. It is only when someone or some group comes to adopt new and different beliefs that one needs a particular explanation of them.

Barnes's position stands or falls to a considerable extent on the question of whether science can be characterised as having a distinct method. This is a complex philosophical issue and cannot be resolved here. His claim, however, that it is only new and different beliefs that need particular explanations, is not entirely credible. In trying to understand magical belief we are attempting to understand under what sort of conditions people are disposed to think magically. Of course, the beliefs are part of a culture passed from one generation to the next. The question is why do they continue to be passed on as part of a culture. What conditions promote their persistence and their credibility? One cannot dismiss the problem in the way that Barnes does. Nevertheless, he makes a very important point in drawing our attention to the fact that it is perhaps illegitimate to set aside our own beliefs as unproblematic while assuming that the beliefs of others require explanation because they do not square with our own.

Criticisms of the neo-Tylorean position have been many. In so far as Horton is concerned they have tended to be centred on his characterisation of scientific culture as 'open', critical and involving alternatives. He has answered many of the points but some have led him to modify his original position (1982). The 'open/closed' dichotomy he admits was too rigidly drawn. Challenges to the current scientific orthodoxy are seen as just as threatening in Western scientific culture as challenges to magico-religious orthodoxy are in traditional societies and are usually resisted by the scientific establishment.

Horton also accepts the reformulation of his position on the presence or absence of alternatives put forward by Gellner (1973). He would now see the contrast not so much in terms of awareness of alternatives but more in terms of the competition between theoretical alternatives. As Gellner pointed out, traditional societies are not so lacking in alternative conceptions as Horton and others have supposed. Also, awareness or not of alternatives is something that has to be said of individuals whereas it is the competition between theoretical perspectives that really characterises modern science in contrast to traditional thought.

If this difference between science and traditional magico-religion is not as clear cut as Horton originally argued, Horton's claim that magico-religion is similar to science seems to be weakened. This does not mean that the neo-Tylorean approach is fatally flawed, however. Ross (1971) and Skorupski (1973a, 1973b, 1976) have pointed out that there is more than one position embodied in contemporary intellectualism. 'Literalism' is the proposition that traditional magico-religious beliefs and practices mean exactly what they say, namely that the rites have instrumental efficacy, and this is what they are fundamentally about. Second, there is the 'theory building' position characteristic of Horton which holds that traditional magico-religion is in many respects like science. Criticisms of the latter position are, according to Ross, generally valid. Science is fundamentally different from traditional magico-religion: it is the product of a long and complex development; it is characterised by parsimony in its explanatory strategies as opposed to the complexity of religion in this respect; it attempts to predict whereas religion seeks only to influence events; religious propositions are generally non-falsifiable; they are not based upon experimental observation; they utilise the same model for everything whereas science uses many.

Skorupski points out that Horton's evidence that traditional magico-religious thought lacks, or is intolerant of, alternatives, which are seen as threatening, is largely drawn from taboo customs and beliefs. His approach, however, would not explain the fact of sacred anomalies. In many tribal societies that which is anomalous, in the sense of being between categories of thought, is often considered to be an abomination. However, it is not uncommon for such things to be treated, in other instances or in other societies, as sacred. In Horton's approach they should all be abominations since all are threatening to the established sense of order.

As for awareness of alternatives, Skorupski claims that while tribal societies do not seem capable of generating alternatives from within, they are, nevertheless, certainly able to conceive of alternatives. New ideas from outside, however, do not simply supplant old ideas but tend to be incorporated alongside in syncretistic fashion. Frequently, rather than become convinced that they were mistaken in their old views, the members of traditional societies absorb new ideas by claiming that the world has changed, so that what used to be true is no longer so; the old gods are seen not as false but to have gone away. Traditional thought, Skorupski concludes from this, lacks a conception of ideas being no more than *ideas* about an *independent* reality. Rather than being like Western science, Skorupski claims, traditional magico-religion is more like Western religion. In both, contradiction and ambiguity are tolerated, both contain mysteries and paradoxes. Horton (1973) has replied denying both that toleration of paradox is at all characteristic of African traditional thought or that Western science lacks it. All systems of ideas, since they will inevitably embody contradictions will also contain a degree of paradox. Neither traditional magic nor science is particularly comfortable with paradox, nor for that matter is Western religion. What does characterise Western religion, however, is the acceptance of mystery. In this it is quite *unlike* traditional African thought. The comparison between science and magical thought remains, therefore, in Horton's view a valid one.

Skorupski's criticisms, if they are valid, do not, however, invalidate the literalist position. In fact, criticisms of literalism, according to Ross, have not proved at all convincing. In any case, Skorupski points out, a symbolist interpretation of traditional magico-religion is not incompatible with the literalist aspect of intellectualism. Skorupski thus suggests the possibility of a synthesis between intellectualism or neo-Tyloreanism and symbolic interpretations.

To achieve such a synthesis it is first necessary to disentangle a number of different types of action which have tended to be lumped together under the term 'ritual'. This Skorupski attempts to do. He points out that much magical and religious ritual consists simply of social interaction in the normal pattern of social interaction with beings and entities – spirits, gods, ancestors – which are within the actor's social field. Religious cosmology often extends the social field beyond its human members. Dealing with such entities is like dealing with other human beings. They can be entreated, persuaded and should be shown respect and deference. The special character of the interaction reflects only the special character of the being concerned or the special nature of the relationship, just as interaction between a king or chief and a subject or subordinate usually has a special character. There is nothing especially expressive or symbolic in this sort of behaviour. The point has also been made by Ahern (1981) who reports that much traditional Chinese ritual took the form of interpersonal interaction between humans and gods in which were used such techniques as would normally be used to influence the behaviour of other human beings. In China this involved forms of 'political control', that is, the utilisation of means of control that were typical in political life such as the exercise of bureaucratic authority which one god may have been believed to have over other lesser spirits, the use of written documents stating the rights of the supplicant and the obligations of the spirit, or the employment of the rules of etiquette by asking in such a way that refusal would be very difficult.

A second type of magical action does involve an element of symbolisation of a certain kind in that the practitioner does symbolically act out what is desired while fully believing that it is being brought about by the magical action. The magician does not, however, attempt to bring it about by the use of symbols but rather whatever is used to symbolise something is perceived to be or to become that thing. The act of symbolising is not, in this account, unlike the interpretations of symbolic/functionalists, the cause of the belief in its efficacy. This Skorupski terms an identificationist interpretation of certain types of magic. What is used to symbolise something is identified with that thing. The wax effigy that the witch uses to symbolise a victim is actually seen to be, to have become, the victim in much the same way that a pepperpot might be used to stand for a vehicle in an after-dinner account of a traffic accident. After all, he points out, a wax effigy does not actually resemble the victim all that closely. It might in fact look like a great many people. The point is that it is made to represent the victim and in the last resort almost anything can serve this purpose. This suggests that what is involved is not homoeopathy in Frazer's sense but identification. Of course the magician will tend to choose particularly appropriate things as symbols if at all possible. But this is not the same as mistaking ideal connections for real causal connections, according to Skorupski. Rather, it makes one thing stand for another – it creates an identity. There are not two series of events with one causally acting upon the other, for example, piercing an effigy with a pin, on the one hand and the experience of pain by the victim, on the other, but only one – the magical act. This analysis leads Skorupski to reject Horton's contention that magic often operates through the power of words, for example, names. It is not that the name is in itself effective but that it is identified with the victim.

Other types of magical action involve the definite idea of contagious transfer of properties. Again there is little that is symbolic about this. There are, after all, Skorupski points out, many instances in which contagious transfer of properties does take place such as the spread of infections or transfer of heat from a warmer to a colder body. It is not at all unreasonable to generalise to a whole range of other things from these sorts of experience.

Finally, some magical acts take the form of operative acts which are not clearly distinguished in the minds of the practitioners from causal effectiveness. An operative act simply states that some state of affairs pertains. For example 'I declare this meeting open', or 'I name this child John'. These are performative statements which bring about a state of affairs by being made but not in any causal manner. Magic, Skorupski suggests, often uses such performative state-ments. The wax effigy in witchcraft may be declared to be the victim.

Operative acts of this kind are often ritualised and ceremonialised. That is to say they are performed in such a way that it is clear to all they are being done. Ceremonial is a way of doing this in a very formal style in order to mark the action out as special. Skorupski suggests that much ritual which is in fact a form of operative ceremony becomes understood in the minds of the participants or observers as having causal power. Absolution, for example, might be interpreted as an act which alters the social relationship between priest and parishioner, and which reaffirms obligations. This sacrament, however, may be interpreted by those concerned as actually bringing about a causal change in the absolved sinner. This is a 'reifying misinterpretation' of such a sacrament in which it becomes a sort of 'transcendental soul cleansing machinery'.

Another writer who points to the strongly performative nature of magical rituals is Tambiah but in his case the point is used in support of a clearly symbolist position (Tambiah, 1973). What Tambiah fails to recognise is that such performative acts do seem, as Skorupski emphasises, to be misconstrued as being causal in nature by practitioners. Tambiah makes the mistake of assuming that because magical acts often have a performative and symbolic–expressive aspect, it is never appropriate to judge them in terms of the 'true/false' criteria of science.

This simply does not follow if Skorupski's point about reificatory mystification is valid.

Skorupski's suggestions, then, offer a way in which an essentially literalist position can account for the symbolic aspect of much magic and ritual, and which might be built into a theory of magic and ritual which acknowledges and accounts for both the instrumental and symbolic dimensions it clearly has but of which one is ignored by each side of the neo-Tylorean/symbolic functionalist debate. Such a theory, however, has yet to emerge in any systematic form. It will clearly need to address the question of the extent to which magical belief and behaviour are linked to the need for meaning in life. Instrumental behaviour designed to produce a definite effect can also embody meanings. The separation of symbolic–expressive action which is not believed or intended to have any effects upon anything as a distinct category set against instrumental action is, as Charles Taylor has pointed out (1982), a quintessentially modern notion. Before the eighteenth century, scientific theories often had an expressive dimension. An example Taylor uses is the language of 'correspondences', used by Bacon and others to attempt to refute Galileo's claim that there were moons orbiting Jupiter. This doctrine held that elements in wholly different domains of being corresponded to each other in virtue of embodying the same principles. For example, since there are seven metals then there must also be seven, and just seven, planetary bodies and the moons of Jupiter cannot, therefore, exist. Taylor refers also to Brecht's *Galileo* in which theologians offer a refutation of the existence of the moons of Jupiter based upon biblical exegesis in which it is 'proved' that they cannot exist, completely disregarding the evidence of the senses provided by Galileo's telescope as irrelevant and illusory. Such ideas seemed perfectly sensible to even the most eminent and clever minds in this age since it was believed that knowledge of the world and coming into attunement with it were one and the same thing. Understanding the world scientifically and uncovering its meaning in terms of human purposes was the same activity. Modern thought has separated them and expects nothing from the former which is relevant to the question of the meaning of reality in relation to human life and existence. Traditional societies have generally sought to explain and to control reality not simply instrumentally but in a way that expresses what is seen to be its meaning. The Azande explanation of illness in terms of witchcraft again serves as an illustration. Illness is not just the arbitrary and accidental consequence of chance for the Azande. It is the consequence of evil intentions of enemies and rivals. Death from sickness is not a meaningless misfortune but understood and confronted in the context of human relationships.

Before leaving the subject of magic and its rationality, however, mention should be made of some of the more concrete attempts by anthropologists to make sense of it. The debate about magic has tended to be dominated by questions of a fairly abstract and philosophical nature and by comparisons between Western and traditional thought and its rationality. Anthropologists such as Bronislav Malinowski and Raymond Firth, however, have tried to set magic in its everyday context, drawing attention to its significance and role in the organisation and regulation of productive activities. Malinowski was one of the first to show that it had such a role. Firth has particularly emphasised this aspect in his studies of the island of Tikopia in Polynesia (see especially Firth, 1939).

Firth argued that magic can throw a cloak of sanctity over technical operations and can create an atmosphere of significance around the task inducing an attitude of seriousness towards it. It sets the pace for the work marking out its various stages and is thus a useful organising device. It gives confidence and alleviates anxiety and in case of failure may provide an explanation and an alibi – the magical procedures can be said to have not been carried out correctly.

Such observations do perhaps help us to understand what might otherwise be very puzzling behaviour as long as we do not take them for a full and sufficient explanation. Magic cannot be said to exist in order to do things without embroiling us in all the difficulties of functionalist accounts discussed above. It is important to remember, however, as Malinowski pointed out, that magic is not just a substitute for technical procedures but an adjunct to them – an auxiliary technique. Whenever possible, tribal peoples do not rely on magic but use mundane empirical techniques. Magic appears to be an aid in the application of empirical techniques – a means of stimulating certain attitudes and of ordering and organising things.

Although Firth follows Malinowski in attributing a confidence-promoting function to magic in situations of uncertainty, he points out that this is not a universal correlation. Only in certain societies do people use magical means in situations of uncertainty and even then only in certain kinds of situation. Magic is only one form of cultural response to situations of this kind. Other types of response mentioned by Firth include reliance upon a beneficent God or spirit, reliance upon probability (another name for science) and simply fatalism. We do not know why this variation occurs.

4 Religion and emotion

Religion, the emotionalists argued, is not a matter of intellectual curiosity, the quest for material mastery, or of cold dispassionate reasoning. The intellectualists had made primitive humanity seem far too rational and had neglected the emotional side in which they sought to locate the fundamental roots of religiosity. Religious beliefs, for these theorists, were not the product of reasoning from observations of the experiences of dreams or of inferences about the connections between things but were derived from emotional or affective states of mind. The fact that tribal peoples do not attempt to rely solely upon magic and religion, overlooked by the intellectualists, pointed to there being particular reasons for the supplementation of ordinary empirical techniques and normal rationality by the use of magic and religion – reasons which had little to do with rationality.

MARETT

Prominent among the emotionalist theorists was R. R. Marett. In *The Threshold of Religion*, published in 1914, he criticised the views of Tylor and Frazer for characterising the mind of early humans as too rational and dispassionate. Religion and magic, Marett argued, are not the product of reason but of emotional or affective states. The fact that ordinary technical activity prevails much of the time among tribal peoples points to a non-rational root in magic and religion. Magical and religious behaviour involves the suspension of normal rationality.

A second criticism made of the intellectualists was that they supposed that religious and ritual activity was motivated or stimulated by beliefs and ideas. For Marett a distinctive characteristic of ritual behaviour was that it stems directly from emotions and not from beliefs. It is ritual action which is fundamental while beliefs are secondary from the point of view of understanding and explaining religion and magic since emotions give rise to action rather than reflection. As Marett puts it 'savage religion is something not so much thought out as danced out' (1914, p. xxxi). The source of the emotions which underlie religious ritual behaviour is the feeling experienced by 'primitive' peoples of the presence of a strange, mysterious and occult power or force for which Marett used the Polynesian word *mana*. The emotion experienced in the face of things possessing *mana* he characterised as a blend of fear, wonder and attraction, summed up by the term awe. *Mana* pervades many things. It is not confined to specific objects although certain things have more of it than others. The sort of things that may have *mana* includes ritual objects, powerful or important individuals, special words, corpses, symbols, special places and locations, rocks, stones, trees, plants, animals. Things which possess mana are generally set apart from ordinary mundane things by the use of taboos.

This type of experience, Marett argued, predates and is more fundamental than belief in spirits. It represents the earliest and original form of religious experience and is older than animism. Marett accepted Tylor's account of animism but criticised his claim that this was the earliest form of religion. It was, for Marett, a later development of those impulses which sprang originally and spontaneously from emotions generated by the experience of *mana*.

Marett's account of magic was based upon similar assumptions to his theory of religion, namely that it was equally a product of emotions and sprang spontaneously out of emotional tension. He thought, in fact, that in the pre-animistic stage magic and religion are not clearly differentiated and used the term 'magico-religious' to refer to it. Whereas the religious impulses sprang from the experience of *mana*, the magical impulses were stimulated by strong desires or fears in situations where ordinary means for fulfilling the desires or alleviating the fears were lacking. Resort is made in such situations to magical make-believe in which mimetic rites figure prominently. Rather in the same manner as Tylor and Frazer, Marett believed that magic is substituted for practical and effective action where the latter seems not to be available. For Marett, however, it is the emotional tension generated by such situations that gives rise to it, not practical aims. If such situations occur frequently and typically, the magical response becomes standardised and customary. This is what Marett calls developed magic as opposed to rudimentary magic which lacks standardisation and the backing of social custom. In developed magic the actor does not really believe that the action produces the desired end but is aware that it is only symbolic. However, giving symbolic expression to desires and fears has a cathartic effect which is recognised by the practitioner. It alleviates tension, stimulates courage and hope, and strengthens resolve. Consequently, magical techniques continue to be utilised even though they are known to be ineffective. Magic is not, therefore, a pseudo-science as Frazer had argued, but quite a different sort of activity with a quite different basis.

Marett's emphasis on emotion in religion and magic was a necessary corrective to the earlier views of the intellectualists who had provided a rather one-sided account but the type of emotionalist position that he adopted is equally beset with problems. Exactly the same criticism can be made of his claim that there was a pre-animistic stage of religious development as of Tylor's claim that animism was the earliest form, namely that there is no evidence for it at all.

A second criticism of Marett is that he does not show why some things have *mana* and some things do not or why different things in different societies are felt to have *mana*. The nature of and reasons for the specific emotion and kind of tension experienced in the presence of things said to have *mana* remain obscure. Emotions such as love, hate, or anger are felt for definite and usually perfectly understandable reasons. In short, they occur in certain situations and contexts such that when one knows about the situation or context one understands why the emotion is felt (Phillips, 1976, p. 49-50). The trouble with the type of emotion said to be felt in the face of *mana* is that it is a special emotion and it is not at all clear why it occurs or what it is about certain objects and situations which causes it. Many of the things which are said to possess *mana* do so, however, clearly because there is a belief of some kind involved. A name or a place has *mana* because it is believed that it has certain powers or is the dwelling place of a spirit. In other words, most instances of the kind of emotion and phenomenon that Marett is talking about rest upon a prior set of beliefs, that is to say a cognitive factor, and are not the spontaneous experience of emotion and performance of accompanying ritual action that Marett thinks they are. The emotion derives from a belief and the actions similarly. This allows us to understand why some things have *mana* and some things do not and why the set of things which does varies from one society to another – the beliefs vary from one society to another.

Even if there is no obvious belief directly involved in producing the type of experience that Marett places at the foundation of religion, it is likely that there is, nevertheless, a cognitive process which draws upon ideas and beliefs which are part of the religious and intellectual background and culture of the individual undergoing the experience. Many individuals have reported what they describe as an awesome experience of the presence of the divine or the sacred. It is this type of experience which led writers like Rudolf Otto ([1917], 1923) in *The Idea of the Holy,* published only three years after Marett's book, to speak of the basis of religion as being the experience of the holy or the numinous. The interesting question is, however, whether the experience is interpreted differently by different individuals and differently in different cultures. It may well be that some individuals are disposed to interpret certain experiences, emotions or feelings which are intense and awesome in the traditional terms of the religious culture to which they belong, namely, as the presence of God or of the divine. Those who reject the notion of the divine or sacred may interpret their experience in quite a different way. In a Hindu or Buddhist community certain experiences may commonly be interpreted as memories of previous lives or existences since belief in rebirth is a central aspect of the culture. It is not uncommon to find people in such cultures remembering incidents from previous lives. This is relatively rare in religious cultures which lack any strong belief in rebirth or reincarnation. In other words, in making sense of experiences which may be out of the ordinary, people will resort to ideas and beliefs with which they are familiar and which have some credibility. They may even be forced to resort to such ideas and conclusions, perhaps to their own surprise, for the lack of any credible alternative.[1]

A further difficulty with Marett's account of religion is that it is often the case that rather than religious activity being a response to emotion it is the cause of certain emotions. Marett and similar theorists who emphasised the emotional roots of religion were criticised by sociological theorists, such as Durkheim, for not recognising that participation in religious ritual and ceremonies is frequently obligatory and socially expected. For at least some of the participants, and perhaps even all of them, their participation in the ritual will not be the product of emotions. There would be little point in socially sanctioning participation if rituals were the spontaneous expression of emotional tension. The obligatory character of participation implies that some, and perhaps all, members of the relevant group or community would not otherwise be motivated to participate.

A further point made by sociological theorists was that such rituals may induce emotions of a certain kind in those obliged to participate. Rites, rituals and ceremonies are as often, and perhaps even more often, occasions for inducing appropriate emotions in the participants as they are means of giving expression to emotions. In fact, the expression of appropriate emotions is often itself obligatory whether or not they are sincerely felt. The problem with the emotionalist position is that it fails to recognise that the relationship between rituals and emotions is highly variable. There is no necessary or uniform link between specific emotions and religious action. The participants in religious ritual might be elated or bored, awed or blasé, sombre or light-hearted. As Evans-Pritchard points out, it would be absurd to say that a priest is not performing a religious rite when he says mass unless he is in a certain emotional state (1965, p. 44).

MALINOWSKI

If Marett could be criticised for having no direct experience of tribal societies the most important of the emotionalist theorists, Bronislaw Malinowski, certainly could not. Whereas Marett made light of the necessity of fieldwork experience, once remarking that to understand primitive mentality it was sufficient to experience an Oxford Common Room, Malinowski founded the tradition of direct participant observation in British anthropology which came to be *de rigeur* and, in the view of some, almost a qualifying initiation ritual for entry into the anthropological community. Malinowski is famous for making the Trobriand Islanders of Melanesia well known, spending several years in the field living with the people, learning their language and participating in their daily lives. Yet the conclusions he came to concerning their religious and magical life were not at all dissimilar to those of the armchair anthropologist, Marett. There is a strong emotionalist element in Malinowski's interpretation of magic and religion even though he is usually thought of as belonging to a sociological and indeed functionalist school influenced by the work of Durkheim. His functionalism is also prominent in his writings on religion and magic but the emotionalist element is sufficiently strong to lead Evans-Pritchard to classify him as a psychological and emotionalist theorist (Evans-Pritchard, 1965).

Whether Malinowski came to similar conclusions to Marett because Marett was actually right about Oxford Common Rooms or because Malinowski was influenced by his ideas and simply saw in the field what he expected to find, or interpreted what he saw so as to confirm prior theoretical predilections (this was certainly true of other aspects of his work as far as the influence of Freud was concerned), must remain a matter of speculation. Malinowski, however, does not base his ideas about magic and religion on the notion of *mana* but, because of his direct observation in the field, roots them in the contingencies, anxieties and uncertainties of day-to-day existence in tribal societies and by extension, all societies.

Religion and magic belong to the realm of the sacred which Malinowski distinguishes from that of the profane, following Durkheim. His characterisation of the sacred is reminiscent of Marett in that it is bound up with an attitude of awe and respect. While his concept of the sacred derives from Durkheim, however, the way he distinguishes between magic and religion is quite different. We saw in the previous chapter that for Malinowski magic is related to concrete purposes or definite outcomes which its practitioners wish to achieve while religious rites have no such concrete purpose or end result but are performed for their own sake.

Despite this fundamental difference between magic and religion Malinowski explains them in a similar way. Both are seen as essentially cathartic. They have their roots in emotional stress and tension to which they give release. The sources of this tension are to be found in the fact that human life is uncertain and stressful. Religion, Malinowski tells us, is deeply rooted in the necessities of human life and 'the stresses and strains of life, and the necessity of facing heavy odds' (1936, p. 59-60). It involves both a belief in Providence and in Immortality. The former consists in a belief in the existence of powers sympathetic to man and which can help him in his life. Such beliefs assist in enhancing man's real capacity to act effectively in the face of difficulty. A belief in Immortality is similarly indispensable for mental stability and for maintenance of social stability. The fact that religious ritual is a means of dealing with tension, anxiety and uncertainty explains why it usually accompanies the major life crises of birth, initiation into adulthood, marriage, and death.

A universal and by far the most important source of the emotional tension which underlies religious rites for Malinowski was the fact of death. A great deal, if not all early religion derives from it, he claimed. 'I think that all the phenomena generally described by such terms as animism, ancestor-worship, or belief in spirits and ghosts, have their root in man's integral attitude towards death' (1936, p. 27).

The religious act *par excellence* for Malinowski, then, is the ceremonial of death. The rituals which universally surround death and bereavement illustrate the cathartic function of religion very well, he argued. Mortuary rituals derive from the natural human fear of death. When a death occurs strong fears and emotions are generated in those close to the deceased. Such emotions can be dangerous and disruptive. A death disrupts relationships, breaks the normal pattern of people's lives and shakes the moral foundations of society. There is a tendency for the bereaved to sink into despair, to neglect their responsibilities and to behave in ways harmful to themselves and others. Group integration and solidarity tend to be undermined.

Mortuary rituals serve to channel such disruptive emotions along constructive rather than disruptive paths. It relieves the anxieties generated by the event and restores a degree of equilibrium. It often does this partly by reaffirming and strengthening a belief in immortality of the soul or spirit and thereby gives assurance to the bereaved that they are not doomed to everlasting extinction – a feeling always aroused by the experience of bereavement.

Malinowski, however, was aware that such rituals are not simply individual responses to events but are public and social affairs which involve communities. They, consequently, involve a wider circle than the immediate relatives and close associates of the deceased. In other words, Malinowski accepted the points that had been made against emotionalist theorists such as Marett that they had ignored the social dimension of religion. Malinowski sought to explain this public and social nature of religious rites once again in terms of their cathartic function. The involvement of the wider community lends force to the rituals and strengthens their effect in combatting disruptive emotions. 'Public pomp and ceremony take effect through the contagiousness of faith, through the dignity of unanimous consent, the impressiveness of collective behaviour' (Malinowski, 1974, p. 63).

Magic also arises in situations of emotional tension, Malinowski argued, but here the source of the tension lies in uncertainty about the outcome of practical activities. When some task, of which the outcome is uncertain, is undertaken, resort is made to magical techniques. Malinowski used what has become a famous example to illustrate this, namely the difference between lagoon and deep-sea fishing in the Trobriand Islands. The former is relatively reliable in terms of the catch that can be expected and there is little danger, whereas the catch from fishing in the open-sea is always very uncertain and there are many dangers involved. It is significant, then, that there is little magic attached to lagoon fishing but a great deal involved in open-sea fishing designed to ensure a good catch and ward off dangers (Malinowski, 1936, p. 22; 1974, pp. 30–1). Whenever, in the pursuit of practical ends man comes to a gap 'his anxiety, his fears and hopes, induce a tension in his organism which drives him to some sort of activity' (1974, p. 79). In such a situation of anxiety and tension he cannot remain passive; he has to do something. He is driven to engage in some form of substitute action in the face of his impotence to do anything directly practical; 'the most essential point about magic and religious ritual is that it steps in only where knowledge fails' (1936, p. 34). The activity substituted is generally some sort of acting out of the desired end. 'His organism reproduces the acts suggested by the anticipations of hope, dictated by the emotion so strongly felt' (1974, p. 79). Magic is founded upon the natural human response in situations of intense desire, fear or anxiety, namely 'the spontaneous enactment of the desired end in a practical impasse' (1974, p. 80). This spontaneous action creates a conviction in the minds of the practitioners that the rites have a concrete effect upon the world because it relieves the emotional tension in the circumstances of un-certainty. The practitioner, also, since he actually feels more confident as a result of this conviction and more calm as a result of the release of emotional tension, may well perform his tasks the more effectively.

Magic, however, as was perfectly evident to Malinowski in the field, is not wholly spontaneous. Its procedures are standardised, socially recognised and customary. Malinowski was well aware, in other words, of the social nature of magic. It may originate as spontaneous action but becomes part of a culture, standardised, learned and passed on from generation to generation. Effective magical rites, in the sense of being genuinely cathartic, are chanced upon or created by creative innovators, men of genius. Being particularly appropriate for circumstances commonly encountered, others take them up and in this way they become part of the culture and tradition. Its fundamental source is, however, in the emotional tensions of life. 'Magical ritual, most of the principles of magic, most of its spells and sub- stances, have been revealed to man in those passionate experiences which assail him in the impasse of his instinctive life and of his practical pursuits.' Malinowski, then, saw magic as 'founded on the belief that hope cannot fail nor desire deceive' (1974, p. 87). The function of magic, he said, is to 'ritualise man's optimism' (1974, p. 90).

Although this is clearly a psychological and emotionalist approach, Malinowski was strongly influenced by the prevailing intellectual fashion of functionalism and, in fact, considered himself to be a follower of functionalism. Consequently, he appended to his essentially emotionalist account of religion and magic a sociological and functionalist addition. He did not rely entirely upon the motives and dispositions of the individual in his analyses of religion and magic but supplemented this with an explanation in terms of the social functions of beliefs and rituals.

His functionalist side can be clearly seen if we take his analysis of initiation rituals for example. Of them he said:

> Such beliefs and practices, which put a halo of sanctity round tradition and a supernatural stamp upon it, will have a 'survival value' for the type of civilisation in which they have been evolved . . . they are a ritual and dramatic expression of the supreme power and value of tradition in primitive societies; they also serve to impress this power and value upon the minds of each generation, and they are at the same time an extremely efficient means of transmitting tribal lore, of ensuring continuity in tradition and of maintaining tribal cohesion.
>
> (1974, p. 40)

And to take the example of mortuary ritual once again, by counteracting the forces of fear, dismay and demoralisation it provides, he says, 'the most powerful means of reintegration of the group's shaken solidarity and the re-establishment of its morale' (1974, p. 53). Magic too has important social functions. Through its cathartic and confidence-generating functions it enables people to perform their tasks the more effectively and this is crucial for the stable conduct of social relations and social life.

Clearly, Malinowski's emotionalism is not open to the same kinds of criticism that Marett's is. Malinowski identifies quite clearly the type of situation in which emotional tension is experienced in a way which makes it perfectly comprehensible why the emotion is felt. What his approach fails to do, however, is to give an adequate account of the specific forms and variety of belief and ritual practice. An emotionalist approach, as we have seen, neglects the dimension of belief in attempting to move directly from emotion to behaviour. It overlooks the fact that there is no necessary link between a specific emotion and a specific action or form of behaviour. As a result, it does not adequately explain the specific form of religious or ritual behaviour and therefore does not explain why rituals differ from one society to another. Emotion and anxiety might possibly explain why some form of ritual is carried out. They do not explain the specific *form* of the ritual. Emotion and anxiety might explain why *something* is done in the situation but they do not explain *what* is done. There is nothing in the emotion of hatred *per se* which would suggest that by making a wax effigy of the hated person and piercing it with a needle, harm can be done to that person, as was allegedly the practice in Europe. There is nothing in the emotion of anxiety about an important outcome which would suggest that touching wood, to take a familiar example from our own culture, will bring about the desired outcome. Neither of these actions stem directly from the emotion alone. The specific form of action derives from a belief that the action will produce the desired result and the beliefs involved are culturally and historically specific.

Malinowski, as we have seen, suggests that actions sometimes do stem directly from emotions when he claims that rituals act out the desired end. As Nadel puts it, for Malinowski magic 'is nothing but the figurative anticipation of the longed for events' (1957, p. 197). There are two problems with this. First, as Malinowski himself states, not all magical or religious rites act out the desired end. In *Magic, Science and Religion* he makes reference to 'ritual proceedings in which there is neither imitation nor forecasting nor the expression of any special idea or emotion' (1974, p. 73). Second, even in the case of rites which do imitate the desired end, since there are many ways of doing this, it is no explanation of the particular form of the rite to say that it acts out the desired end. Malinowski provides only a possible account of the general form of some magical and religious rites but no account of the specific form. In any case, as Nadel points out, since magical rites are standardised, customary and learned they must be based upon more than simply emotion but also upon certain principles and arguments which make them persuasive and give them objective appeal. They must, in short, 'contain something in the nature of a *theory* . . . akin, however remotely, to scientific theories' (1957, p. 197, original emphasis). It is, in fact, surprising that Malinowski did not see this point more clearly or manage to relate the emotional and cognitive dimensions of religion and magic more effectively, since in characterising magic as a form of behaviour which acts out the desired end in the belief that it will occur as a result is similar to Frazer's claim that in magical thinking connections which exist in the mind are mistaken for connections which exist in reality. In fact Malinowski fully and explicitly accepts Frazer's ideas in this respect (1974, p. 72 and pp. 86–7). Where he differs from Frazer is that he rejects the view that the mistake derives from ignorance or naivety but believes that the root source of the error lies in emotional tension and the need to relieve it. What he failed do was to integrate this intellectualist emphasis on the theoretical aspect of magic and religion with its emotional aspect.

Finally on this point, Malinowski's claim that rites began as the inventions of men of genius is highly speculative and quite without the backing of empirical evidence – the very criticisms he and his contemporaries made of the intellectualists.

Malinowski's functionalism presents a different set of problems from his emotionalism but they are, for the most part, the problems which functionalist explanations in general suffer from and, since these will be confronted later when dealing specifically with functionalist approaches they will not be discussed in detail at this point. One point to note here, however, is that given his account in terms of emotional tension Malinowski's functionalism seems superfluous and unnecessary. It seems to be simply a reflection of his general espousal of the functionalist approach prevalent at the time he was writing rather than a considered and essential element of his treatment of magic and religion. The consequence of his dual emphasis on emotion and social function, as Nadel has pointed out, was that he failed to strike a balance between the individual and social aspects of religion. Nadel suggests that this was because in reality for Malinowski 'the decisive weight', when it came to religion and magic, 'lay with the psychological, and in this sense individual, sources of religion' (1957, p. 203). Despite his awareness of the social as well as the individual side of religion, he tended to attempt to reduce it to a single type of cause and never managed to fully grasp it as a many-sided phenomenon.

This is shown most clearly in Tambiah's (1990) criticism of Malinowski's neglect of the expressive dimension of magical rituals which relate not so much to those situations which give rise to anxieties for the individual but to those which generate anxieties pertaining to social values. This point can be demonstrated from Malinowski's own material. In contrasting deep-sea and lagoon fishing he fails to tell us, Tambiah points out, that only deep-sea fishing provides sharks which have a high ritual value for Trobriand Islanders. More clearly, the cultivation of taro and yams is surrounded with magic while the cultivation of mangos and coconuts is not. Yet taro and yam cultivation is a matter of great pride and the good gardener of them enjoys great prestige. There is a high degree of control involved. Differences in the degree of control and uncertainty of outcome cannot explain differences in the degree of magic involved in garden practice. What does seem to be relevant is the fact that taro and yam constitute the bulk of important payments a man must make to his sisters' husbands in fulfilment of his affinal kinship obligations to them. Such payments become a test of his capacity, through skill in gardening, to fulfil crucial social obligations. Important men in the Trobriand Islands conspicuously display stores of surplus yams until they rot in order to demonstrate their prestige and power. Yams and taro are at the centre of social evaluations and concerns which the magic addresses and expresses rather than any technical uncertainties.

A second aspect of Malinowski's version of functionalism again warrants mention at this point since it presents specific problems which derive from his attempt to locate the social functions of religion in its function for the individual. To take the example of mortuary ritual where he argues that in calming potentially disruptive emotions it promotes group cohesion, he has to assume that actions which stem ultimately from intense emotions will have beneficial effects for the individual. Clearly they will often do so. For the most part people will behave in ways which benefit themselves. But where intense emotions are felt it is by no means certain that people will always behave in ways which are either beneficial to themselves or to the social group. Situations of emotional tension are quite likely to produce behaviour which is disruptive of relationships, destabilising, and even self-destructive. Even the standardised and customary nature of ritual is no guarantee that it is essentially beneficial to individuals or to society. As Yinger has pointed out (1970) the fact that, in most cases, mortuary rituals affirm a belief in immortality does not necessarily mean that they are beneficial since such a belief may have the effect of producing resignation to suffering and injustice and prevent action to remove such things.

Despite the many problems that Malinowski's approach presents, it was a valuable contribution to our understanding of religion since it rightly emphasised an aspect, emotion, which the earlier intellectualists had neglected and it did attempt to analyse the nature of the emotions involved and the circumstances that generated them. Malinowski's contribution was also invaluable in showing that magic is not just a mistaken form of rational behaviour or a pseudo-science but an expression of hope and desire. He showed too that magic runs parallel to 'science' existing alongside it as an adjunct to it and not a substitute for it.

FREUD AND RELIGION

Despite their unique characteristics Freud's theories of magic and religion belong in the emotionalist category. Because of such characteristics, however, it is impossible not to treat them separately. There are three aspects to Freud's work in this area; a theory of magic, a general theory of religion, and specific theory of the origins of religion in totemism and its subsequent evolution.

Magic

Freud attributed magical practices to what he called the omnipotence of thought. By this he meant essentially that primitive human beings thought that they could manipulate the real world just by thinking about it – by willing certain things to happen. This is quite reminiscent of Tylor and Frazer's claim that in magical thought ideal connections are mistaken for real connections. Freud was, in fact, strongly influenced by Frazer's work. For example, in his essay *Animism, Magic and the Omnipotence of Thought* he says: 'Objects as such are over-shadowed by the idea representing them; what takes place in the latter must also happen to the former, and relations which exist between ideas are also postulated as to things' (1938, p. 136).

However, for Freud the omnipotence of thought was far from being just a mistake in reasoning or the false product of an inherent tendency to speculate about the world and to generalise as it was for Frazer. For Freud it had little to do with rational processes at all.

Magical acts, he argued, are like the actions of neurotics; they are akin to obsessional actions and protective formulae which are typical of neurotic behaviour. Just as the latter are the consequence of repressed thoughts, fears and desires so with magical acts the 'mistakes' are more than mere mistakes and have their source in irrational impulses.

It is important to note that Freud did not say that magical practices are the same as obsessive actions or neurotic behaviour. What he argued was that they are alike and that there is a parallel between them such that we can understand magic by examining the causes as he saw them of neurotic behaviour. Freud was quite aware that it would be absurd to claim that the entire populations of many tribal peoples are neurotic or suffering from individual mental disorders.

The parallel between magical and neurotic behaviour exists because in the course of human development the individual goes through certain stages which are the same stages that the whole species has gone through in the course of its emotional and psychic development. There is, as Freud put it, a parallelism in ontogenetic and phylogenetic development. The neurotic individual is stuck at an infantile stage of development. Aberrations which occur in later life can be attributed to events in the course of early development in childhood which have arrested emotional and mental development.

Thus magical thought and practice represent an early stage of the development of the species reminiscent of an early stage in the development of the child and of the behaviour of the neurotic arrested at the same stage. It is characterised by the attempt to solve difficulties in fantasy rather than realistically, to overcome them in thought and imagination – hence the belief in the omnipotence of thought.

Freud claimed that the human individual goes through four stages of development from birth to adulthood. These he termed auto-erotism, narcissism, object selection and finally maturity. These stages are stages in sexual development or, to be more precise, stages in libidinal development, which, while fundamentally sexual, includes also much of emotional and affective development in general. Freud believed that the sexual impulse underlies a great deal of emotional life in its various manifestations, and he used the term libido to refer to this impulse.

In the first stage, that is the auto-erotic stage, the libidinal impulses of the human infant are not yet directed towards any object. The child seeks and obtains gratification and pleasure in its own body and bodily functions.

In the narcissistic stage the sexual impulses find an object but it is not yet an external one. It is at this stage that the infant develops a conception of a self or in other words an ego. This ego becomes the object of libidinal impulses in the narcissistic stage.

In the stage of object selection the child turns its libidinal impulses towards external objects. At this stage the external objects which are of greatest concern and interest to the child are the parents. It is here that the roots of the Oedipal complex are found. The tendency is for the libidinal impulses to be directed towards the parent of the opposite sex. The parent of the same sex becomes a rival and feelings of hostility towards that parent develop in the child. This in turn generates feelings of guilt. In other words, the feelings of the child towards the parent of the same sex are characterised by ambivalence. In the male the father is seen as both a protector and provider and yet a rival for the affection of the mother. Also, because the libidinal impulses are directed externally they now become subject to repression. The instinctual desires and wishes are opposed by the real world and its pressures. They are disallowed and must be repressed. This produces further tension, aggression and hostility, guilt and ambivalence.

In the final stage, maturity, the individual adapts to reality and to the external world and accepts the limitations it imposes upon desires. A realistic attitude is adopted towards problems.

Corresponding to the stages of narcissism, object selection and maturity in the development of the individual there are three stages in the development of the species, respectively the magical, religious and the scientific. (There is no stage which corresponds to auto-erotism.) The similarity of this scheme to that of Frazer is not accidental.

Magic, then, corresponds to the narcissistic stage of the development of the individual. It is the technique associated with an animistic mode of thought and this mode of thought is characterised by the omnipotence of thought. The infant at the narcissistic stage of development when unable to satisfy desires in reality tends to seek to satisfy them in fantasy and imagination. Thought is substituted for action. Similarly, the magical stage of development is characterised by the attempt to produce desired results by the use of techniques based upon association of ideas. Again, thought is substituted for action. The neurotic, arrested at the narcissistic stage of development, also responds to problems in an unrealistic way. Both the neurotic and the magician overestimate the power of thought. Omnipotence of thought is most clearly manifested in cases of obsessional neurosis, Freud tells us. It is characterised by superstition. Just as the magician is afraid of offending spirits and demons, the neurotic is often fearful that something awful will happen if the dictates of obsessions are not observed. Everything must be checked over and over again. The state is often characterised by hypochondria, fear of infection and of dirt, or obsessional washing and cleaning. But in all forms of neurosis, Freud argues, 'it is not the reality of the experience but the reality of thought which forms the basis for the symptom formation' (1938, p. 139). In short, both the magician and the neurotic attribute far more to their ideas and thoughts than is admissible.

Of the spirits and demons that the animist postulates, Freud says that they were 'nothing but the projection of primitive man's emotional impulses; he personified the things he endowed with effects, populated the world with them and then discovered his inner psychic processes outside himself' (1938, p. 146).

So the magical approach to the world derives from a sense of frustration and emotional tension. The projection of inner psychic processes onto the outer world

– animism – offers psychic relief. Magic is a form of wish fulfilment through which gratification and relief are obtained through fantasy.

Religion

The religious stage of human development corresponds to the object selection stage of the development of the individual which is characterised by ambivalent feelings towards the parents. In *The Future of an Illusion* Freud argued that life inevitably entails privation. Since civilisation itself is based upon a renunciation of instinctual drives and impulses, the inescapable consequence is that the individual suffers frustration. Civilisation entails social order and regulation and cannot but impose privations upon us. Also, we impose privations upon one another because in any society some dominate others, some exercise power over others. In addition to these privations nature itself holds many threats and imposes many limitations and therefore many privations. It is the purpose of civilisation and culture to combat such threats which it helps to do only at the cost of a different set of privations.

In the religious phase of development the tendency is to attempt to cope with the threats and limitations imposed by nature by humanising it. The natural world is seen in human terms, as if it had the characteristics of human beings. If nature is seen as impersonal it cannot be approached and dealt with and contact with it cannot be established. If it is seen in anthropomorphic terms, i.e. as having a will, desires, purposes and intentions, it can be influenced, appeased, adjured, bribed, or persuaded. It is great relief and consolation, especially in the conditions of primitive society in which religion first emerged, to think of nature this way and, Freud argues, actually a step forward in dealing with the world.

This way of dealing with frustration and privation is based, according to Freud, upon the model of the child-parent relationship or more specifically the relationship between child and father. The individual attempts to interact with the world in much the same way as the child interacts with the father. Freud expresses it as follows:

> For this situation is nothing new. It has an infantile prototype, of which it is in fact only the continuation. For once before one has found oneself in a similar state of helplessness; as a small child, in relation to one's parents. One had reason to fear them, and especially one's father; and yet one was sure of his protection against the dangers one knew. Thus it was natural to assimilate the two situations . . . a man makes the forces of nature not simply into persons with whom he can associate as he would with his equals – that would not do justice to the overpowering impression which those forces make on him – but he gives them the character of a father. He turns them into gods.
>
> (1961, pp. 29–30)

In time the gods become, by degrees, more autonomous from nature. The idea arises that the gods themselves are subject to their own fates and destinies. At this stage the compensatory function of gods is emphasised. They are believed to provide compensation for the privations that culture imposes as a result of its repression and regulation of instinctual drives. Religion now becomes bound up with morality.

> It now became the task of the gods to even out the defects and evils of civilisation, to attend to the sufferings which men inflict on one another in their life together and to watch over the fulfilment of the precepts of civilisation, which men obey so imperfectly. Those precepts themselves were credited with a divine origin; they were elevated beyond human society and were extended to nature and the universe.
>
> (1961, p. 18).

Religion provides compensation by presenting a picture of a world order in which everything has meaning, everything fits into place and nothing is arbitrary and accidental. All sins will be punished in the long run. Those who seem to prosper by wrongdoing will receive their punishment in due course. Their actions do not invalidate or undermine the moral order. Without this type of belief, Freud argues, the moral order would break down.

This aspect of Freud's approach contains a clearly functionalist element but it is not fundamental. It does not warrant treating him as a functionalist as some have done (for example, Scharf, 1970, p. 82). Freud states, in fact, that the consoling and reconciling functions of religion are not sufficient to explain it. His explanation is essentially in terms of a psychological process which he terms wish fulfilment. Religion, he says, is an illusion. He defines an illusion as any belief, true or false, which is held not because there are good grounds for holding it but because there is a strong desire or need to believe it. Religion is made up of such beliefs. It is a form of wish fulfilment or self-delusion which derives from an overpowering will to believe – a will stronger than the reason.

It is, therefore, a psychological process which explains religion and not fundamentally its socially beneficial effects. Although religion may be functional for social order its root source lies in individual needs and in the psychology and motives of individuals.

For Freud, then, the religious stage parallels the stage of object selection of the development of the individual characterised by ambivalent feelings towards the father and the Oedipus complex. Religion would thus be 'the universal obsessional neurosis of humanity; like the obsessional neurosis of children, it arose out of the Oedipus complex, out of the relation to the father' (1961, p. 43).

Again, however, Freud is not arguing that all religious believers are actually neurotic in the same way that some individuals are. Quite the contrary, 'their acceptance of the universal neurosis spares them the task of constructing a personal one' (1961, p. 44).

Totemism

Freud's theory of totemism is perhaps the most celebrated of his work in the sphere of religion. It is an extraordinary story of the origins not only of religion but of the whole of human civilisation. The term 'story' is not used inappropriately. Evans-Pritchard (1965) calls it a 'just so story' and a 'fairy tale'. Here then is Freud's fairy tale. Once upon a time, a very long time ago, primitive man or perhaps it was the pre-human ancestors of man, lived in what Darwin had called the primal horde. This was alleged to have consisted of a dominant male who monopolised a number of females, greedily keeping them all to himself. The other males of the troupe, largely the sons of the dominant male and offspring of the females, were kept away and relegated to the periphery of the group by the stronger, jealous and violent father.

One day, however, the peripheral males, a group of brothers and half-brothers, joined forces and killed the dominant father – an act they could never have achieved singly. The very first act of cooperation was to commit parricide.

Freud goes on to heap one horrific event upon another. 'Of course', he says, 'these cannabalistic savages ate their victim.' One wonders whether Freud used the introspective method to arrive at this conclusion. The reason for this act of cannabalism, according to Freud, was that the brothers believed that by eating the victim they would absorb his strength and power into themselves. The first ever celebratory feast, then, was a cannabalistic one. It was the forerunner, Freud argued, of the totemic feast in which the totem animal, normally taboo, is ritually slaughtered and eaten.

After their triumph, however, the brothers would have been seized by remorse for what they had done. They may have resented and hated the dominant father when he was alive but at the same time they admired him and loved him. While he was alive the negative aspect of their ambivalent feelings tended to predominate in their consciousness but once dead they came to realise the strength of their positive feelings and were overcome with guilt.

In an attempt to undo and to atone for their terrible deed they invented two prohibitions. They found a symbolic substitute for the father in the form of an animal species. This claim is based upon Freud's analysis of the displacement of feelings and emotions onto substitute objects, a phenomenon analysed by Freud in clinical studies of childhood phobias relating to animals. They then placed a taboo upon killing or eating the totem animal. Second, they renounced the fruits of their victory by denying to themselves the liberated females. In this way, Freud argues, the two fundamental institutions of totemic society were established – the taboo against killing the clan totem and clan exogamy. These taboos represent the two repressed wishes of the Oedipus complex, namely to kill the father and sexually possess the mother.

The taboo against killing the totem animal is interpreted by Freud as an attempt to strike a bargain with the dead father. He would watch over them and protect them while they pledge not to repeat their act of parricide by not killing the totem animal. Thus totemic religion derived from a sense of guilt and an attempt to atone for it and to conciliate the injured father through subsequent obedience. These factors are at the root, in fact, of all religion according to Freud, who says:

All later religions prove to be attempts to solve the same problem, varying only in accordance with the stage of culture in which they are attempted and according to the paths which they take; they are all, however, reactions aiming at the same great event with which culture began and which ever since has not let mankind come to rest.

(1938, p. 222)

The old antagonistic attitude towards the father, however, does not entirely disappear. Attitudes to him remain ambivalent. So, once a year the great triumph over him is commemorated in the form of the totemic feast – the totem animal, standing for the father, is ritually killed and eaten. His strength is once again absorbed by the participants. Freud claims that this theory of totemism has distinct advantages over others that were prevalent at the time. For example, one such was that of Robertson Smith (1889), an early theorist who had treated the sacrificial totemic feast as a means of communicating with the tribal deity. The feast, he argued, was seen as the sharing of a communal meal with the tribal god by which means members of the tribe could establish a close relationship with him; they could become identified with him in common solidarity. This is all very well, Freud says, but how does this idea of a tribal god arise in the first place? His own theory, he claims, can account for the belief in a tribal god. Psychoanalytic theory shows that 'god is in every case modelled after the father and . . . our personal relation to god is dependent upon our relation to our physical father, fluctuating and changing with him . . . god at bottom is nothing but an exalted father' (1938, p. 225).

Freud goes on to trace certain aspects of the development of religion from totemism and to show how the original events upon which it is founded have left their traces in myth, legend and religion generally. The first step is that the totem animal loses its sacredness. It becomes more of an offering to the gods and less a representation of the god.

The sacrifice becomes less a re-enactment of the original parricide and takes on an aspect of self-denial and of an offering in expiation of the original crime. The sacrifice of an animal is not, however, adequate expiation for the murder of the father and does not allay the feelings of guilt. Nor is it a true re-enactment of the original crime. It follows, Freud argues, that only a human sacrifice would be really adequate to these purposes. He goes on to interpret the ritual sacrifices of kings who had grown old, alleged to occur among the Latin tribes and other peoples in antiquity, as acts representing the ambivalent emotions of the members of the tribe in relation to the father.

It was such customs that Sir James Frazer was ostensibly concerned with explaining in his book *The Golden Bough* and which had stimulated the writing of that massive study. Freud saw such sacrifices as partly a re-enactment of the original parricide and partly an expiation for it. The original animal sacrifice, can, with this development, be seen for what it was – a substitute for a human sacrifice. So, along with parricide, incest and cannibalism Freud now adds human sacrifice to the catalogue of customs upon which civilisation and culture are founded.

The ambivalent emotions felt towards the father, guilt on the one hand, defiance on the other, continue throughout history, Freud argues. It is manifested in a great many myths and legends, he claims. Figures like Attis, Adonis, Tammuz and many others commit incest with the mother in defiance of the father. They often suffer punishment through castration, as in the case of Attis, or at the hands of the father in the form of an animal – a boar in the case of Adonis.

Finally, Freud examines Christianity and finds in it also evidence for his psychoanalytic theory and presents a psychoanalytic interpretation of certain of its distinctive features. Why, he asks, should Christian doctrine speak of an original sin which had to be atoned for by the sacrifice of a human life and, furthermore, the life of the son of God? He argues that an offence against a father which can only be atoned for by the life of the son must have been murder – it must have been parricide. Christian belief thus reveals the influence of the momentous event which took place in the remote past and from which has sprung so much of our culture and belief.

> Thus in the Christian doctrine mankind most unreservedly acknowledges the guilty deed of primordial times because it now has found the most complete expiation for this deed in the sacrificial death of the son. The reconciliation with the father is the more thorough because simultaneously with this sacrifice there follows the complete renunciation of woman, for whose sake mankind rebelled against the father. But now also the psychological fatality of ambivalence demands its rights. In the same deed which offers the greatest possible expiation to the father, the son also attains the goal of his wishes against the father. He becomes a god himself beside or rather in place of his father. The religion of the son succeeds the religion of the father. As a sign of this substitution the old totem feast is revived again in the form of communion in which the band of brothers now eats the flesh and blood of the son and no longer that of the father, the sons thereby identifying themselves with him and becoming holy themselves. Thus through the ages we see the identity of the totem feast with the animal sacrifice, and the Christian eucharist, and in all these solemn occasions we recognize the after-effects of that crime which so oppressed men but of which they must have been so proud. At bottom, however, the Christian communion is a new setting aside of the father, a repetition of the crime that must be expiated. We see how well justified is Frazer's dictum that 'the Christian communion has absorbed within itself a sacrament which is doubtless far older than Christianity'.
>
> (1938, p. 236–7)

Criticisms of Freud

Freud's theories of magic and religion are highly ingenious and challenging yet open to innumerable criticisms and replete with difficulties of many kinds. Let us take the theory of magic first. Being an emotionalist theory it is open to many of the criticisms of such theories discussed above. The distinctive aspects of Freud's approach, however, create problems of their own. Perhaps the most distinctive aspect of Freud's approach is that it generalises from observations of a limited number of individuals whose behaviour is abnormal. Generalisations made upon this narrow and dubious basis are applied to the whole of humankind and to the intellectual and emotional development of the entire species.

It is important to note, in this respect, that Freud, of course, did not perceive the alleged parallelism between individual development and that of the species. He could never have perceived the development of the species but had to infer it on the basis of his observations of individuals who were suffering from mental and emotional difficulties. This is a highly suspect way to proceed.

There are, also, logical difficulties in likening magical behaviour to neurotic behaviour. The notion of neurotic behaviour depends for its sense upon a notion of normality. It is logically parasitic upon the idea of normality (Phillips, 1976, pp. 58–9). Now in the case of individuals whose behaviour is considered to be abnormal, it may well be possible to characterise it as neurotic by contrasting it with normal behaviour and show that it deviates from this in specified and typical ways. In the case of the practitioner of magic it is not possible to do this. The actions of the magician are perfectly normal in the society in which he operates. Freud, however, is not, admittedly, saying that the magician is individually abnormal. He is saying that the whole of the culture of the magician and all cultures like it are abnormal in relation to modern rational empirical ways of dealing with the world. But what can abnormal mean in this context? Against what is the cultural tradition of magic being contrasted such that it can be said to be abnormal? Can the greater part of the history of human culture and the majority of human societies that have so far existed be legitimately or meaning-fully thought of as being abnormal? Can long stages in the development of the intellectual and emotional life of the human species be seriously characterised as abnormal? The parallel between magic and neurosis appears very shaky indeed when seen in this light.

There is one distinctive aspect of Freud's approach which, it might be thought, overcomes the difficulty of emotionalist approaches mentioned above – that they cannot explain the particular form of religious beliefs and practices. Psycho-analytic theory provides a way of analysing symbols and religious beliefs and rituals might thus be amenable to treatment in the same way as psychoanalysis deals with what it regards as the symbolism of dreams. Freudians have often attempted such analyses. Reik (1975), for example, in his book *Ritual* tries to make sense in psychoanalytic terms of many ritual practices including, to take just one example, that of the *couvade* in which the husband of a woman under-going labour will manifest all the symptoms of labour himself and be treated by all those around him as if it were he and not his wife that was about to give birth. Failure to observe this custom is often believed to have the consequence of bringing harm to the yet unborn child. The custom is widely distributed in societies throughout the world including traditional Basque society. What it symbolises, Reik argues, is the desire for self-punishment on the part of the husband, by taking on the pain that his wife must endure. This desire for self-punishment is a consequence of the guilt he inwardly feels because of repressed feelings of aggression towards the child about to born and a wish for its death, since it is a potential rival for the affections of the mother and a challenge to his masculine authority.

The problem with psychoanalytic theories of this kind is that it is difficult to know whether the interpretation of the symbolism is correct. Symbolic meaning can be read into almost anything and there is no way of checking if the interpretation is correct independent of the theory itself. Consequently, different interpretations of the alleged symbolism are possible. There can be quite different psychoanalytic interpretations associated with different schools of thought within psychoanalysis. Freudian interpretations, for example, will differ markedly from Jungian ones. There is no easy way to resolve these differences, no means of appealing to the evidence; one is simply a Freudian, a Jungian or neither.

Another difficulty with the psychoanalytic theory is that it fails to deal effectively with the social nature of magic, the fact that it is customary, standardised, learned and socially recognised, perhaps even obligatory. Freud was well aware of the social character of magic and interprets it as a collective response to those situations which involve frustration and emotional ambivalence. Magic is a collective fantasy, he said. But how can a collective fantasy come about? How could comforting self-delusions have become socially recognised and even obligatory? Freud does not answer such questions. The problem is that there is a certain tension between a psychological approach to magic in terms of the mental characteristics or states of individuals on the one hand, and the social nature of magic, on the other, which is not resolved by psychoanalytic theorists.

There is, however, a possibility that the psychoanalytic approach, assuming that it is not without any validity at all, might be addressing itself to quite different aspects of magical belief compared to sociological approaches. It might be that the two approaches simply ask very different questions about a complex and many-faceted type of behaviour.

An example of how a psychoanalytic approach might complement a sociological analysis is given by Leach (1958) in his discussion of the psychoanalyst Charles Berg's treatment of customs concerned with hair, the dressing of hair and its significance in rituals. Berg argued that head hair can be a symbol of the genital organs. Cutting hair and shaving the head can be seen, therefore, as symbolising castration. This symbolic castration is an attempt, he argued, to control primary aggressive impulses. Berg derived these conclusions from clinical studies which he then applies to ethnographic data which, Leach points out, was of rather limited quality. Taking rather better data Leach concludes that the psychological and the anthropological interpretations could coexist side by side without contradiction since they are concerned with rather different aspects of the same rites. The rituals are performed for social reasons and embody social meanings. The particular symbols used in such rituals may, however, be chosen because they have a potency derived from the fact that they relate to those powerful and dangerous thoughts and impulses of which the psychoanalysts speak and which are normally repressed. Thus the explanation of social rituals has to make reference to social structures and social processes in order to understand why they are carried out at all. But the particular symbolism involved may require an explanation in psychological and perhaps psychoanalytic terms. Rituals may be socially effective because they make use of and make public potent symbols which have a private and internal, if not fully realised, meaning for the participants.[2]

Turning now to Freud's theory of religion, what are we to make of his claims that God is an exalted father, that religion is the humanisation of nature on the pattern of the child-father relationship and that religion is a form of wish fulfilment that gives consolation to men at an immature stage of development?

For someone of Christian background there does, at first sight, seem to be a lot in Freud's account that is plausible. The Christian religion does speak of 'God the Father'. God is usually conceived as a paternalistic figure but also a stern disciplinarian. It is a very human characteristic to believe what is comforting to believe. Perhaps this is what some Christians mean by faith. Finally, as we have seen, at least one anthropologist has defined religion as the extension of human interaction beyond the confines of human society. It is conceivable that the pattern for such interaction could be that of the child-father relationship.

However, if much of what Freud said about religion might be said to fit Christianity quite well, can it be generalised to suit other religious traditions? Could Freud's theory account for the variety of forms that religious belief and behaviour take? It would seem not. The diversity of religion across different cultures is so great that it seems very doubtful that there is, underlying such diversity, a uniform pattern which derives from universal characteristics of human nature. Take, for example, female deities. Freud himself admitted that female deities do not fit into his theory at all well, for obvious reasons. Female deities have, however, been an important feature of many religious traditions. Also, Wulff (1991) points out that empirical studies have found that the concept of God correlates more highly with the concept of the mother than that of the father. There is a marked tendency for both men and women to associate the idea of God with the preferred parent which for both sexes is more often the mother.

It would seem, then, that Freud was somewhat ethnocentric in his approach. He did not know very much about, or at least overlooked, a great deal of the variety and diversity of religious belief. He tended to generalise from the type of religious tradition with which he was familiar and to see features of this tradition and of his own culture as universal and inherent traits of human beings *per se*. He tended also to reduce all social forms to basic universal psychological processes. The problem is that it is difficult to see how the diversity of social forms can all derive from the same source. Freud ignores the specific social contexts in which emotional tensions exist and arise. Emotional tension and ambivalence of a particular kind cannot just be assumed to be there, inherent in all human beings and in all societies. For one thing, societies are structured very differently and the tensions and emotions which occur typically in a society will reflect, to a considerable degree, the particular character of the social structure. An example would be matrilineal kinship organisation, such as that of Malinowski's Trobriand Islanders, where the father is relatively unimportant, is not a disciplinarian, and has no real responsibility for his children for whom the mother's brother is the figure of authority and the child's real superior and guardian. Clearly, emotional ambivalence towards fathers in such a society is likely to be much less intense than that in the nineteenth-century, middle-class Victorian family in which Freud grew up.

However, this may simply mean that Freud's ideas require only modification in such a way as to be more generally applicable rather than outright rejection. The essential hypothesis of such a generalised Freudianism would be that religious beliefs are a function of the type of domestic situation in which socialisation occurs in a given society. Gods and deities, if this approach is correct, should look like projections of the characteristics of parents bearing in mind that parents will behave in different ways towards children in different societies. A number of studies have been carried out in order to test this sort of hypothesis. The evidence has so far proved to be contradictory. Few studies have found much evidence for Freud's original ideas but some have found evidence favourable to a generalised version of it.[3] The most useful studies of this kind are those which take a cross-cultural perspective. One such came to the conclusion that there exists 'an extraordinary analogy between the Oedipus structure and the structuring of the religious attitude' (Vergote *et al.*, 1969, p. 877).

Some theorists who have been influenced by Freudian ideas do not see the origins of religion as arising out of relationships between parents and children and patterns of child rearing but rather use such factors to explain the persistence of religious ideas in a population.[4] Beliefs, they acknowledge, are learned and part of a cultural tradition. They come, however, to have a hold upon people and are felt to be credible because they conform to the psychological forces within the typical individual in a given society. The private fantasies of individuals conform to the culturally determined and acquired beliefs. In this way this approach allows for the social and cultural dimension of religious belief. Psychology is brought in only to explain why individuals accept and perpetuate the cultural tradition.

Of course, the fact that images of gods and deities match, to a large extent, parental images, if they do, would not in itself prove that the source of religious belief does lie in experiences in the family situation. The neo-Freudians have far from demonstrated their case as yet.

Another criticism that can be made of Freud's theory of religion is that it fails to do justice to the expressive character of religious ritual which other emotionalist theories bring out more effectively. Freud tended to see religion as essentially pragmatic, an attempt to control the world so as to produce definite practical results. There is much more to religion than this. Freud is very close in his attitudes to the typical nineteenth-century view of religion as a mere illusion based upon false reasoning.[5]

Another weakness of Freud's approach can be seen in his attempt to account for religious development. In its initial phase, Freud tells us, religion is the humanisation of nature in an attempt to control it. But it is the privations that civilisation and social regulation of the instinctual drives impose that are the source of those ambivalent emotions and tensions which underlie the Oedipus complex rather than the privations imposed by the natural world. Since this is so, why should religion take the form of humanisation of nature? Also, it is difficult to see why this humanised nature should come to have the responsibility of compensating human beings for the privations that civilisation imposes upon them. Why should an anthropomorphised nature become concerned with upholding morality and justice? There is little coherence or plausibility, then, in this aspect of Freud's account. There is a certain sleight of hand in it; the Oedipal theory first applied to relations with the natural world is rather surreptitiously generalised to social relations and morality.

Finally, we come to Freud's discussion of the origins of religion in totemism. It is hardly necessary to dwell on this. It is, of course, highly conjectural and there is not the faintest trace of evidence for it. The information on totemism on which it was based has since been shown to be largely false or misleading. There is no evidence that totemism was the earliest form of religion or that other religions have evolved from it. Totemism as a distinct form of religion had, in fact, been shown, even at the time Freud was writing, to be a myth. The various elements of totemism, clan exogamy, belief in clan descent from the totem animal, tabooing of the totem animal, the totemic feast, all occur separately in different societies and in various permutations but only very rarely all together (Levi-Strauss, 1962).

There is no evidence, either, for the claim that early human or pre-human social organisation took the form of the primal horde. Even in primate species where there is a horde-like structure of dominant and peripheral males the dominant males do not monopolise the females (Freeman, 1969).

Finally, the theory was based upon a notion of an inherited racial memory of the original events which continued to exert its influence in every subsequent generation, an idea now wholly discredited by modern biology.

KARL JUNG

Before leaving psychoanalytic theories of religion a brief mention of the work of Karl Jung should be made. Jung at first accepted Freud's claim that religion was a comforting illusion but slowly came to believe that religion in fact expressed a kind of truth – a psychological truth. He came to believe that religion had positive value for the individual.

Jung broke with Freudian theory in rejecting the notion of libido being primarily a sexual impulse. He modified the concept, seeing it as a sort of diffuse psychic energy or drive. Neuroses, for Jung, resulted from the blocking of this energy. The neurotic response, he claimed, had a positive side to it and he saw it as an attempt to produce a solution to problems arising out of the blocking of psychic energy. This solution consists in finding new channels for the psychic energy and is accomplished through the medium of symbols, the symbols of dreams, for example. Symbols raise the psychic energy to higher levels and often to a religious level. Religious symbolism is a way of exploring new possibilities and of discovering new ways of coping with personal difficulties relating to emotional development. For Jung religion was psychotherapeutic – it gives meaning to existence and suggests paths for adaptation for the future.

It is a characteristic of symbols, Jung argued, that they have no fixed meaning. Symbols are multi-faceted and their meanings may remain unrealised until revealed by analysis. They are products of the unconscious and the process of analysing them throws up new possibilities for the psychic and emotional development of the individual. Very often Jung believed that he discovered in the dreams of patients a religious symbolism which he interpreted as the unconscious mind attempting to show the individual ways to overcome personal problems.

This implies that there is more to the unconscious than just suppressed wishes, thoughts and experiences as Freud had said. Jung is famous for his postulation of a collective unconscious and of the 'archetypes'. The unconscious, he said, is divided into two parts. First, there is the personal unconscious which includes things forgotten during life, subliminal perceptions and all psychic contents incompatible with conscious attitudes, i.e. things which are for one reason or another inadmissible and consequently pushed out of consciousness and re-pressed. Second, there is the collective unconscious which includes things which are not restricted to the individual. These complexes, as Jung calls them, are universal, that is, common to all human beings. The collective unconscious is inherited by all members of the human species and contains its collective experience.

It is these elements of the collective unconscious which produce the symbolism of dreams in which religious solutions are being suggested. He calls these elements the archetypes. They are manifested not only in dreams but in myths and legends, stories and in many aspects of culture. Examples include the wise old man, the mother figure, the cross, and the hero.

When some element of the unconscious rises into consciousness it is felt by the individual to be uncanny and strange. It does not seem to come from within the individual but to come from outside. It is also fascinating and awe-inspiring. Jung interprets the experience of spiritual powers and belief in spirits as elements of the collective unconscious rising into consciousness. Members of a tribal society who have such experiences will say that a spirit is bothering them.

Such experiences are particularly common when society undergoes a profound change of a social, religious or political nature. At such times elements of the collective unconscious rising into the conscious mind cause many people to see strange things, or experience visions. The sighting of UFOs and flying saucers might be a contemporary form of this phenomenon. The collective unconscious is attempting to provide possibilities for adaptation to the changing circumstances and the problems this creates for individuals and the society. These experiences are religious experiences and religion is thus a progressive and adaptive force, according to Jung.

All this may seem very mysterious and indeed much of Jung's writing is. It is difficult, also, to grasp without a good grounding of his complex psycho-analytical system, which it is not possible even to outline here.[6]

NEO-FREUDIANISM: MELFORD SPIRO

While the psychoanalytic approach to understanding religion, and the Freudian approach in particular, is not accepted by many theorists in its original form, a number of writers have developed modified, less ethnocentric versions of it and most prominent among these is Melford Spiro.

Spiro (1966) believes that it is not, in fact, possible to develop a single comprehensive explanation of religion because it is too diverse and complex a phenomenon. We must develop separate explanations for its various aspects. The fact that every theory we have examined so far seems to have some element of truth in it would support Spiro's claim. Some aspects of religion, Spiro argues, require a modified Freudian understanding.

Spiro first considers beliefs as opposed to practices and asks why people believe what they do believe. On what grounds are religious propositions believed to be true? He considers that a psychological theory is necessary to understand this aspect of religion. He is aware that beliefs are part of a cultural tradition and handed down from generation to generation; he accepts, in other words, that an explanation of the content of beliefs cannot be essentially or primarily psychological. His concern, however, is not with the content of the beliefs or with their origins but with why they are believed at all, why they persist and have credibility. Cultural tradition is not adequate to answer this. In other words, Spiro implies that people do not believe religious propositions simply because they are socialised into them. He believes that certain psychological processes are behind the acceptance of beliefs.

Nor does Spiro attempt to explain beliefs in terms of any need to believe. Because people need to believe in something, this is not a sufficient reason for them believing it or explanation of why they do believe it. Nor does any need in the sense of a functional requirement of society explain belief. It does not follow that if society needs its members to believe something that they will believe it.

Spiro proposes a broadly Freudian interpretation of belief – one which is generalised from Freud's own ethnocentric model. He argues as follows. It is a child's experiences in the family which dispose him or her in later life to accord credibility to beliefs in powerful beings which are sometimes benevolent and sometimes malevolent, or some similar set of beliefs. This is because it is in the family that beings who have such characteristics are experienced. A child learns that various actions on his or her own part can induce powerful beings, the parents, to act either benevolently or malevolently; in this way the efficacy of ritual is learned since for the child the actions required by adults seem ritualistic.

Spiro suggests that this is a better hypothesis to account for beliefs in super-human beings and for ritual than other theories because it can account for cross-cultural variations whereas most others cannot. If childhood experiences are different in different societies then we would expect to find differences in beliefs to be correlated with family structures and methods of child rearing. Empirical test of this theory, then, is clearly possible. Various studies, Spiro claims, have confirmed the hypothesis.

Turning to the question of religious practices, Spiro argues that in general terms people engage in various actions because they wish to achieve various ends and satisfy various desires and believe that the activity will accomplish this. In short, to understand religious practices we must examine the motives people have for engaging in them; 'an explanation of the practice of religion must be sought in the set of needs whose expected satisfaction motivates religious beliefs and the performance of religious ritual' (1966, p. 107).

Although Spiro speaks of the satisfaction of needs by religion as being its social and psychological functions, he is not really a functionalist. He does not seek to explain the existence of the practices in terms of the needs (see Chapter ten). As in the case of belief, the same applies to practice, need does not ensure occurrence. Spiro explains practices in terms of motivations on the part of individuals who experience certain needs and respond to this situation in a certain way. If, for example, it is necessary to promote social cohesion and it is claimed that this is done by means of religion, the existence of the religious beliefs and practices is only explained if it is recognised by believers and participants that it is necessary to promote cohesion, if they desire to promote it and if they accept the beliefs and engage in the practices in order to promote it. In short, an explanation in these terms is possible only if the participants recognise, desire and intend that the alleged function be fulfilled.

With this clear, Spiro goes on to examine the 'functions' that religion, in his view, has which explain it. He distinguishes three types of function, adjustive, adaptive and integrative and corresponding to these there are three types of desire which are satisfied by religion, cognitive, substantive and expressive.

Religion satisfies cognitive needs by providing explanations of puzzling phenomena in the absence of competitive explanations. Religion satisfies the desire to know and to understand and is resorted to when more mundane means of explanation fail.

The substantive needs that religion satisfies concern concrete and material desires which cannot be satisfied in other ways. Religion satisfies them in the absence of competing technologies. In doing so it reduces anxiety by giving confidence that desires will be fulfilled and goals achieved.

The substantive functions of religion are both recognised and intended, according to Spiro. They are, however, not real, that is, they do not produce the results they are believed to. Their function is only apparent, that is, one which is not empirically confirmable. Rain-making ritual, for example, has only an apparent not a real function. The fact that much religious ritual has no real function has made it seem irrational which has led to the tendency to attribute social functions, such as integration to it. Rain-making ceremonies are said to integrate society. But even if they do, they cannot be explained in this way. Spiro claims that to say that their functions are unreal is, however, not to say that they are irrational.

Religion meets expressive needs by allowing the symbolic expression of certain painful drives and motives. Spiro here is referring to those drives involving fears and anxieties which psychoanalysis has revealed to us and which can be disturbing and destructive. And by painful motives he means those which are culturally forbidden including aggressive and sexual motives. These drives and motives become unconscious but still seek satisfaction. Religion reduces these drives and motives by symbolically giving expression to them.

All three of these sets of desires that religion satisfies, cognitive, substantive and expressive refer to the motives underlying religious behaviour, that is, to a psychological variable. Yet the sources of these motives are often related to social factors. Again the crucial social context in which such motives are generated, according to Spiro, is the family. We ought, therefore, to be able to correlate different family structures with variations in religious practices. Spiro has undertaken studies of this kind which, he claims, support his basic hypotheses.

Spiro, then, seeks to integrate psychological and social dimensions and to provide a theory which is couched in terms of both cause and function. 'Function', in his approach, is, however, very different from the concept as it is used in traditional functionalist theory. For Spiro 'function' means only certain actual or putative effects

A point to note about this type of causal/functional approach is that it would, of course, explain not only religion but anything that would satisfy cognitive, substantive and expressive desires. The question arises why these desires are satisfied by religion rather than in some other way. Spiro recognises that the desires might not be satisfied by religion but by some alternative means. This is why he stresses that religious means are resorted to in the absence of more mundane means. As he puts it 'the importance of religion would be expected to vary inversely with the importance of other projective and realistic institutions' (1966, p. 116). But this does not tell us why religious means are used in the absence of alternatives. All Spiro says is that in such circumstances religious means are the means *par excellence*, but he does not tell us why that is so. Perhaps it has something to do with the origins of religious conceptions – a question he declines to examine. The theory, then, is only a partial one. It is a theory, however, which Spiro has sought to apply in his substantive work in the sociology of religion and particularly his work on Buddhism which is examined in the next chapter.

5   Buddhism

We saw in Chapter one that Theravada Buddhism poses dilemmas for the attempt to define religion because belief in god or gods is not a central tenet of Buddhist faith which is often said, in consequence, to be atheistic.

According to orthodox teaching the Buddha was not divine, although a very remarkable man, he no longer exists, and cannot help us to achieve salvation. He only pointed the way, when alive, for others to follow. His teaching consisted of the Four Noble Truths. First, life entails suffering (*dukkha* in Pali, the language of the Buddhist scriptures – a term which means, more accurately, the opposite of well-being. The closest word in English that anyone has so far been able to suggest is 'unsatisfactoriness'). Second, the source of suffering is desire and craving. Third, suffering can be ended by extinguishing desire and fourth, this can be achieved by following the eightfold path of the *Dhamma* (Sanskrit, *dharma*)[1] – the path of Buddhism. This results in the attainment of *nibbana*, a blissful state in which desire has been extinguished. As in Hinduism, the Buddha Gottama, taught that true salvation meant escape from the cycle of rebirths.

Rebirth is the inevitable consequence of *kamma* (Sanskrit, *karma*) which is intentional action, that is, action which springs from desire. Action which is good results in a better rebirth. Action which is bad results in a worse rebirth. Escape from this endless cycle of rebirths and inherently unsatisfactory material existences may be achieved by following the noble eightfold path of right views, right aspiration, right speech, right conduct, right livelihood, right effort, right mindfulness and right contemplation. The first two 'steps' refer to the necessity of seeking salvation and acceptance of the *dhamma*. The next three concern morality and may be stated also in terms of the five precepts – abstention from taking life (*ahimsa*), from stealing, from illicit sex, from taking intoxicants, and observance of honesty. On holy days and during the Buddhist 'Lent' further precepts should be observed – abstaining from food after midday, from theatrical entertainments, from wearing adornments and perfume, the enjoyment of luxury and often the handling of money. Monks must observe all these precepts all of the time and must observe them more strictly (no illicit sex becomes complete celibacy) and beyond the novice stage the remainder of the 227 rules specified in the *vinaya*. The final three steps of the eightfold path concern meditation and through it the achievement of tranquillity and the attainment of wisdom.

Meditation leads to ultimate salvation – *nibbana* (Sanskrit, *nirvana*). This is achieved when wisdom is attained – the wisdom that the self or soul is really only an impermanent flux. The Buddha taught that nothing is permanent and that all is transitory. There is no self or soul which endures; this is known as the doctrine of *anatta*. Rebirth is not the rebirth of the soul in a new body since there is no enduring soul to be reborn. It is simply an effect in the future of karmic causation or consequence of actions performed in the past. Meditation reveals the truth of this and enables the extinction of desire which falls away when the illusory nature of the soul is realised. Even meditation will now be done without desire, even for salvation, and will be without karmic consequence.

Spiro, in his study of Buddhism in the daily lives of villagers in Upper Burma (1971), distinguishes between the set of beliefs described above, which he calls *nibbanic* Buddhism and which is the canonical or 'normative soteriological' form and a modified adaptation or popular form of Buddhism which he terms *kammatic* Buddhism. While Nibbanic Buddhism, Spiro argues, was the religion of a world-weary privileged stratum, Kammatic Buddhism (from the Pali *kamma*), or non-normative soteriological Buddhism, is the religion of relatively disprivileged strata. Since it is a selection and modification of normative Buddhism it is still Buddhist, according to Spiro.

Kammatic Buddhism has considerably modified the doctrines of Nibbanic Buddhism. It does not renounce desire but seeks satisfaction of desire in a future worldly existence. Suffering is not considered to be inherent in life but only temporary. Kammatic Buddhism, then, seeks a better rebirth, a worldly goal, not nibbanic salvation. Gombrich (1971) reports also that in Sri Lanka the aim of *nirvana* is not sought by most villagers at least in the near future. Like St Augustine who prayed that God would make him chaste and continent – but not just yet, village Buddhists were happy to have *nirvana* deferred almost indefinitely. In Burma, if *nirvana* is sought it is not conceived of as extinction of the self. The doctrine of *anatta* is not well understood by most followers of Kammatic Buddhism or they are psychologically incapable of accepting it. Their ideal is a form of salvation in which the self endures.

Kammatic Buddhism holds that a better rebirth is achieved by good *karma*. Deliverance from suffering, therefore, is achieved not by the extinction of desire and *karma* but by increase in good *karma*. Suffering is due to bad *karma* and immorality must be avoided because it brings bad *karma*. Good *karma* comes from meritorious actions. Salvation is achieved by the accumulation of merit not extinction of *karma*. If it is desirable to meditate it is because it is meritorious not because it brings wisdom. But merit mostly comes from giving in a religious context – feeding monks, donations towards the building and upkeep of monasteries and pagodas.

In Kammatic Buddhism merit can be transferred from one person to another. It can, for example, be transferred to a dead relative during the days immediately after death through the performance of meritorious acts by the living to increase the good *karma* of the deceased and earn him or her a better rebirth. Strictly contrary to the doctrine of *karma*, this fact is simply not perceived or is ignored by most villagers. Others rationalise it within the principles of karmic causation by claiming that the rituals performed give the deceased an opportunity to applaud the living for their desire to share merit. The act of applauding this is itself meritorious so merit is not actually transferred but earned by both parties. Such rationalisations of what appear to be practices contrary to orthodox Buddhist doctrine are common.[2]

These beliefs, Spiro argues, are consistent with the perceptual and cognitive structure of the Burmese – they fit the experience of the Burmese of how things in reality are. This experience and view of reality are laid down in childhood. Spiro here draws upon a school of thought associated with Kardiner and Whiting which argues that religious and other conceptions reflect childhood experience and child-rearing patterns.

The important elements of the notion of *karma*, Spiro points out, are first, that one can rely on oneself and one's own actions for salvation, and second, that there is in fact no saviour one can rely on – one has to rely on oneself. Spiro claims that the belief that one can be saved by the efforts of a compassionate saviour, a divine figure, can only carry conviction where, in the formative stage of experiencing what the world is fundamentally like, namely in infancy, that experience is one of persistent and enduring love and emotional nurturance. The child is assured that he or she is not alone and a cognitive structure is created isomorphic with belief in saviour gods.

Such a cognitive structure would be difficult to acquire in Burma, Spiro claims. Early on infants are treated with the greatest nurturance. Their need for affection is constantly satisfied and dependency indulged. This nurturance is rather abruptly and unpredictably withdrawn at a certain age and after infancy physical expression of affection is rare and verbal praise and expression of affection slight in order not to spoil the child. Children may become victims of much teasing and are compelled to carry out many small chores. Strict obedience is expected of them and punishment is often severe. 'Burmese socialisation is characterised by an important discontinuity between the indulgent nurturance of infancy and its rather serious withdrawal in childhood' (1971. p. 133).

There is thus no experiential model for the development of the notion of a divine saviour. The only view which carries credibility and conviction is that salvation must be attained by one's own efforts. The belief that one can save oneself is equally strongly fostered.

Salvation for the average villager, we have seen, is largely achieved by feeding and providing for monks. Monks, Spiro argues, stand in the same position relative to laymen as infants do in relation to adults – dependent, provided for and in a state of blissful irresponsibility. Magical reciprocity suggests that feeding monks will place the laymen himself eventually once again in the blissful position of infancy.

There is an inevitable uncertainty in the notion of *karma*. No one can ever be sure of the fate that awaits because no one knows what acts performed in the past have affected the karmic balance. Misfortunes can be explained in terms of bad *karma* acquired in past lives but the price is that the future is always uncertain.

This also fits the Burmese experience – as a child affection was unpredictably withdrawn and the world is experienced, therefore, as an unpredictable place.

It is important to note that Spiro's theory is not one of origins of belief systems. It is a theory of why beliefs carry conviction. Mahayana Buddhism reached Burma as early as Theravada but did not take root. Neither has Christianity had much success in the Theravada countries of South East Asia. These religions, with their emphasis on saviour figures, carry no conviction given the Burmese cognitive structure. Whatever the reasons for the emergence of the particular form of Theravada belief, the exposure of Burma to it is largely an accident of geography but once exposed to it this type of belief carried conviction. Only the generic notion, then, that salvation must be attained by one's own efforts is promoted by this particular cognitive structure. The particular form of the doctrine is accidental. In short, the cognitive structure which is favourable to such a belief is a necessary but not a sufficient condition for the prevalence of the belief.

Spiro's analysis of the nature of Theravada Buddhism is further developed in his treatment of the monks, the sangha. The monkish way of life is held in the highest esteem by lay Burmese. The monk is largely concerned with seeking salvation for himself. He is not an intermediary and does not administer sacraments. His main role is not to serve a congregation; he is not a priest.

The monk–layman relationship, Spiro argues, is the reverse of that between priest and layman in Christianity. The Buddhist layman supports the monk and therefore assists him in attaining his primary aim of salvation. In Christianity it is the priest who assists the layman to achieve salvation by his sacramental function.

Monks are supposed to spend a great deal of time meditating in the quest for wisdom and enlightenment but few, Spiro reports, do so. Gombrich (1971) also reports that Sri Lankan monks find frequent meditation to be impractical and uncongenial. The routine of Burmese monks consists largely of the daily round of alms begging and some teaching of the village children. The alms begging was performed largely for the benefit of the villagers in order to allow them to acquire merit. The monks rarely ate the food they collected but had much better provided for them by wealthier members of the community prepared and cooked at the monastery. Ryan (1958) reports much the same in Sri Lanka where monks had, in fact, largely given up the daily round, the food being provided by organised rotation of donors. In the Burmese village where Spiro worked the monks seemed bored most of the time and slept a great deal. Most came from poor rural families. The monastery gives them status and a higher standard of living than they would otherwise enjoy. Tambiah (1976, pp. 356-7) reports the same for Thailand where entry into the *sangha* is an important route for upward mobility and the acquisition of education. In Burma, where there was no state education in rural areas, the monastery has greater influence and ability to attract recruits than in the town where monastery education is looked down upon.

As for the particular individuals who become monks, Spiro argues that monks have a certain personality. It is, he believes, the general type of the Burmese personality but in a more extreme form. Spiro claims that monks manifest a strong 'need for dependence'. The monk–layman relationship places the monk in the structural position of the child and the layman in the position of the parent. In Christianity the priest is called 'father' by the layman whereas in Burma, Spiro reports, the monk calls the layman 'father'.

As a result of Burmese child-rearing practices, Spiro claims, there is a strong unconscious wish to return to blissful infancy. The monastery is an institutionalised means for realising this fantasy. It is a form of regression symbolised by the physical appearance of the monk. His shaven head gives a foetalised appearance. The celibacy required of monks is interpreted by Spiro as an institutionalised and symbolic resolution of the Oedipus complex. All women are forbidden mothers and all men fathers. In exchange for this renunciation the monk can enjoy the benefits of infancy.

Spiro's interpretation echoes to some extent that of Tambiah (1968). Commenting on the common practice whereby most Thai youths spend a period of time in the monastery as monks, as they do in most of the countries of South East Asia including Burma, he interprets it as a form of *rite de passage* marking the transition from childhood to adulthood. Those young men who take up the yellow robe acquire merit by doing so and also confer merit upon their parents. Merit produces good *karma* and is essential for a better rebirth.

There is, then, a kind of reciprocity between the generations and between monk and laymen here. The older generation persuades its youth to temporarily give up worldly pleasures and pursuits. The rule for monks is an ascetic one; they must remain celibate, renounce personal possessions and observe all 227 rules of the *vinaya* code governing the life of monks. Youth is asked to give up its vitality and sexual potency in order to follow this ascetic way of life. This is a kind of sacrifice of sexual vitality, according to Tambiah, made by young Thais in order to produce in its place an ethical vitality which counters and combats the effects of bad *karma* and thereby suffering.

Fortes (1987) interprets the reciprocity between monk and layman in a similar way. It is, he argues, a symbolic, ritually legitimated working out of repressed rivalry and mutual hostility. The renunciation of sexuality is seen by him as an expression of filial submission and a form of symbolic castration before regression to a state of infantile-like 'back-to-the-womb' dependence on parents and sexual innocence as a member of the monastery. Filial piety expressed through the institution of monkhood is thus a customarily legitimate device for converting repressed hostility into socially respectable humility.

Monks also, Spiro claims, manifest a lack of sensitivity to the needs of others and a preoccupation with self. They are characterised not by egotism but by narcissism. Often a man will abandon wife, children and other dependents, leaving them with no support in order to enter the monastery. Monkish life provides, Spiro says, a legitimate means for indulging this abdication of responsibility and narcissism.

We may conclude, then, that the Buddhist emphasis on redemption from suffering permits the monastery, in addition to its other functions, to serve as an institutionalised solution to the problems of all kinds of men including those who, from a secular perspective, are (or would become) misfits, neurotics, and failures.

(Spiro, 1971, p. 350)

The monastery, in fact, does not only protect them from potential neurosis but allows them to achieve an honoured status in the society. Monks are not abnormal because their behavioural pattern conforms to culturally prescribed norms and values (Spiro, 1965). The monastic order acts as a collective saviour in Theravada Buddhism.

Monks are indeed highly venerated because of their ascetic way of life. Despite a low intellectual level, a tendency to narcissism and vanity, their moral standards are very high and they keep the precepts of the *vinaya* strictly. This asceticism is seen by laymen as being extraordinarily difficult and greatly admired and it is often thought to give monks extraordinary qualities and powers – in Weber's terms magical charisma. Monks are also essential for the layman to acquire merit. By giving to monks, laymen can improve their karmic balance and their rebirth.

Spiro's neo-Freudian interpretation of Theravada Buddhism has been challenged by Gombrich (1971) and Southwold (1983) who criticise Spiro for basing his charge of narcissism on a very small sample of monks (21) who are not typical of the *sangha* in general but only, Southwold argues, of those monks who practise Spiro's 'normative' Buddhism.

Gombrich has also questioned the claim that child-rearing practices promote Theravada beliefs. Spiro presents no evidence for the alleged character traits of the Burmese which are postulated to be the reason for their commitment to Theravada beliefs but deduces them, in fact, from their beliefs. 'Spiro seems to . . . have built up a picture of what Burmese personality ought to be like, given their religious systems' (1972, p. 485). In any case, does it seem plausible that differences in child-rearing practices could explain differences in religious conception? All babies are given unconditional nurturance. Are we to conclude that belief in saviour figures is only possible when this is maintained through childhood? Should we not find the basic elements of Theravada belief, if in different form, in many other cultures? How could we account for religious change such as that which occurred in India on the part of the majority of the population from the belief that everyone is wholly responsible for their own salvation to that of devotion (*bhakti*) to a saviour god? Surely not in terms of a change in child-rearing practices.

One might also question Spiro's characterisation of the personality and motives of monks. Their alleged narcissism is, nevertheless, as we have seen, tolerated by laymen. Spiro believes this toleration of and reverence for the monk is the reflection of the laity's own inner desire to return to the infantile state. The character of the monk is that of the Burmese writ large. Most people do not become monks, however, because they could not follow the ascetic regime. An alternative interpretation of lay tolerance might, however, be that the pursuit of salvation is seen by laymen as indeed of overriding importance for those who are fortunate enough to be able to pursue it. If existence is defined as unsatisfactory and meaningless, as it is in Buddhism, them one can hardly be too concerned with the plight of others. The fact that monks avoid attachments because they involve risk of hurt is interpreted by Spiro as emotional timidity. There are two possible motivations, Spiro argues, from which the relinquishing of attachments may stem – that which is sacrificial and heroic and in which attachments are given up for the greater goal of salvation, and that which is overcautious, timid and fears pain. This, surely, is too great a contrast. 'Fear' of attachment may be just the other side of the coin of 'sacrifice'. It does not follow that to give up attachments, even out of fear of pain, is to make no sacrifice at all. No one, in any religion, makes sacrifices for the sake of it but precisely to achieve a higher or greater goal.

Gombrich has further challenged Spiro's interpretation of popular Buddhism. Both he (1972) and Southwold (1983) reject Spiro's contention that *kammatic* Buddhism is an adaptation of canonical *nibbanic* Buddhism and a deviation from orthodoxy. Gombrich shows that this view is founded upon a misunderstanding of the doctrine of *karma*. Spiro erroneously states that even good and meritorious action always results in rebirth since it has karmic consequences so that salvation is only achieved by the extinction of *karma*. Gombrich points out that canonical Buddhism holds, in fact, that only action performed from desire produces rebirth. The merit in an action depends upon the intention behind it. Good actions performed from the desire for reward have karmic consequences. Disinterested actions, as long as they are good, do not. Salvation is achieved by the extinction of desire. Good action is a step on the way to salvation and is considered to be spiritual progress. The consequence of this is that popular Buddhism is as canonical as *nibbanic* Buddhism and not a heterodox adaptation of it. The peasants who pursue merit are doctrinally quite correct in their understanding of Buddhism. Nevertheless, Gombrich acknowledges that there is a difference between *kammatic* and *nibbanic* Buddhism. He prefers, however, to express this difference in rather simpler terms than Spiro – as simply the discrepancy between what people say they believe and what the behaviour tells us they believe. It is this distinction which informs his own detailed ethnographic study of Sri Lankan Buddhism (Gombrich, 1971). Spiro presents the two forms of Buddhism as distinct cognitive structures. Gombrich's correction of Spiro's misinterpretations of the doctrine of *karma* means, he claims, that the cognitive structure which he calls *kammatic* Buddhism is really only in part *nibbanic* Buddhism and in part an extrapolation of people's actual behaviour. Burmese villagers do not behave as if they really did believe all life entails suffering. Because of this Spiro attributes to them a different form of Buddhism. Gombrich argues that they are simply not very good Buddhists, a fact which is no more remarkable than that most professed Christians or Muslims are not very good Christians and Muslims. The values of Buddhism represent, as Spiro himself puts it, 'what the Burmese think they ought and would like to be – but aren't' (Spiro, 1971, p. 475).

Southwold makes a similar point in his treatment of the alleged lack of interest of most laymen in attaining *nirvana* but goes further than Gombrich to whom his remarks equally apply. We cannot assume that the popular lack of interest in the goal of *nirvana* is a deviation from canonical Buddhist teaching, he claims. The fact is that *nirvana* is simply not available to most people, if anyone, for a very long time – not until the coming of the next Buddha, Maitreya – a very distant prospect. There is, Southwold claims, no lack of scriptural backing for this view. Village Buddhists are uninterested in *nirvana* largely because it is something they have no hope of attaining in any case. They are very rationally and understandably prioritising proximate and ultimate goals. It is perfectly reasonable and not a deviation from orthodoxy to place a very low priority on something which has very low probability of attainment and to defer concern with something which can only be achieved in the distant future. Emphasis on *nirvana* as a primary and immediate aim of Buddhism is in any case, Southwold claims, largely a middle-class interpretation of Buddhism which not even many monks share, as Spiro's and Gombrich's studies confirm. Furthermore, this middle-class Buddhism has itself been largely shaped and influenced by prestigious Western interpretations of what the essential features of Buddhism are which have fed back into the understanding of both monks and laymen in Buddhist countries. The layman's viewpoint is, if anything, more consistent with scripture than that of middle-class Buddhism which is guilty of a misreading of them.

Nevertheless, the distinction between *nibbanic* and *kammatic* Buddhism, or that between what people profess to believe and what their actions tell us they believe remains valid whether or not the latter is a deviation from or adaptation of the former. These two forms of Buddhism broadly address the transcendental and pragmatic needs that Mandelbaum (1966) distinguishes. Yet the latter are also catered for by non-Buddhist pagan beliefs and practices in all Theravada countries – for example, *nat* cults in Burma (Spiro, 1978) and spirit cults in Thailand (Tambiah, 1970). Obeyesekere (1966) has shown that in Sri Lanka cults centring on various deities and demons are nevertheless integrated with Buddhist belief to some extent. The ultimate source of power and authority of these gods is said to be the Buddha who has delegated power to them. The Buddha is associated with other-worldly concerns whereas the gods and lesser supernaturals are concerned with material and this worldly matters. Ames (1964a; 1964b) similarly argues that magical practices and Buddhism do not stand in contradiction but are complementary even though pagan beliefs and practices are clearly distinct from popular forms of Buddhism (see also Evers, 1965). Both Ames (1964b) and Obeyesekere (1963) argue that the relationship between canonical Buddhism and popular Buddhism is not that between a great and a little tradition along the lines of Redfield's (1956) well-known distinction. Buddhism, Ames states, whether canonical or popular, belongs to the realm of the sacred – *lokottara* in Pali. Magic and worship of gods belongs to the realm of *laukika* or the profane. Popular Buddhism is concerned with earning merit while magical practices are not but with practical, immediate mundane ends. Obeyesekere argues further that the concepts and values derived from the 'great' tradition of

Theravada Buddhism are by no means merely a thinly formed veneer over a mass of non-Buddhist popular concepts which constitute the true religion of the masses, as interpretations of the great–little tradition distinction often suppose. The concepts of Theravada Buddhism, even the popular interpretations of them, constitute the frame of reference by which the deeper and fundamental facts of existence are understood.

6 Religion and ideology: Karl Marx

Freud's theories of magic and religion like most psychological theories examined in Chapter three have the greatest difficulty, as we have seen, in dealing with the social character of religious belief and practice. Yet Freud's theories are often compared with those of the first sociological theorist we shall discuss, namely Karl Marx. There are indeed some similarities between them. Both saw religion as a compensating and comforting illusion which would eventually be dispensed with as human beings lost their need for illusions. Neither saw religion as an integral part of human society or life *per se* and can be contrasted in this respect with typical functionalist theorists to be examined later. Yet Marx's theory is essentially a sociological theory and not a psychological one.

Religion for Marx was essentially the product of a class society. His ideas on religion are part of his general theory of alienation in class-divided societies. Religion is seen as both a product of alienation and an expression of class interests. It is at one and the same time a tool for the manipulation and oppression of the subordinate class in society, an expression of protest against oppression and a form of resignation and consolation in the face of oppression.

In pre-class societies, Marx believed, human beings are at the mercy of nature. Primitive peoples had little control over nature and little knowledge of natural processes. They attempted, consequently, to gain control over nature through magical and religious means. When society became characterised by class division, human beings were again in a position where they were unable to control the forces which affected them and in which their understanding was inadequate. In class society the social order itself is seen as something fixed and given which controls and determines human behaviour. Yet the social order is nothing but the actions and behaviour of the members of society. It is in fact their creation in the sense that they maintain it by their own actions. In short, in class society human beings are alienated and have a mystified view of reality. Human products are not seen as such but as being the creation of external forces. They take on an independent reality which is seen as determining rather than being determined by human action.

It was the philosopher Ludwig Feuerbach, Marx considered, who had shown that the characteristics of gods are really nothing other than the characteristics of man projected beyond man into a fantastic realm where in an elevated and exaggerated form they are thought to lead an independent existence and actually control men through their commandments. To this Marx added the observation that Christians believe that God created man in his own image whereas the truth is that man created God in *his* own image. His own powers and capacities are projected onto God who appears as an all powerful and perfect being.

Religion is, therefore, a reversal of the true situation because it is a product of alienation. Feuerbach had shown the true nature of the religious illusion; the next step was to show how this illusion could be understood in terms of the structure of the society. For example, Marx says in the *Theses on Feuerbach* that:

Feuerbach starts out from the fact of religious self-alienation, the duplication of the world into a religious, imaginary world and a real one. His work consists in the dissolution of the religious world into its secular basis. He overlooks the fact that after this work is completed the chief thing remains to be done. For the fact that the secular foundation detaches itself from itself and established itself in the clouds as an independent realm is really only to be explained by the self-cleavage and self-contradictoriness of this secular basis. The latter must itself, therefore, first be understood in its contradiction and then revolutionised in practice by the removal of the contradiction.

(1957, p. 63)

The criticism of religion, then, is also the criticism of the society which produces religion.

There is no systematic treatment of religion in Marx's writings. What he had to say consists of many scattered passages throughout his works. The most extensive passage occurs in his *Contribution to the Critique of Hegel's Philosophy of Right* which contains in highly condensed form his overall approach to the analysis of religion. It is worth quoting in full before discussion of its elements.

The basis of irreligious criticism is: *Man makes religion*, religion does not make man. In other words, religion is the self-consciousness of man who has either not yet found himself or has already lost himself again. But *man* is no abstract being squatting outside the world. Man is *the world of man*, the state, society. This state, this society, produce religion, a *reversed world-consciousness*, because they are *a reversed world*. Religion is the general theory of that world, its encyclopaedic compendium, its logic in a popular form, its spiritualistic *point d'honneur*, its enthusiasm, its moral sanction, its solemn completion, its universal ground for consolation and justification. It is *the fantastic realization* of the human essence because the *human essence* has no true reality. The struggle against religion is therefore mediately the fight against *the other world*, of which religion is the spiritual *aroma*.

Religious distress is at the same time the *expression* of real distress and the *protest* against real distress. Religion is the sigh of the oppressed creature, the heart of a heartless world, just as it is the spirit of a spiritless situation. It is the *opium* of the people.

The abolition of religion as the *illusory* happiness of the people is required for their *real* happiness. The demand to give up the illusions about its condition is the demand *to give up a condition which needs illusions.* The criticism of religion is therefore *in embryo the criticism of the vale of woe,* the *halo* of which is religion.

Criticism has plucked the imaginary flower from the chain not so that man will wear the chain without any fantasy or consolation but so that he will shake off the chain and cull the living flower. The criticism of religion disillusions man to make him think and act and shape his reality like a man who has been disillusioned and has come to reason, so that he will revolve round himself and therefore round his true sun. Religion is only the illusory sun which revolves round man as long as he does not revolve round himself.

(Marx, 1957, pp. 37–8)

Religion, then, is a 'reversed world-consciousness' because it is a product of a reversed world. In this claim we see the characterisation of religion as essentially ideological. Ideology, for Marx, is a form of thought in which 'men and their circumstances appear upside down as in a *camera obscura*' (Marx, 1957, p. 66). This is so because, in a sense, in a class-divided society – a society in which we see ourselves as essentially determined rather than as determining agents, in which we actually are determined by our social creations to a degree – things are upside down. Engels expressed the idea in this way: 'Religion . . . is nothing but the fantastic reflection in men's minds of those external forces which control their daily life, a reflection in which the terrestrial forces assume the form of supernatural forces' (1957, p. 56).

At first it was the forces of nature which were so reflected, but with the emergence of class division social forces became supernaturalised in this way. When Marx says religion is the general theory of this reversed world, he is referring to this fantastic reflection which involves an explanation and account of society and its nature because men in such a society cannot be clear about or grasp the truth of the matter.

But religion is also the 'universal ground for consolation' and 'the opium of the people'. The clear implication here is that whatever consolation religion may give to those who suffer or who are repressed, it is the kind of consolation one gets from drugs which give only temporary relief and at the cost of blunting the senses and having undesirable side effects. It provides no real solution and, in fact, tends to inhibit any real solution by making suffering and repression bearable. Religion thus plays its part in helping to perpetuate the very conditions which produce it. It promotes resignation rather than the search for means of changing the world.

But religion is more than simply compensatory and in being the 'universal ground for justification' of this reversed world, religion is more than simply an explanation of it. It is a force which legitimates it. The very thing that gives consolation and produces resignation is also used to convince those classes that might benefit from change that their condition is not only inevitable but has been ordained by a higher non-human authority. The submissiveness of the exploited and oppressed classes is reflected in their submissiveness to the commandments of religion. Religion offers compensation for the hardships of this life in some future life but it makes such compensation conditional upon acceptance of the injustices of this life.

However, not only the oppressed classes are religious. Members of the ruling class are often equally so. Religion is not a mere manipulative device to control the exploited groups in society. To some extent religion may be upheld by the ruling class because consciously or unconsciously it is seen as a force for social control but it may be followed also because the ruling class is itself alienated to a considerable degree. The need to take various measures to maintain privilege leads this class to see the social order as something other than simply the way human beings have chosen to organise themselves and, in a sense, 'in the nature of things'. Their perception is, of course, not that privilege is being preserved but that good order and stability must be maintained. Inequality, superiority and subordination, the distinction between rulers and ruled are all perceived as inevitable features of human society. This is not just rationalisation. Commitment to such ideas and their religious legitimation results from the ruling class's own fear of social disruption and its own dependence upon forces which seem to be, and to a degree are, beyond its own control. It stems from the feeling that it is constrained to do what must be done in the interests of stability and social order.

Marx also suggests that religion can be an expression of protest against oppression and distress experienced in a class-divided society as well as something which promotes acceptance of such a society. It is a form of protest, however, which cannot help the oppressed to overcome their conditions of oppression – a palliative drug not a cure. This acknowledgement that religion is 'the sigh of the oppressed creature' in Marx has led to a tradition of analysis of certain religious movements, particularly millennial movements, as essentially political protest and class-based movements expressed in a religious idiom. They are seen as socialist movements before their time and consequently doomed to failure. This approach will be discussed in the following chapter but one point to make here is that in seeing them as representing an incipient class consciousness it seems to ignore Marx's emphasis upon the opiate-like and mystificatory character of religion.

Finally, religion, Marx says, must be abolished as the illusory happiness of the people before they can achieve real happiness. But, since religion is the product of social conditions it cannot be abolished except by abolishing those social conditions. The institution of a communist society will, therefore, abolish religion. In such a society men will control their own society rather than being controlled by it, alienation will be overcome, and mystified views of reality will no longer prevail. Like Tylor, Frazer and Freud, Marx believed religion had no future. Religion is not an inherent tendency of human nature but the product of specific social circumstances. Marx makes the point clearly in the seventh thesis on Feuerbach where he says 'the "religious sentiment" is itself a *social product*' and 'the abstract individual . . . belongs in reality to a particular form of society' (1957, p. 64).

CRITICISMS OF MARX

The first major criticism that can be made of Marx's approach to religion concerns his characterisation of it as an expression of class interests and a form of ideology useful to the ruling class. There can be little doubt that religion can and has been used in that way. One could certainly argue, also, that in class-divided societies it is very likely that it will be used in such a way. The dominant ideas in any age, as Marx said, are generally the ideas of the ruling class, including religious ideas which, as a consequence, are likely to legitimate their position and to discourage any challenge to it. Religious leaders and organisations have often accommodated themselves to this situation accepting an alliance with the secular powers in which religious legitimation is exchanged for state support and even state-maintained monopoly in religious matters. But given all this, the question remains as to whether religion can be said to be essentially ideological and manipulative or whether it is only used in this way in certain circumstances. Because a set of beliefs can, and often is, put to certain uses, does this mean that it is nothing more than a device to support a particular social order? Critics of Marx would say it is not. Marx himself suggests that it is not. If religion were fundamentally a manipulative device one would expect it to stem largely from the dominant class in society. But Marx, in seeing religion as a product of alienation, recognises that it springs from those who are most alienated, the subordinate classes. He emphasises its compensatory function and the fact that it is a form of expression of protest.

Certainly, once in existence, religion may lend itself to ideological uses. To say, however, that religion can be turned into an instrument of manipulation is no more to explain it than saying that because art or drama can be utilised for ideological purposes this explains art or drama. The explanation of religion as ideological manipulation can, at best, explain only why it takes certain forms or receives certain emphases and interpretations. It does not explain religion as such.

In short, the analysis of religion as ideological is to some extent in conflict with its attribution to alienation. This shows itself in Marx's interpretation of religion as simultaneously an expression of protest and a means of legitimation which defuses protest. It is able to be both of these things, of course, because as an expression of protest it is ineffectual in Marx's view. It does not lead to alteration of the conditions which produce it but, in fact, serves to perpetuate them. In removing the solution to a fantastic plane it forms no threat to the status quo but is, rather, in channelling aspirations into 'harmless' paths, a prop to it. Not only does this seem far too convenient a position to take for the critic of religion, but it tacitly acknowledges that religion is fundamentally grounded in the circumstances of the subordinate class and that its ideological aspects are secondary.

This immediately raises the possibility, one never considered by Marx and Engels, that religion might be something more than mere opiate-like and resignation-generating compensatory fantasy. Might it not, for example, be a means of preserving a sense of meaning and dignity in the face of difficult circumstances? After all, Marx did not believe that it was possible in most class societies for the oppressed class to fundamentally alter their conditions of existence. This only becomes a possibility in late capitalism. Why then should one expect the prevailing world-view to be anything other than one which accepts the status quo and attempts to help people adjust to it and to come to terms with their lot? Whether or not one accepts that there is a degree of mystification in the religious world-view stemming from a condition of alienation, it does not follow that it is merely compensatory. Much more could be involved than this. The Marxist approach tends to ignore many aspects of religion, to oversimplify a complex phenomenon, and to make sweeping generalisations. The fact that religion may be an attempt to struggle with universal questions, inherent in the human condition, concerning the meaning of suffering, life and death, is never entertained by Marx and his followers. These are questions which transcend class interests and specific social situations. The implication is that such concerns only trouble people in tribal societies, where they are at the mercy of nature, and in class-divided societies. In a communist society people will not be disposed to dwell on such questions but concern themselves only with material matters and religion will atrophy. It would seem less than plausible, however, that the removal of those problems which stem from the specifically capitalist organisation of production by the institution of a different social and economic order will of itself also remove all those factors and forces which underlie the religious view of the world.

Perhaps Marx would have acknowledged that there is more to religion than his account seems to suggest if the point had been put to him. To some extent the fault in Marx on the question of religion is one of omission. It is what he left out of his account that renders it problematic. Marx was, however, largely concerned to offer a critique of religion and to analyse those aspects of it which bore upon his major purposes, namely to provide a critique of exploitation in class society and particularly capitalism which would play its part in its overthrow. Marx rarely wrote out of purely academic interest but generally had political purposes in mind. It did not serve those purposes to analyse all aspects of religion but only those which seemed to stand in the way of those purposes. Marx, therefore, did not attempt to produce a comprehensive analysis of religion (McKown, 1975; Plamenatz, 1975, p. 228). In not being explicit about this, however, Marx left the impression that what he said about religion was the essence of the matter and, therefore, that his view was rather a crude, one-sided, careless and unsophisticated one.

Marx's ideas on religion can also be examined in the light of the predictions they suggest. They imply that with the growth of class consciousness there would be a turning away from religion and concentration on the part of the proletariat on purely political forms of action. In short, one should expect increasing secularisation generally, greater secularisation in the more advanced capitalist societies and greater secularisation among the proletariat.

Most observers would agree that there has been such a process of secularisation in many countries. However, secularisation does not seem to be closely correlated with the level of maturity of capitalism as measured by the degree of industrial advance nor with the level of class consciousness of the industrial proletariat as measured by support for left-wing and particularly communist parties. The most advanced capitalist country, the United States, shows one of the lowest levels of secularisation among industrial nations, at least as measured by church affiliation and membership, and a low level of class consciousness. Holland and Belgium have tended to be somewhat less secularised than other equally advanced industrial nations, although the differences seem to be diminishing, while Britain, Northern Germany and the Scandinavian countries have tended to be more so. Class consciousness does not appear to differ very much between these cases. Also, within particular countries secularised life-styles are often by no means confined to the proletariat but extend throughout the society.

All this suggests that the relationship between religiosity, class consciousness and level of industrialisation is more complex than the Marxist theory supposes even if it does fit some of the facts. There are also a host of problems, glossed over in the generalisations set out above, relating to what is meant by secularisation and how it can be measured – problems which cannot be examined at this point but which will receive discussion in a subsequent chapter. To illustrate the Marxist approach in more substantive terms the next chapter will look at Marxist and other approaches to millennial movements.

7 The coming of the millennium

Marx and Engels, and particularly Engels, applied their ideas to many aspects of religion and especially to the analysis of religious movements such as early Christianity and to millennial movements, attracted, it would seem, by the revolutionary, world-changing potential of such movements and their frequent association with rebellion and revolution on the part of the oppressed and downtrodden sections of society. In this chapter we shall examine their treatment of millennial movements of the Middle Ages and the way their ideas concerning such movements have been developed by more recent writers and applied to a variety of such phenomena, both historical and contemporary.[1]

The millennial movement is a phenomenon more often found in Third World and developing countries or in the past and which, in consequence, has received more attention from anthropologists and historians than sociologists. There are, then, broadly two types of study in the literature on millennial movements, the historical which utilises sociological concepts and approaches and the anthropological studies, many of which are based on first-hand observation and have been able to document the conditions in which they have arisen in some detail. These two types of study have tended to produce somewhat different interpretations but as a result complement one another. They provide, also, a broad comparative basis for the development and testing of theories of this type of religious movement. The study of them is, then, not only fascinating in its own right but of considerable theoretical importance. For the most part they tend to fade away when the promised millennium fails to materialise but sometimes they grow into important religious traditions. Christianity was a millennial movement is its early phase and within the Christian tradition a millennial undercurrent has survived throughout its history.

The millennial movement expects a complete overturning of the present world order. There are perhaps five main characteristics of the millennial view as to how this transformation will come about and its nature. Cohn (1970) and Talmon (1966) identify much the same set of characteristics which the latter incorporates into a useful definition. Millennial movements are 'religious movements that expect imminent, total, ultimate, this-worldly, collective salvation' (Talmon, 1966, p. 166). Cohn leaves out the 'ultimate' aspect but adds that this salvation will be brought about by miraculous means.

In the millennial movement, then, the present world order is expected to be transformed at any time. It may be thought to be only days, weeks or months away. The transformation will be complete and total and is often thought to be the result of a final catastrophe which will destroy the present world order. A perfect world will come about in which men and women are freed from all troubles and difficulties. There will be peace, justice and plenty. There will be no evil or unhappiness. Often this perfect world is seen as the final and ultimate stage of history. There can be no further development since a perfect world will exist and it is a world not essentially different from the existing material world except that it lacks its faults. It is a this-worldly salvation, not an other-worldly one. The believers do not seek escape from this world but a perfect life within it. The millennium, finally, is usually seen as something that applies to a whole society or group within it, that is, to a collectivity rather than to individuals. It is a collective form of salvation.

A common and important additional feature is the central role of a prophet or leader who may have experienced revelations concerning the imminence of the millennium and may believe that he has been specially selected for his mission. Sometimes this prophet is seen as a cultural hero returned from the dead or a supernatural figure in human form – in tribal societies sometimes a returned ancestor. In this case the movement can be said to be messianic. Also messianic are those movements which believe that when the final catastrophe occurs a messianic leader, again often a past hero, will appear and bring about this event.

Another common feature of such movements is the high degree of emotion generated. These movements are often ecstatic and frequently hysterical. They tend to spread at an alarming rate and to involve totally those who fall subject to their influence, whose whole lives become bound up with the millennial expectations. There is often a complete break with previous ways of life. All past morality, all the old rules, norms and customs may be abandoned. Very often the millennial expectation is so strong that people abandon normal productive activities. They may abandon homes and fields and in some cases have destroyed property and livestock convinced that they will have no need of such things.

In the case of the cargo cults of Melanesia the usual belief is that with the onset of the new order the natives will be inundated with the consumer goods of Western civilisation. A common practice in such movements is feverish activity in building airstrips or wharfs so that these goods, the cargo, can be delivered, perhaps by ancestors. The natives frequently come to believe that they have somehow been cheated by the white men of their share of the cargo which comes from the ancestors who will now put things to rights.

Another common feature of these movements is a deep sense of guilt or responsibility for the plight in which the followers find themselves. Often in Melanesia, the natives feel that it is somehow their own fault that things have gone wrong. They may be cheated but this has only been possible because they have been foolish or wrong in their ideas and behaviour. The millennium comes about when someone finds a way of putting things right. In his discussion of early Christianity, Engels identifies a similar sense of guilt and personal responsibility for the malaise of the Roman Empire, expressed in terms of original sin and the inherently sinful nature of mankind who can, nevertheless, be redeemed by God's goodness and sacrifice in the form of the messianic saviour. This echoes a familiar theme, seen often in discussing the character of tribal religion, of misfortune and its association with personal responsibility or with the state of moral relations within the group or community.

This bring us to the question of the underlying conditions which generate and promote the millennial response. Most writers on this question have seen a very strong connection between millennialism on the one hand and deprivation and oppression on the other. Because of this there is usually a very close relationship between millennial movements and the political aspirations of those who are caught up in them. For this reason the study of millennial movements has been bound up with the study of the emergence of political awareness and activity among peoples and social strata which have not previously manifested an interest in political activity.

A number of such studies have been carried out from a Marxist perspective. One of the earliest accounts in sociological terms of a millennial outburst was Engels' account of the movement centred around Thomas Müntzer during the peasant wars in Germany during the Middle Ages (Engels, 1965). This type of interpretation began a long tradition which sees millennial movements as essentially incipient political movements arising from class antagonism, oppression and exploitation. Hobsbawm (1971) and Worsley (1970) in particular have contributed to this tradition. They tend to emphasise the positive contribution of millennialism to the development of realistic political movements among the lower classes in society. Such a view could be contrasted strongly with that of Marx himself, however. Marx saw all religions, and perhaps millennial ones more so than most, as opiate-like, fantastical and likely to preclude the possibility of the realisation of any real, practical, concrete political aims.

A different approach is that which emphasises the essentially irrational and desperate character of these movements (Cohn, 1970). The difference between these two approaches is that one sees millennialism as essentially a social phenomenon while the other, while recognising the importance of social factors, sees it as an essentially psychological response.

One could consider the approach of Burridge (1969), who stresses psychological factors to a certain degree, while seeing the movements as part of a transition from one set of values and assumptions to a completely new set, in a radically altered social situation, as in some ways a synthesis of these two approaches.

To begin with the Marxist approach, Engels (1965) characterised the role of Luther in the German Reformation as first encouraging the peasants in their demands for an improvement in their conditions but then deserting them when they went too far in demanding too far-reaching changes. Luther had given the peasants a powerful weapon in having the Bible translated into the vernacular because they could now read about early Christianity for themselves and about its millennial promise which they tended to apply to their own situation. But

Luther himself represented the interests of the propertied classes and the lesser nobility. The peasant and plebeian interests were actually expressed by Thomas Müntzer who early on in his studies came under the influence of millennial ideas concerning the Day of Judgement, the downfall of the degenerate Church and of a corrupt world.

Müntzer soon became involved with the millennial Anabaptist sect. He travelled all over Germany preaching violently against the Church and the priesthood, rapidly becoming more and more political and revolutionary in his preaching. He advocated the establishment of the Kingdom of God here on earth and by this he meant a society without class differences, according to Engels – a society without private property and without any central authorities independent of the members of society.

Müntzer aroused much interest and attracted many followers but Engels says that he went far beyond the immediate ideas and demands of the majority of the peasants. He created a party of the elite and the most advanced elements of the revolutionary groups in society which remained, however, only a small minority of the masses.

The time was not ripe for his ideas. Many fragmented and uncoordinated peasant rebellions and uprisings swept across Germany but all were defeated and brutally suppressed. Müntzer became a prophet of the revolution spurring the peasants on. He was recognised as leader of one of the uprisings centred on Mühlhausen in Thuringia. This too was defeated by the Landgrave Philip of Hesse and Müntzer's followers were massacred and Müntzer himself was captured, tortured and decapitated.

Engels emphasised the communism and egalitarianism of Müntzer's teachings and tends to play down the fantastical and truly millennial element in them. He also presents the millennial aspirations of Müntzer as a kind of forerunner of communism, centuries before its time and necessarily expressed in terms of religious ideas and concepts because in the Middle Ages it was not possible to think in any other terms. Müntzer is seen as a hero and a martyr and one of the first revolutionary figures to promote class war. This has been the general tendency of Marxist historians in interpreting such movements. In this way Engels founded the tradition of interpreting millennial movements as really incipient political movements with a class basis and as forerunners of modern class-conscious revolutionary political movements.

Cohn is very critical of this approach and presents a very different picture of the movements centred on Müntzer. He emphasises the mystical nature of Müntzer's thought and his obsession with millennial fantasies. His writings are full of the most fantastic claims and beliefs. One account of the final battle tells us that Müntzer claimed to have conversed on its eve with God himself and had been promised victory and that he would catch the enemy's cannon balls in the sleeves of his cloak. His followers certainly seem to have believed that some extraordinary miracle was about to take place.

As for Müntzer's communism and his concern for the plight of the peasantry, Cohn claims that he was indifferent to the material welfare of the poor. Müntzer, according to Cohn, simply utilised social discontent in a fantastic and hopelessly unrealistic programme to bring about his perfect society.

Originally, and Engels himself acknowledges this, Müntzer appealed to the princes and rulers to institute his perfect society, but not surprisingly they showed little interest in his ideas. Only then did Müntzer turn to the disaffected peasantry. Even then the great majority of them were not in the least interested in his millennial ideas. There had been and later there were to be frequent millennial outbursts associated with displaced social groups suffering relative deprivation, but the mass of the German peasants at Müntzer's time were actually better off than they had previously been. Their militancy was actually the consequence of a newly acquired self-confidence and they were attempting to remove obstacles that still remained in their way. This is true, Cohn claims, at least of those groups that took the initiative in the peasant uprising. Consequently, Müntzer and his ideas had no appeal for them. Their demands were realistic and political and they were sometimes able to make limited gains through bargaining with the princes. When they did come into open conflict it was often because the princes drove them to it in order to have an excuse to crush them. The peasants and their traditional rights stood in the way of some of the princes' aims of establishing absolutist regimes, imposing new taxes and laws and of bringing local administration under centralised control. Engels himself describes a long series of such conflicts in which there is no hint of millennialism.

The role of Müntzer, then, was one which, according to Cohn, has been greatly exaggerated by Engels and others. He played no part in the majority of uprisings, nor did his aspirations or programme appear in the demands of the majority of the peasant revolts. Here, as in the case of his analysis of Christianity, Engels shows his tendency to find class-conscious revolutionary movements among the lower orders of society at various periods of history without much justification. In fact, if religion acts as an opiate which inhibits the lower orders from furthering their real interests, as Marx said, Engels' interpretation of millennial movements is hardly a Marxist one. Millennial movements demonstrate a total lack of awareness and understanding of the real conditions and what is possible given them. They demonstrate a thoroughly mystified religious way of thinking which expects a social transformation not by the efforts of human beings themselves but by the intervention of supernatural powers or other fantastical means.

It was not poverty or material deprivation *per se*, Cohn argues, that stimulated such millennial fantasies in the Middle Ages. The ordinary peasants, who lived the traditional life however hard and poverty-stricken it was, were not particularly disposed to join the outbursts that occurred from time to time. It was rather the displaced groups and those on the margins of society that provided the following of such movements – landless peasants, unemployed journeymen, beggars and all those who could find no assured and recognised place in society.

It was in conditions of change and uncertainty, also, that the millennial response tended to occur, stimulated by the break up of the old order and familiar patterns. Particularly important was the loss of credibility and authority on the part of the Church. This left emotional needs unfulfilled and many people tended to turn to prophets and miracle workers.

Cohn emphasises the fact that these movements also tended to arise amidst some more political and wider uprising which was more realistic in its aims. The millennial prophet attempted to use such situations to raise support and to gain a following during a time of unrest. Millennial movements in the Middle Ages were thus not early stages of political movements but outbursts of fantasy and mania.

Cohn considers that those who got caught up in such movements were in a pathological state of mind and that on the whole they were irrational outbursts. When they collapsed there was no necessary tendency for things to take a more realistic political direction. They were highly ephemeral movements incapable of making any headway in dealing with the social and economic problems of those affected.

On the whole Cohn seems to be right concerning the importance of social displacement, insecurity and emotional anxiety in these movements and about their essentially fantastical character. It is less easy to accept that they were the product of mass psychological disturbance or pathological mental states. The social character of them refutes such a claim.

But do they pave the way for more realistic political movements? Are they early exploratory stages of a growing political awareness? This is the kind of claim that writers like Worsley (1970), from an analysis of the Melanesian cargo cults, and Hobsbawm (1971), writing on nineteenth-century movements in Southern Europe, make. Worsley also links the movements to the oppressed and the displaced elements in society and sees them as essentially revolutionary movements which reject the rule, power and values of the dominant group and inevitably come into conflict with it. This may be a dominant class or a different ethnic group as in the case of the colonial situation of Melanesia.

Usually, this kind of movement occurs among peoples who are divided into small isolated units lacking adequate political institutions or existing means of organisation for coping with the situation in which they find themselves. This is true of many primitive societies and especially of Melanesian societies where there were no permanent institutions of chiefship or wider political structures other than the small lineage groups. Also the terrain was such as to produce a patchwork of numerous very small tribes and linguistic groups with little contact or communication with one another. What the millennial movement can do in such a situation is to integrate these fragmented units into some degree of unity. The common situation vis-à-vis the colonial rulers promotes this tendency towards unity and the means is very often a millennial cult.

Another common situation where such movements tend to emerge is that of feudal organisation where the peasants and urban plebeian strata lack forms of political organisation which would enable them to effectively oppose the political authorities.

Marx likened the rural peasantry to potatoes in a sack. They are all in the same situation and have common interests but do not form a true class and lack any organisations for furthering their interests. Leaders tend to be thrown up claiming to represent their interests but these leaders inevitably become new masters. In more advanced types of society the tendency is towards Bonapartism or Caesarism. In backward societies prophets promising a mystical resolution of problems tend to emerge. And in Worsley's view such millennial movements are early phases of political movements and forms of political activism among peasants.

A third type of situation in which millennial ideas flourish is that where political institutions representing the interests of all groups in society exist but where the society is in conflict with a vastly superior power and suffers a series of defeats and disappointments. Frequently, recourse to millennial hopes and dreams is the result, all else having failed. This has occurred in Africa and was, of course, the situation in Palestine when Christianity emerged. In these cases, when the old structures and the old political organisations will have been destroyed, the millennial movement can weld the fragmented society together on a new basis.

But having unified a people in these ways millennial movements, according to Worsley, tend either to develop into secular political organisations which divest themselves of their millennialism or they become passive, quietistic, escapist sects. The conditions under which a cult is likely to become passive are first, where it has been defeated and second, where political aspirations are no longer expressed in religious forms and where political parties supplant religious organisations. In other words, while some are politicised those elements which retain their millennial outlook after defeat and after the majority has gone over to secular politics adopt a response which ceases to really confront the dominant powers of the current world order. They lose their revolutionism and drive and blame things on their own sinfulness or on mankind as a whole rather than on the dominant elements in the society.

Worsley's account and interpretation are, then, a good deal more sophisticated than that of Engels. His account is based, also, upon a much wider range of material and data. And there is a good deal in it that is sound, especially the points about integration of fragmented communities. But Worsley may go too far in claiming that these movements are early forms of political movement or that they grow into secular political movements. It seems rather that they are replaced by the latter when more realistic assessments of the situation are grasped in time. The millennial movement, as Cohn argues, is essentially fantastical and attempts to solve problems through fantasy due to a general lack of appreciation of the realities of the situation. In this, Marx seems to have had a better understanding. Worsley sees them as early attempts at realistic action which are successively replaced when tested against the realities and found to fail. This perhaps over-rationalises the process. It also assumes a spurious succession. The various movements that have occurred in Melanesia do not seem to have formed any overall progressive development.

These movements may give the authorities a good deal of concern and cause them some trouble but unlike genuine attempts to bring about political change they never really threaten the established order and are much easier to deal with than real rebellion or insurrection. If Melanesian natives insist on engaging in feverish activity building airstrips so that the ancestors may fly in the cargo, this does not unduly worry the authorities. It is a nuisance rather than a threat since all it does is to take the natives away from their normal jobs and work. Such activities could be seen as relatively harmless outlets for frustrations which do not last long.

Another problem with Worsley's approach is that it is probably more often the case that millennial movements follow a period of straightforward political activity than precede it. They are more often post-political than pre-political and follow a period of despair after normal political means have failed. This was clearly the case with the emergence of Christianity and among the North American Indians when the Ghost Dance cult swept through many of the tribes after a long period of military resistance and warfare. (We may take warfare to be political activity in the wider sense of the term; politics carried on by other means, as Clausewitz said.)

Political and military resistance to invading powers is the understandable initial response and, therefore, the more usual and normal one. Insurrection seems the more likely response of oppressed and displaced peasantry in agrarian societies. Worsley acknowledges that this kind of situation may occur but he does not recognise it as the more usual response.

In the case of Melanesia, political and military resistance to the colonial powers was impossible from the start so small-scale and fragmented were the peoples living there when contact was first made and so superior were the colonial societies that brought these regions under their administration. Where resistance is impossible, a millennial response may well occur at the outset due to the total hopelessness of the situation and the total lack of comprehension of it. In the North American situation, where colonial penetration occurred much earlier, the technological and cultural superiority of the colonists was not as great. Communications were less difficult and the Indian tribes used the horse and therefore had the means of rapid mobility across wide areas of the plains. It was difficult to isolate and control them. They were sometimes able to form large-scale alliances and to engage in full-scale warfare with the colonial settlers. Although military action on the part of the North American Indians was often encouraged by new prophetic religious cults, only when hopelessly defeated did they come to rely wholly on millennial hopes (Wilson, 1975).[2]

It is the situation of despair that seems to be the key point in understanding the nature of such movements. Cohn, as we have seen, attempts to deal with the emotional nature of them by resorting to psychological factors and by characterising them as pathological. More enlightening is the approach of Burridge writing about the Melanesian cargo cults (1960, 1969). In Melanesia the cults generally involve a high degree of emotion and even hysteria at times. The disruption of traditional patterns of life has been of a severe nature but it is not so much the material suffering of the native people that has been significant as the tremendous blow to their self-respect and dignity. The cults obviously centre upon white man's goods because these things are in themselves desirable and the natives feel deprived of them. But these things are also a symbol of the power of the white man and of the superiority of his culture.

More than this, traditional material goods and their ceremonial distribution and exchange for the purpose of acquiring prestige by men who sought a leading role in the society – big men – are a key institution of Melanesian society. Such goods are given away to rivals and their followers in the hope of humiliating them by making it impossible for them to make an adequate return. The ceremonial gift exchange system embodied all the most central values of the Melanesians relating to dignity and prestige. Suddenly, however, they found themselves excluded from possession of the most desirable goods – white man's goods. Their position as a culture stood in the same relationship to the white man's culture as an individual native who played no role in ceremonial gift exchange stood in relation to a big man. Such a man was known in many tribes as a 'rubbish man'. The Melanesians were forced into the awful realisation that in relation to white man's culture theirs was a 'rubbish culture'. The clearest expression of the fact was that the white man would not exchange his goods with the natives on the traditional basis. They were not even considered players in the game.

In the cargo cult, as in the Middle Ages, what seems to be happening is that the disaffected are desperately trying to restore a sense of dignity and self-respect. They are seeking a way of placing themselves once again at the centre of things, to make themselves people who matter and who have a role to play in the world. Hence the emotion, the fanaticism and the hysteria. All this goes much deeper than desire for material goods. It goes beyond politics.

Related to this and also extremely important in these movements is the attempt to understand what is happening. The impact of white civilisation, the defeat or futility of all resistance, the displacement of traditional patterns, all this is confusing, bewildering and incomprehensible. In this situation people use whatever intellectual resources they possess to account for the situation – traditional mythology, the Bible, the religious tradition, or new ideas that arise. In pre-industrial societies any attempt to construct a coherent view of the world and man's place in it will tend to take a religious form and often one which seems fantastic to the outside observer. Given the cultural context and the people's perception of their situation such attempts can be seen not to be irrational or the product of collective mental disturbance but reasonable and, for those involved, a credible response given the tradition of ideas and ways of thinking.

Very often the initial response in primitive societies is couched in magical or thaumaturgic terms, according to Wilson (1975). In Africa troubles are often blamed upon witches, for example. A rise in witchcraft accusations is common in situations of rapid change and disruption of traditional patterns. Witchfinding cults and movements may flourish as a result. In the Middle Ages, as Cohn documents, as well as millennial outbursts there were frequent persecutions of Jews.

Early stages of millennial movements are often simply thaumaturgic or magical cults applied to the collectivity as a whole. It is not just individuals who perceive themselves as under threat from evil but the whole community or society. From this the truly millennial movement may develop under certain circumstances – war, suppression of magical movements by the colonial authorities, or despair.

Wilson agrees with Worsley that such movements can create unity where it was lacking before because they are reflections of a common situation. But he places much less emphasis on them as early forms of political action. He too considers them to be very much emotional responses to a loss of integrity and status and of feelings of inferiority. He emphasises also their attempts to make sense of a confusing situation going beyond merely political aims. They do, in his view, however, create a new consciousness of the possibility of change and an expectation of it. In this way they establish a new framework of order. A new conception of the social organisation of the community is created. The religious tradition which sanctioned a particular social order is now utilised to initiate changes and to justify them.

In some ways this is the beginning of a more secular view of things. As Wilson puts it 'it is within *religious* phenomena that secularisation must first appear' (1975, p. 497). Millennial movements may be fantastical in their ideas and outlook but they do create the concept of change in cultures that had never before looked at the world as changing and changeable. In time, such a radically new way of thinking can give rise to realistic and rational demands for change based upon an appropriate comprehension of the situation.

8 Religion and solidarity: Emile Durkheim

The most outstanding 'sociological' theorist and one who has exercised an enormous influence on the sociology of religion is Emile Durkheim. Some of his ideas and aspects of his approach were influenced by those of the earlier but rather less well known W. Robertson Smith in his study of ancient Semitic religion in *Lectures on the Religion of the Semites* published in 1889. Before examining the view of Durkheim himself a brief exposition of those of Robertson Smith will serve to set the background of Durkheim's contribution.

Robertson Smith emphasised practices rather than beliefs. It is the practices of religion which are fundamental, he argued – its ceremonies, rites and rituals and not the beliefs. To understand religion one has to analyse first and foremost what people do and not what they believe. Practices are primary and beliefs secondary. This is why beliefs are often rather vague, inconsistent and contradictory. People are not so much concerned about doctrine but with rituals and observances. The sociologist must therefore pay attention primarily to what they do and not what they say.

Robertson Smith was perhaps rather extreme and one-sided in this emphasis but he did have a point. There is often a tendency to focus upon the scriptural and doctrinal side of religion whereas in the lives of its followers it is the practices which matter rather than the finer points of dogma. On the other hand, the point of view of Robertson Smith entails the danger that the actor's conception of what he or she is doing will be overlooked or insufficiently taken into account by the sociological interpretation of the actions concerned which may, consequently, misunderstand and distort them.

A second point to note about Robertson Smith is the emphasis he placed upon the obligatory nature of religious observance in most societies. Religion is not, for the most part, a matter of individual choice but instilled into the members of the society and required of them. Religion is part of what Durkheim would later call the collective representations of the society. The emphasis Robertson Smith placed on this aspect of religion relates to his views on the close connection between religion and political allegiance. Religion is an affair of the group and the society and these are essentially political entities.

Religion, Robertson Smith claimed, has two functions; regulative and stimulative. Regulation of individual behaviour is important for the good of all, or in other words, the group, and it is religion which has been largely responsible for this regulative task in the history of human societies. Sin, Robertson Smith said, is an act which upsets the internal harmony of the group. Religion also stimulated a feeling of community and unity. Ritual is a repetitive statement of unity and functions to consolidate the community. The function of the sacrificial totemic feast that the ancient Semites were alleged to have practised, the most basic and elementary form of religion it was believed by many at the time, was to sacralise the group and promote its unity and solidarity. Clearly, then, Robertson Smith was opposed to the view that sees religion as springing from within the individual. Religion, he said, is not to do with the saving of souls but with the consolidation of the group.

Robertson Smith based his analysis upon very flimsy and unreliable data. Durkheim had rather better data to work upon, relating to the totemic system of certain Australian aboriginal tribes, particularly the Arunta, collected by the fieldworkers Spencer and Gillen. In the very first sentence of his major work based upon this material, *The Elementary Forms of the Religious Life*, he announces that the purpose of the study is to look at the most primitive and simple religion known to us which he believes to be the totemism of these Australian tribes. First, however, he undertakes to characterise the nature of religion and to define his subject matter, offering the definition quoted in Chapter one above where the concept of religion was discussed. He also sets out his methods of study and subjects theories of religion current in his day to trenchant criticism.

He is particularly concerned to challenge the prevalent notion that religion is largely false and illusory. How could it have survived so long, he asks, if it were mere mistake and illusion? While the tenets of various religions may seem odd and strange, we have to see them as essentially symbolic in nature and we have to go beneath the symbolism to appreciate what they are really expressing. When we do so we find, Durkheim says, that 'in reality there are no religions which are false. All are true in their own fashion' (1915, p. 3). So in examining what he takes to be the most primitive and simple religion as a means of understanding all religion, he is not doing what other writers had done. He is not reducing religion to its origins in mistaken and false conceptions of primitive societies and thereby discrediting it. On the contrary, even the most primitive religion expresses a kind of truth even if, as we shall see, this truth is not quite what the believer thinks it is.

Durkheim goes on to set out the rationale of his own approach. In looking at the most primitive form of religion he is looking for that which is constant and unvarying in religion, its essential features. This is best done by looking at the simplest cases one knows of and in which, also, the relationships between the facts are more apparent, rather than more developed and complex instances where what is essential is difficult to disentangle from and tends to be lost in secondary elaboration and accretion.

This is not all Durkheim sets out to do in *The Elementary Forms*. It is also a study in the sociology of knowledge. The basic concepts and categories of thought, such as those of space, time, number and cause, are born in religion and of religion, Durkheim claims. And since religion is something which is eminently social it follows that the basic categories of thought are derived from society. It is only because we live in society that we conceptualise the way we do, according to Durkheim.

After these preliminaries Durkheim embarks upon the analysis of Australian aboriginal totemism. He describes the clan organisation of aboriginal society and the association between each clan and a sacred totem animal or plant species. The totems are represented by stylised images drawn on stones or wooden objects called *churingas* which, since they bear the image of the sacred totem, are also sacred. They are surrounded by taboos and treated with the utmost respect. In fact, Durkheim argues, since they are even more taboo than the sacred species itself they are actually more sacred than it is. These totemic symbols, Durkheim says, are emblems of the clan in much the same way as a flag is the emblem of a country.

Durkheim goes on to show how the totemic system is also a cosmological system and how such basic categories such as class, that is, the idea of a category itself, is tied up in its origins with totemism and the clan structure said to characterise early human society. First, he notes that human beings also partake in the sacred. As members of clans with sacred totems and who believe themselves to be descended from the sacred totem, they too are sacred. An Australian aborigine will say not that he or she belongs to the white cockatoo or black cockatoo clan, for example, but that he or she *is* a white cockatoo, or a black cockatoo. In other words, they are in some sense of the same essence as the totemic species and, consequently, sacred.

In the same way, in the totemic system of ideas, since all known things are associated with one or other clan totem, they too partake in the sacred. For example, rain, thunder, lightning, clouds, hail, winter and so on, are all associated with the Crow clan among the Arunta. Similarly, each clan has associated with it a range of natural phenomena so that 'all known things will thus be arranged in a sort of tableau or systematic classification embracing the whole of nature' (Durkheim, 1915, p. 142). These totemic systems of classifications were the first in the history of human thought and are thus modelled upon social organisation. They have taken the form of society for their framework. It is, consequently, clan social organisation which has made the basic categories of thought and, thereby, thought itself possible.

Where else could this notion of class or category and of a system of categories come from, asks Durkheim. It was not, he claims, given to our minds *a priori*. It must have been suggested by something in experience. It was the experience of collective life that generated such ideas and concepts.

After reviewing current theories of the origins of totemism Durkheim sets out his own. The variety of natural things associated with the totems, as we have seen, all partake of the sacred. This is so because all partake of a common principle. Totemic religious practice is really addressed to this common totemic principle rather than to the individual clan totems. 'In other words totemism is the religion not of such and such animals or men or images but of an anonymous and impersonal force, found in each of these beings but not to be confounded with any of them' (1915, p. 188).

This impersonal force turns out to be the familiar *mana*. Durkheim says of it:

> This is the original matter out of which have been constructed those beings of every sort which the religions of all times have consecrated and adored. The spirits, demons, genii and gods of every sort are only the concrete forms taken by this energy or 'potentiality' . . . in individualising itself.
>
> (1915, p. 199)

What is this *mana* and in what does it originate? Why do certain things have it? Not, Durkheim says, because of their intrinsic nature but because they are symbols of something else. This is shown by, among other things, the fact that it is the symbolic representation of the totem, the *churinga* that is the more sacred. What is this something else? We have seen that the totem stands for two things; first, this abstract and impersonal force or totemic principle and second, the clan. Durkheim therefore concludes that 'if it is at once the symbol of the god and of the society, is that not because the god and the society are only one?' (1915, p. 206). He goes on 'The god of the clan, the totemic principle, can therefore be nothing else than the clan itself, personified and represented to the imagination under the visible form of the animal or vegetable which serves as totem' (ibid.).

How did such a thing come about? Why should there be this equation between god and society? Durkheim answers as follows:

> In a general way, it is unquestionable that a society has all that is necessary to arouse the sensation of the divine in minds, merely by the power that it has over them; for to its members it is what a god is to his worshippers.
>
> (1915, p. 206)

The characteristics of gods are that they are superior to men who depend upon gods and are subject to their will and commandments. Society also gives us this feeling of dependence, according to Durkheim. Durkheim characterises the nature of society and the relationship between it and the individual in the following way:

> Since it has a nature which is peculiar to itself and different from our individual nature, it pursues ends which are likewise special to it; but, as it cannot attain them except through our intermediacy, it imperiously demands our aid. It requires that, forgetful of our own interests, we make ourselves its servitors, and it submits us to every sort of inconvenience, privation and sacrifice, without which social life would be impossible. It is because of this that at every instant we are obliged to submit ourselves to rules of conduct and of thought which we have neither made nor desired, and which are sometimes even contrary to our most fundamental inclinations and instincts.
>
> (1915, p. 207)

This highly characteristic passage from Durkheim well illustrates the primacy that he always gave to the social over the individual and his conception of society as a reality *sui generis* subject to its own laws and with its own requirements and needs.

This predominance of society is not, however, based so much upon material or physical restraints but upon moral authority. We are induced to obey the dictates of society by a moral authority exercised by society rather than because we reason that it is in our interests or wise to obey. We obey, Durkheim says, because our will is overcome by an outside pressure. When we feel such a pressure we feel at the same time a deep sense of respect for the source of it.

For Durkheim, then, the dictates of society form the basis of morality. Actions are moral because society demands them of us. Of moral precepts Durkheim says 'It is society who speaks through the mouths of those who affirm them in our presence; it is society whom we hear in hearing them; and the voice of all has an accent which that of one alone could never have' (1915, p. 208). On occasion this moral supremacy of society is brought home to us in a striking way. 'In the midst of an assembly animated by a common passion, we become susceptible of acts and sentiments of which we are incapable when reduced to our own forces' (1915, p. 209).

Because this moral sensibility is experienced as an external pressure, human beings came to conceive of the society which exercises this pressure as an external force or power which took on also a spiritual and sacred nature since it was quite unlike any ordinary external object or force. In this way reality was perceived to be of two radically different natures or, in other words, divided between the sacred and the profane.

Religion, then, for Durkheim, is nothing other than the collective force of society over the individual. Religion 'is a system of ideas with which the individuals represent to themselves the society of which they are members, and the obscure but intimate relations which they have with it' (1915, p. 225). Religion, then, is not an illusion; it is not inherently false. When believers believe they depend upon and are subject to a moral power from which they receive all that is best in themselves they are not deceived; 'this power exists, it is society' (1915, p. 225).

But religion is not simply a system of beliefs and conceptions. It is a system of action; it involves rituals. What is the significance and role of ritual in religion according to Durkheim? Religion, he argued, is, in fact, born out of ritual. It is in participating in religious rites and ceremonies that the moral power is most clearly felt and where moral and social sentiments are strengthened and renewed.

Durkheim illustrates this function of ritual from the Australian aboriginal data. Most of the year the clan is scattered in the form of small hunting bands. During a certain season the bands gather together at a certain place and at this time a series of rites are performed in which great excitement is experienced as well as feelings of exaltation, or, as Durkheim calls it, effervescence. It is these rites, he argues, that generate, strengthen and renew religious sentiments and their sense of dependence upon an external spiritual and moral power which is in fact society. It is the collective nature of such gatherings which is responsible for effervescence and which gives the participants a sense of the importance of the group and the society couched in religious terms. Ritual thus generates and sustains social solidarity and cohesion.

Durkheim seeks to show how his approach can explain a great variety of religious beliefs and practices. For example, the idea of the soul is really, he argues, 'nothing other than the totemic principle incarnate in each individual' (1915, p. 248). It is a recognition that society exists only in and through individuals. The soul, he points out, partakes in divinity. In this it represents something which is other than ourselves but yet within us. This is no illusion Durkheim insists. The soul represents the social aspects of the human being and, in a sense, society is something external to us yet internalised within us. We do incorporate a sacred element in the form of the social in that we are social creatures. The soul, also, is immortal because it is the social principle. Individuals die but society continues and the belief in the immortality of the soul expresses this.

Belief in various spirits and gods is explained by Durkheim as being derived from belief in ancestral spirits which are actually the souls of ancestors and, therefore, the social principle manifested in particular individuals.

Ritual taboos and prohibitions are derived, he argues, from an attitude of respect for sacred objects and their purpose is to maintain this attitude. He derives the whole ascetic outlook, common to many religious traditions, from these ideas of taboo, sacredness and respect. From these arose the values of prohibition and self-denial which express the notion, also, that social order is only possible if individuals suffer denial of their wishes to some degree.

Sacrifice is, of course, closely related to self-denial but Durkheim asks why are gods so often hungry for sacrificial offerings. It is because gods cannot do without worship, which sacrifice expresses, and this reflects the understanding that since gods are nothing other than society they cannot do without worshippers, no less than society can do without individual members.

Rituals, as we have seen, are for Durkheim, essentially about maintaining group cohesion but frequently they are believed by participants to bring about some desirable state of affairs or prevent an undesirable one. Such is the case with the aboriginal *intichiuma* ceremony, the express purpose of which is to ensure the reproduction and abundance of the totemic species. Durkheim seeks to explain this putative instrumental efficacy of religious rites as the result of their moral efficacy. Because of this moral efficacy, which is real, a belief in their physical and material efficacy, which is in fact illusory, can be supported. The rites give a profound sense of elation and well-being and this generates a confidence that the rite has succeeded in its purpose. In other words what the participants think is happening is not happening; something quite different is happening which is not perceived by the participants; 'the true justification of religious practices does not lie in the apparent ends which they pursue, but rather in the invisible action which they exercise over the mind and in the way in which they affect our mental states' (1915, p. 360).

Rituals are thus explained in functionalist terms. Durkheim says of them that 'they are as necessary for the well working of our moral life as our food is for the maintenance of our physical life, for it is through them that the group affirms and maintains itself' (1915, p. 382). It is not surprising that Durkheim has been likened in this aspect of his work to Marx. As Turner puts it 'it is often difficult to distinguish between the Durkheimian conception of religion as social cement and the Marxist metaphor of religion as a social opium' (1991, p. 78).

Durkheim notes that different aboriginal ceremonies are all essentially variations on a basic theme. They are all the same ceremony adapted for a variety of purposes. This is also true of other religious systems, he observes, for example, the Catholic mass of which there is a form for marriages, funerals, etc. Durkheim concludes from this ambiguity that the real function of such rites is not the expressed aim. This is only secondary; 'the real function of the cult is to awaken within the worshippers a certain state of soul, composed of moral force and confidence' (1915, p. 386). Consequently, it does not matter what form the rite takes or what its expressed purpose is. The real function of it is always the same. It does not matter what the members of group assemble to do; all that matters is that they assemble and do what they do collectively. 'The essential thing is that men are assembled, that sentiments are felt in common and expressed in common acts; but the particular nature of these sentiments and acts is something secondary and contingent' (1915, p. 386).

> What essential difference is there between an assembly of Christians celebrating the principal dates of the life of Christ, or of Jews remembering the Exodus from Egypt or the promulgation of the decalogue, and a reunion of citizens commemorating the promulgation of a new moral or legal system or some great event in the national life?
>
> (1915, p. 427)

CRITICISMS OF DURKHEIM

There have been many criticisms of Durkheim's account of religion[1] but they can be broadly divided into three kinds, methodological, theoretical, and ethnographic/empirical. To take the methodological difficulties first, the fact that Durkheim bases his whole study on a very limited range of data, that pertaining to a few Australian aboriginal tribes, gives cause for concern. He considered that it was only necessary to examine one case in detail since his purpose was to find the essential nature of religion. Is it then possible to generalise this to all religion? The problem is that it is not possible to be certain that the essence of the particular religion examined is the essence of religion in general. To determine that it would be necessary to examine a wide range of cases which Durkheim does not do. If he had done this it is unlikely he would have observed the close relationship between religion and social groups that he does in the case of the Australian aboriginal tribes in question. In many primitive societies there is strong relationship between a given set of effective social units, usually kinship based, and most aspects of life including such things as religion, political action and economic structures. This is not necessarily so in more economically advanced, larger-scale societies. Or to put it another way, in the latter type of society individuals belong to a multiplicity of single-purpose groups and their religious lives may overlap very little with their economic and political activities, at least as far as the sets of people involved are concerned.

Also dubious is Durkheim's claim that if one takes a society at a very simple level of technological development one can observe the simplest form of religion. It does not follow that because the level of technology is simple, other things such as symbolic and religious systems will also be simple and unelaborate. 'Simple' should not, in any case, be equated with 'essential' or 'fundamental'. These points are supported by the fact that the religious and symbolic systems of hunter-gatherer societies like that of the Australian aboriginal societies vary considerably in character including their degree of elaborateness and complexity. It is not the case that all such societies have clan structures or totemism nor is there any correlation between totemism and clan structure.

This brings us to criticisms on ethnographic and empirical grounds. Evans-Pritchard (1965, pp. 64–6) sums up the many criticisms of this kind that have been made of Durkheim as follows:

1 There is no evidence that totemism arose in the way Durkheim speculated that it did or that other religions are derived ultimately from it.
2 The distinction between sacred and profane is one which will not fit many systems of belief, a point made earlier when discussing definitions of religion.
3 The Australian aboriginal clan is not the most important group in the society. It is not a significant corporate group. These are the horde or hunting band and the tribe.
4 Totemism of the Australian aboriginal type is untypical and the totemism of the Arunta and related tribes is even untypical of Australia.
5 A relationship between totemism and clan organisation is not common.

The first theoretical point to be made about *The Elementary Forms* concerns Durkheim's central theoretical claim that society has everything necessary to arouse the sensation of the divine in our minds and that the divine is not, therefore, illusory but refers to something real, namely society. Of course, it would hardly be surprising to discover that there is a close connection between religion and society but what is contentious in Durkheim's theory is that he goes much further than this in arguing that the object of religious concern, the divine, is nothing other than society. It is perfectly acceptable to describe similarities between religious conceptions and the nature of the social but can one leap from the observation of such similarities to the conclusion that religion is nothing other than the symbolic representation of society and the way in which the members of a society represent to themselves the relationship they have with it? Even if the parallel between the character of society and the divine were as close as Durkheim makes it out to be, and this is very questionable since he selects only those aspects of each which support his case, it does not follow that it is society that *is* the source of religious conceptions or the object of religious concern. There are many reasons why religious conception might reflect aspects of social structure other than the claim that Durkheim makes.

At the heart of the problem with Durkheim's thesis, then, is the way he characterises the nature of the divine and of society and the relationship between them. His characterisation of the nature of society and the relationship individuals have with it can most clearly be seen to lead to problems in the context of his discussion of morality. Such is the force or pressure that society exercises over us, and this, remember, is essentially moral pressure, that we are capable of acts we would not otherwise be capable of, and of someone who is inspired by moral/social pressure he says:

> Because he is in moral harmony with his comrades, he has more confidence, courage, and boldness in action, just like the believer who thinks that he feels the regard of his god turned towards him. It thus produces, as it were, a perpetual sustenance for our moral nature.

> (1915, p. 210)

If social pressure can inspire acts of heroism, however, it can also inspire acts of atrocity. Durkheim's seems a strange conception of morality. Does the social and collective pressure that the crowd situation exerts, for example, guarantee moral action or is it more likely to lead to the suspension of our moral sensibilities and their replacement with mob mentality? Collective passion is no guarantee of moral behaviour by most criteria of morality. Is it not the case, also, that the great moral heroes of history are precisely those who have stood against the majority or against those with power and authority and suffered as a consequence?

In a sense, of course, morality is a matter of social relationships. In this sense society could be said to be the source or at least the subject of moral concern and Durkheim is right to point out that a society is a moral community. The trouble is that he jumps from saying this to the conclusion that morality is nothing other than the voice of society.

The fact that our moral sense might make us go against the majority, the society, or authority, shows that we are not quite so dependent upon or creatures of society as Durkheim claims. Society, powerful as it is, does not have the primacy that Durkheim believes it has. Ironically, it often seems to be the case that religious beliefs can have a much greater influence upon and hold over the individual than society does since it is often out of religious convictions that individuals will fly in the face of society or attempt to withdraw from it, as in the case of many sectarian movements.

The emergence of sectarian movements and of religious pluralism and diversity within a society is, of course, something that Durkheim's theory has great difficulty dealing with. Also, religious differences frequently lead to tension and conflict, a fact which seems to undermine his functionalist account of religion as an essentially integrating force. Religion has as often been as divisive a force as an integrating one. As Aron has pointed out, if Durkheim were right 'the essence of religion would be to inspire in men a fanatical devotion to partial groups, to pledge each man's devotion to a collectivity and, by the same token, his hostility to other collectivities' (1970, p. 68).

However, the cynic might argue that this is precisely what religion does and it is a strength of Durkheim's thesis that it recognises this. But this would indeed be too cynical a view despite the conflict and suffering that has occurred in the name of religion since it neglects the universalism that transcends group allegiances that is also a genuine and fundamental aspect of many great religious traditions, and it is precisely this universalism that Durkheim's approach fails to do justice to or account for.

A further problem with Durkheim's theory relates to his functionalism. He does not only seek to explain religion by demonstrating that it embodies fundamental truths in symbolic form but also in terms of the role it plays in integrating society. Functionalism is a perspective which owes a good deal to the influence of Durkheim. It came to dominate British social anthropology through figures such as Malinowski and Radcliffe-Brown during the early part of this century and American and British sociology during the 1940s and 1950s. Functionalism essentially states that a social institution can be understood in terms of the contribution it makes to the survival of a society or to its social integration and solidarity.

Functionalist explanations are beset with problems and functionalist explanations of religion particularly so (see Chapter ten). This is because the discrepancy between the functionalist account of the given social behaviour and the interpretation of the participants themselves is at its greatest in the case of religion. The consequence of Durkheim's explanation of religion is that he places himself in the position of claiming to know what the participants in a religious ritual are really doing and that the participants are mistaken in what they believe they are doing. Durkheim does not only claim a privileged position in regard to ritual of course, since to say that God is real, that he is society, is to say that although religious belief embodies a truth of a sort, believers are nevertheless deluded about the nature of this truth. Participants in religious rites do not consider that what they are doing has much to do with integrating the group, or if it does do this in their eyes this is, at least, not its primary purpose and not what it is fundamentally about. The participants also, of course, do think it really matters what they do and would not accept that all rites are fundamentally the same. For the Arunta the aim is not to promote clan solidarity but to ensure the abundance of the totem species and it is crucial to do just the right things to achieve this aim.

The implication of Durkheim's view that all rituals are essentially the same, then, is that the beliefs of the participants and the expressed purposes of the rites have nothing to do with what happens. This is a strange conclusion to reach. It seems unavoidable that in attempting to understand religious behaviour we have to pay attention to the beliefs the participants have about their behaviour and that this must be significant in accounting for it. This is not to say that there can never be any factors other than the participants' own understanding of what they are doing and that when one has understood that one has understood everything, as some would argue. It is equally extreme, however, to argue, as Durkheim does, that what the participants think they are doing plays no significant part in an explanation of what they are doing.

A further consequence of Durkheim's dismissal of the importance of the particular form of rites is that he is left with no real basis for explaining the particular form they take. If it does not really matter what people do, then how can one explain what they do?; how is it they come to do one thing rather than another?

To be fair to Durkheim, he was not a naive functionalist and realised that it is not enough to point to the function of a social institution in order to explain it but that an account of its origin is also needed. He attempts in *The Elementary Forms* to construct hypothetically the way in which the aboriginal cult practices could have arisen and in the course of which he says 'Men who feel themselves united, partially by bonds of blood, but still more by a community of interests and tradition, assemble and become conscious of their moral unity' (1915, p. 387).

The trouble with this is that Durkheim has already said that the fact of assembling and the performance of a collective ritual are the cause of the common bonds and feelings of unity. We now find him arguing that the rites originate from these feelings. The origins of the rites is explained in terms which presuppose a social order, a community of interests, or a tradition. The rites are necessary for the continuation and stability of society but without there first being a social order of some kind there can be no rites. While it is easy to see that once a social order exists, part of which is a religious and ritual system, that social order might be sustained by it but this does not explain the genesis of the religious and ritual system.

This kind of logical contradiction is very typical of Durkheim's work. It occurs in his account of the origins of religious and moral ideals and of the basic concepts of thought. In the former case he argues that the notion of the ideal and of the perfect arise in the course of collective ritual. The intense emotion generated on such occasions produces a sense of the extraordinary in which the participants feel themselves transformed and experience the everyday environment as similarly transformed. In order to account for this, extraordinary powers and qualities are attributed to otherwise ordinary things and, as we have seen, the notion of the sacred is generated. This is seen as an ideal and perfect dimension of reality. The notion of an ideal world is, then, generated in and through collective life and the experience of the social; it is not innate but a natural product of social life. If religion upholds certain ideals and is concerned with what ought to be, this itself is a social product. The ideal constitution of society grows out of and is a product of the real, concrete and actual existing society.

The problem again is how any society could function at all without some prior set of notions about what ought to be and to happen – in short, a set of ideals. How can the set of ideals which is necessary for social order and stability be generated in the experience of social life when such life presupposes a set of norms and standards for behaviour? The ideal constitution of society could not grow out of its real constitution but must exist alongside it from the start.

Similarly with the basic categories of thought. These are generated in and through the experience of the social, Durkheim argues, and sustained by collective ritual, but how could there be any social order without the prior existence of the essential concepts with which human beings think and make sense of the world (see Runciman, 1970)?

Durkheim has been criticised, as we have seen, for his equation of religious sentiments with the emotions generated in collective gatherings. Apart from the charge that this misrepresents the nature of religious sentiments, discussed above, this has left him open to the accusation that *The Elementary Forms* runs counter to his own 'rules of the sociological method' which state that social facts cannot be derived from psychological sources. Religion is, for Durkheim, an eminently social fact yet he bases it on what Evans-Pritchard calls crowd psychology and crowd hysteria (1965, p. 68). This is little better, Evans-Pritchard argues, than deriving it from hallucination, delusion and error, an idea upon which Durkheim himself poured scorn.

Finally, Evans-Pritchard points to a final contradiction in Durkheim's approach. If his analysis in *The Elementary Forms* is correct, then religion is exposed to the believer for what it really is and as something other than what it was thought to be. It loses any basis of credibility. Yet religion is necessary for social order and stability. Durkheim's way out of this dilemma was to admit that traditional forms of religion were unsupportable in the contemporary world but that new creeds would arise to take their place – secular doctrines which would yet fulfil the functions of religion. It will always be possible to invent new doctrines as was the case with French Revolution and its cult of Fatherland, Liberty, Equality, Fraternity and Reason. Durkheim is thus the forerunner of those who claim that there is and always will be something in society to which the label religion can be attached which fulfils an essential integrative function and who tend, thereby, to defend their functionalist theory against any test of evidence. Like Durkheim they solve the question of religion by definition rather than by empirical demonstration. Religion is whatever happens in fact to integrate the society; it is whatever unites into a moral community. There never could be a moral community without religion by this conception and the claim that religion exists because it integrates is rendered inevitably true by definitional fiat.

9   The birth of the gods

A contemporary writer who has attempted to apply Durkheim's ideas in a general study of religion[1] is Guy Swanson in his book *The Birth of the Gods* in which he examines a range of comparative data to put the theory to empirical test. He takes up Durkheim's basic idea that it is the experience of society which generates feelings of dependence expressed in symbolic form. He reasons that since it is experience of social life that generates religious belief, different types of social condition would give rise to different types of religious conception. It is the particular experience of people in differing social circumstances that produces their various concepts of supernatural and spiritual beings or entities.

Swanson finds it necessary, however, to make some modifications to Durkheim's views. First, he asks what exactly is the society that is venerated according to Durkheim. 'Is it the composite of all the effects which contacts with one another have on people's conduct? Is it the pattern of such contacts? Is it but one special kind of social relationship to which people may belong?' (1960, p. 17).

Swanson suggests that we must look to certain key features or relationships in the social organisation for the clue to the particular religious conceptions held. He also raises the question of how gods associated with nature and natural forces, such as the wind, sun, or sea, could refer to social forces in a symbolic guise when such forces are quite clearly not controlled by society. Finally, he points out that not all spirits are venerated or respected – for example, demons and devils – while others may be ignored, ridiculed, or even punished by those who feel some grudge against them. Durkheim's theory does not account fully for this variety of relationships between human beings and gods.

What has to be done, he argues, is to link religion not to society in the very general way that Durkheim does but to look carefully at the particular characteristics of gods, spirits and other religious agencies and then to see what specific kinds of social relationships have corresponding characteristics.

First, he notes that spirits are purposeful beings. They have desires and intentions and produce effects in accordance with those intentions. This implies that the corresponding social relationships are those where there is an evident connection between intention and effect, or in other words distinct purposes.

Second, spirits are immortal so we must concentrate on social relationships or groups that persist beyond the life-span or involvement of particular members or sets of members. Such groups are usually those into which members are born and in which they die.

Finally, the fact that gods and spirits differ in their purposes and are concerned with and govern specific aspects of nature, or seek particular forms of attention from human beings, implies that we should look for social groups with specific and differing purposes. He sums up all this by saying 'the characteristics of spirits suggest that we identify them with specific groups which persist over time and have distinctive purposes' (1960, p. 20). These groups, Swanson argues, are of the kind which have sovereignty in some specific sphere of life which is not delegated from some superior authority but which originates from within the group itself. In so far as a group has sovereignty it is likely to provide the conditions in which concepts of spirits and gods originate.

These, then, are the fundamental assumptions of Swanson's study. Spiritual beings are conceptualisations of the constitutional structures of social life. Constitutional structures are those which define the purposes of groups, and set out their spheres of competence and their proper procedures.

Within any group, however, in addition to its constitutional structure, there will be a whole range of interactions not governed by constitutional procedures. Swanson calls this aspect of the patterning of relationships in groups the primordial structure. This does not give rise to conceptions of specific spirits or gods or any discrete religious entity but to that vague, unspecific and mysterious power or force – *mana*.

To test out these claims Swanson undertook an extensive comparative analysis examining the ethnographic data on some fifty societies for details of social organisation and religious conceptions. These elements were coded and a statistical analysis carried out to uncover patterns and relationships in the data. A number of statistically significant correlations between religious factors and aspects of social organisation were found. The religious factors found to relate to social structures included monotheism, polytheism, ancestor worship, reincarnation, ideas of the soul, witchcraft, and certain aspects of morality.

Perhaps the most important finding is that concerning the belief in high gods, as Swanson calls them – that is, those which are considered to be ultimately responsible for all things whether as creator or director or both. The idea of a high god is one which gives a sense of order to the world and its diversity, he argues. Belief in a high god explains everything and makes the world seem a determinate and ordered place. The social situation which corresponds to this belief is where a sovereign group reviews, judges, or modifies the actions of subordinate groups. Belief in a high god is the consequence and expression of a hierarchical structure of superordinate and subordinate groups.

The other significant relationships found in the data may be summarised as follows:

1 Polytheism is related to the existence of class divisions and differentiation based upon the division of labour. The number of superior deities is correlated with the degree of class division.

2 Ancestral spirits are associated with the occurrence of a kinship organisation which is more embracive than the nuclear family.

3 Reincarnation is associated with a settlement pattern of neighbourhoods, nomadic bands, extended family compounds or other small but continuing social units. This has something to do with the importance of individuals in small territorially-based social groups according to Swanson.

4 Witchcraft is associated with conditions in which people interact with one another on important issues 'in the absence of legitimated social controls and arrangements' (1960, p. 151) governing such interaction.

5 Moral sanctions are of a supernatural nature where there is inequality in wealth.

From this Swanson concludes that 'the belief in a particular kind of spirit springs from experiences with a type of persisting sovereign group whose area of juris-diction corresponds to that attributed to the spirit' (1960, p. 175). In other words, his comparative investigation is claimed to support a broadly Durkheimian theory. The data do not support other theories, he claims. No significant relation-ship was found between religion and deprivation in general nor does the latter seem to account for any particular type of religious belief. Swanson argues that if there is a relationship between religion and deprivation it is that once a particular religious belief has arisen it is put to compensatory use. The beliefs do not arise as a result of the condition of deprivation.

No relationship was found, either, between religious beliefs and attitudes towards the father. The data contradict the claim that monotheistic gods are projections of the experience with the father in childhood.

Finally, Swanson tackles the problem of religious decline in contemporary industrial societies. If Durkheim were right should we not expect the structures of such societies to be represented in thought in terms of gods and spirits? Disbelief in modern industrial societies, he argues, is associated with one or more of the following conditions:

1 A lack of contact with the primordial or constitutional structures of the society on the part of its members.

2 Alienation from those structures.

3 The assumption that all, or most significant features of those structures are knowable and controllable by human effort and will.

With this last condition Swanson introduces a completely new factor which radically alters the nature of his theory (Robertson, 1970, p. 154). It clearly implies that once we are able to reflect upon and to understand social structures we are freed from religious modes of thinking. If this is so, any one-way deterministic model in the sociological approach to religion cannot succeed.

It is worth pointing out a number of similarities between Swanson's ideas and the Marxist approach to religion. Both regard religion as something which declines when we are no longer controlled by social arrangements but can our-selves control them. Religion is a product of the failure or inability to conceive of and become aware of the fact that we create our own social arrangements.[2]

On the other hand, Swanson differs from Marx in that for the latter, consciousness of human ability to control social arrangements is the outcome of a class situation and emerging class consciousness, whereas for Swanson it seems to be simply a product of the growth of knowledge and understanding and not embedded in any particular kind of social organisation or situation. In fact Swanson declines to attempt to answer the question of under what circumstances the assumption arises that human social arrangements are controllable. Consequently, he does not make it clear why it is that all past societies have *not* made such an assumption and why it has been possible only in recent societies. As with Durkheim, there is no satisfactory answer to the question of why it is the case that in traditional societies social structures are conceptualised in a religious/symbolic way at all. It is far from obvious why the experience of a given social structure should be expressed symbolically, let alone in terms of religious conceptions. Swanson's answer to the question of how his theory can account for, or be compatible with, contemporary secularisation is, therefore, inadequate and because of this so is his theory.

A final criticism that can be made of his approach is that it places too much emphasis on statistical correlations and concludes from them more than is warranted. It is not so surprising that different social structures are associated with different religious conceptions (especially in certain types of social structure) or that the religious beliefs found in a type of structure are closely related to aspects of it but it is long way from this to the conclusion that the beliefs are no more than symbolic expressions of those structures. The statistical relationships he finds certainly do not prove this; it is still only Swanson's interpretation of what the correlations mean and how they come about and there may be other possible interpretations. Also, while there may be a relationship between social structures and religious conceptions in many traditional societies, the fact that this is not necessarily true of contemporary industrial societies leads us to question Swanson's interpretation.

10 Religion and solidarity: the functionalists

Emile Durkheim's *The Elementary Forms of the Religious Life* had a great deal of influence and many sociologists and particularly anthropologists took up and applied Durkheim's ideas. One such was A.R. Radcliffe-Brown who did much to establish functionalism as the dominant perspective in anthropology and sociology. His essential ideas on religion are contained in his ethnographic monograph of his fieldwork in the Andaman Islands (1922) and in his Henry Myers lecture of 1945 on 'Religion and Society'. These were applied to totemism (1929) and taboo (1939).[1]

Radcliffe-Brown along with Malinowski and others who adopted a functionalist position strongly rejected the evolutionary schemes of earlier writers and generally criticised the search for the origins of religion which they saw as a futile endeavour, since we could never know much if anything about the religious life of the remote past from which little survives. To them it was also a misguided method, since what mattered was not how things began but the role they play in present-day societies. It was a mistake, Radcliffe-Brown thought, to think that the 'primitive' societies existing today represent unchanged examples of the societies characteristic of the remote past of our early ancestors. Their religious and ritual systems had to be understood in the context of the existing society and their role in that society. They could not be taken as evidence for the way religious ideas and actions originated in some remote past.

Although influenced by Durkheim, Radcliffe-Brown differs from him in a number of ways. Most importantly perhaps he differs in not accepting the idea that religious ideas express a truth even in a symbolic way. He accepts that, for the most part, religious beliefs are error and illusion. Despite this, however, they are symbolic expressions of sentiments necessary for the stability and survival of society. For Radcliffe-Brown false beliefs and erroneous practices nevertheless have valuable social functions. The rituals do not have the effects that the practitioners and participants hope for but they do have effects which have beneficial social value.

> We may entertain at least as a possibility the theory that any religion is an important or even essential part of the social machinery, as are morality and law, part of the complex system by which human beings are enabled to live

together in an orderly arrangement of social relations. From this point of view we deal not with the origins but with the social functions of religions, i.e. the contribution that they make to the formation and maintenance of social order.

(1952a, p. 154)

Radcliffe-Brown follows Robertson Smith in believing that it is religious practice which is primary rather than beliefs. An emphasis on beliefs, and the view that practices are the direct consequence of beliefs, lead, in Radcliffe-Brown's view, to attempts to discover how the beliefs were formed and adopted and this search for origins, as we have seen, encourages neglect of the way in which rites play a vital role in the lives of participants and of the society. It is clear, then, why Radcliffe-Brown is not concerned with the fact that the beliefs are false or with how it is that false and illusory beliefs come to be held. Beliefs do not really matter all that much; it is what people do that is crucial. The relationship between beliefs and practices, he argues, is not causal. 'What really happens is that the rites and the justifying or rationalising beliefs develop together as parts of a coherent whole' (1952a, p. 155).

For Radcliffe-Brown, then, beliefs are rationalisations and justifications of rites. To understand religion, therefore, we must first concentrate upon the rites. It is, then, the social function of rites which gives us the key to an understanding of religion. His approach is summed up in the following passage:

an orderly social life amongst human beings depends upon the presence in the minds of the members of a society of certain sentiments, which control the behaviour of the individual in his relation to others. Rites can be seen to be the regulated symbolic expressions of certain sentiments. Rites can therefore be shown to have a specific social function when, and to the extent that they have for their effect to regulate, maintain and transmit from one generation to another sentiments on which the constitution of the society depends.

(1952a, p. 157)

He also gives us the general formula that religion is everywhere an expression in one form or another of a sense of dependence on a power outside ourselves, a power which we may speak of as a spiritual or moral power. He likens this dependence to that of a child upon its parents. In this aspect Radcliffe-Brown is reminiscent not only of Durkheim but also of Freud.

There is clearly something vital missing from this very functionalist account and all functionalist accounts suffer from the same deficiency. The fact that certain sentiments necessary for social order require reinforcement through ritual expression is not sufficient to account for the fact that they are so expressed. Because a thing is necessary for social order is no guarantee that it will occur and is no explanation of its occurrence. This is especially so when those who perform the rites do not say or believe that they are performing them to maintain social order and when such notions are far from their minds. And, of course, it is by no means clear that such rites and the beliefs associated with them do always contribute to social order – they may, in fact, do just the opposite.

It is not at all clear, in any case, why sentiments necessary for social order require reinforcement. If the participants were sufficiently aware of their importance to stage rites which reinforce them, surely these sentiments were strong enough in their minds in the first place. Unless, of course, they were unaware of their importance; but then how is it the participants come to perform socially necessary rites without having the slightest understanding of what they are doing, undertaking the action out of wholly different motives? It seems entirely fortuitous and, indeed, mysterious that actions performed to increase the abundance of a totemic species or to ensure that the actor has a place in heaven should actually have the real and important but unconscious effect of maintaining social order.

In any case, to say that religion is essentially about maintaining social order is to take a very limited view of it. Clearly, most religious traditions have been concerned with order and harmony in human affairs and relations but it does not follow that this is all religion is about.

Radcliffe-Brown's claim that religious doctrines and beliefs are merely rationalisations of practices is also beset with difficulties. Many rites are of a clearly instrumental character. The practitioners say they perform the rite to bring about some definite end – prosperity, protection from danger or whatever and what they do may appear to be very much such an attempt. But if what they do is not the consequence of a belief that this particular set of actions will produce the desired result and the belief is just a rationalisation of what is done, how is it possible to account for what is done, that is, the form of the rite? It is almost as if Radcliffe-Brown is suggesting that after having been unconsciously driven to symbolically express sentiments necessary for social order, the participants come to reflect upon what they have done to find that it appears to have been behaviour designed to bring about some definite result. Why they should have acted in the particular way they did remains completely mysterious since it was not their belief which motivated them nor the desire to ensure social order since they never realise, unless the anthropologist is kind enough to allow them to share in his or her superior insights into their own behaviour, that this is what they have been doing.

Clearly, this will not do. The actions must be the consequence of a desire to bring about the result the actions are said to achieve and the belief that they will do so, or at least of a feeling that the desired end is a matter of some importance and an intention to express this. In other words the actions are stimulated by ideas and beliefs and the latter cannot, at least always or even most of the time, be rationalisations. (This is not, of course, to say they could not sometimes and in certain circumstances be rationalisations.) At the root of the difficulties with functionalist accounts such as that of Radcliffe-Brown, then, is the inevitable discrepancy between the observer's and the actor's account of what is going on and the necessity to dismiss the latter. The functionalist, while dismissing what people say they are motivated to do as largely irrelevant, is left with no way of explaining how they come to do what they are not motivated to do.

RECENT FUNCTIONALIST APPROACHES

Intellectualist, emotionalist, and sociological theories have each illuminated our understanding of religion despite their deficiencies. Each provides a partial insight into the nature of religion but only a partial one because religion is a far more complex phenomenon than any of these approaches supposes. A comprehensive theory of religion thus needs to incorporate the insights of all of these approaches into some synthesis in which the complex interplay of intellectual, emotional and sociological factors is fully encompassed. More recent functionalist theories have gone some way towards doing this.

Some functionalist-oriented theorists, recognising the deficiencies of the purely functionalist approach, have introduced a psychological dimension in their analyses and attempted to integrate it with their functionalism. Modern functionalists became aware that the existence of a social need for religion is not adequate to account for it and have attempted to complete their functionalist analyses by seeking to root religious belief and behaviour in certain fundamental aspects of human nature. They have tended to see religion as arising from basic, universal human needs and circumstances. They have, therefore, introduced a strong psychological component into what is essentially a sociological approach and there is in their analyses a dual emphasis in which, on the one hand, religion is seen to be the product of psychological factors inherent in all human beings, and on the other it is seen as providing support for social values and social stability. The two emphases do not always coexist comfortably. Kingsley Davis's once widely used textbook *Human Society* (1948) is a good example. In the chapter on religion, entitled 'Religious Institutions' he lists the positive functions of religion which, he says, justifies, rationalises and supports the sentiments that give cohesion to society. The expression of common beliefs through collective ritual seems to enhance the individual's devotion to group ends. It strengthens his determination to observe the group norms and to rise above purely private interests. It reinforces his identification with his fellows and sharpens his separateness from members of other tribes, communities or nations.

Davis uses the familiar distinction between the sacred and the profane. Things which are sacred symbolise certain intangible phenomena to which religious beliefs and practices refer. Davis calls them 'super-empirical realities'. They are of three kinds: first, subjective states of mind such as 'peace', 'salvation', 'nirvana', and so on; second, transcendental ends such as 'immortality' and 'purification'; and finally imaginary creatures, beings, objects and things such as gods, spirits, heavens and hells. Because these things are intangible they must be represented by concrete objects or actions.

These intangible phenomena and the concrete objects and actions which represent them play a crucial role in maintaining social cohesion in the following way. Society requires that individuals subordinate their desires and drives to the dictates which are necessary for social order. Group goals, ultimate values and so on are not inherent but have to be sustained by some means. To achieve this they must be brought into association with individual drives and it is the function of the super-empirical realities to do this. The necessity and validity of social regulations are brought home to the individual by linking them to an imaginary world. This supernatural or super-empirical world is made to appear to be the source of these ultimate values and ends and through this imaginary world these things appear both necessary and plausible.

The imaginary world, then, justifies and accounts for the ultimate values. The sacred objects which represent the imaginary world convey a sense of its reality. Religious practice, or ritual, functions to sustain beliefs and it is the 'chief instrumentality for reviving the actor's devotion to ultimate values and his belief in the fictitious world' (Davis, 1948, p. 528).

All of this, of course, owes much to Durkheim. Belief in the supernatural world, however, is also a convenient device for propagating the view that good is inevitably rewarded and evil inevitably punished and through the promotion of such beliefs helps to uphold the ultimate values which might be undermined if individuals were to believe that evil may prosper and good go unrewarded; that is, if it were to appear that life and fate are just a matter of chance unrelated to good or bad actions. This implies that religion fulfils a social function through meeting the individual need for psychological reassurance that the world is not arbitrary and meaningless.

The emphasis upon ultimate and supernatural punishment for bad actions and reward for good actions explains, Davis argues, the frequently anthropomorphic character of the religious realm. Reward and punishment imply some will or power which commands or expects certain kinds of behaviour and whose action is conditional upon the expected behaviour being forthcoming. As Davis puts it 'to create the illusion of moral determinism it is necessary to invent a supernatural realm' (1948, p. 531).

The supernatural realm has another compensating function. The goals that society emphasises for this life are usually such that they are unattainable for some people and rarely attainable to an equal degree by all. To prevent them from becoming dissatisfied and disillusioned, society provides transcendental goals which anyone can reach no matter how unsuccessful in this life. Again, religion provides psychological compensation for the apparent injustices of this world.

Later functionalist theorists go much further in introducing a psychological element into their theories. Yinger, for example, tells us that a set of overarching values to live by is essential (1970, p. 8). These values must provide answers to the 'ultimate problems' of human life and, most of all, the problem of death. They must account for and make meaningful such things as frustration, failure, tragedy, suffering, and so on. Certain exceptional individuals, religious innovators, have discovered 'solutions' to these problems. To put it another way, they have discovered the possibility of salvation.

We saw in Chapter one, that Yinger actually defines religion as a system of beliefs and practices addressed to the ultimate problems of life. It is an 'attempt to explain what cannot otherwise be explained; to achieve power, all other powers having failed us; to establish poise and serenity in the face of evil and suffering that other efforts have failed to eliminate' (1970, p. 7). In other words, religion is an attempt to deal with problems that cannot be dealt with in any other way or by any other means.

This approach might be thought to resemble that of Freud and other psychological theories which explain religion in terms of fear, anxiety, frustration and helplessness. But Yinger does not believe that religion will disappear in some future stage of maturity as Freud did. The basic problems will always remain no matter what level of development is reached.

One might argue against this claim that religion is declining in advanced industrial societies. This would not invalidate Yinger's claims, however, because of the nature of his definition of religion. For Yinger any system of belief which aids people in dealing with the ultimate problems of human life is a religion whether or not it looks much like a religion or fits the general common sense or traditional conception of what religion is. In Yinger's view such systems of belief can be found in even the most secular societies. All men and women have some set of absolute values or beliefs, according to Yinger, which provide some sort of answer to the ultimate problems, even if only as a form of escape from them. He would, therefore, consciously include such 'creeds' as communism and nationalism within the category of religion since in his view they do struggle with ultimate problems. Even the belief that science can ultimately solve all problems is, for Yinger, a kind of faith and essentially religious in character.

Clearly, the needs that religion satisfies are fundamentally psychological needs. But Yinger recognises that religion is, at the same time, primarily a social phenomenon. For this reason 'private' beliefs are not considered to constitute a religion; not until doctrine and practice are shared by a group can we speak of a religion. One reason for this is that the ultimate questions to which religious belief and practice are addressed are never simply a matter of individual concern. They are ultimate primarily because of their impact upon human associations. Even death is not fundamentally an individual crisis, in Yinger's view, but a group one. Fear, frustration and uncertainty are socially disruptive unless they can be reinterpreted as part of a shared experience. Also, the desires and drives of the individual must be subordinated to a conception of an absolute good which is in harmony with the shared needs of the group.

Religion thus has a double root in that it meets individual and group needs. It meets group needs largely through its functions for the individual. Yinger echoes Davis in claiming that by emphasising values which are universally and equally attainable, that is non-material values such as salvation, and by accounting for suffering, failure, deprivation, etc., religion upholds the moral order of society.

It is this emphasis upon a 'double root' of religion which is the major source of difficulty in Yinger's approach. Religious allegiance motivated by personal needs may conflict with the needs of social cohesion. As is often pointed out concerning the functionalist approach, religion is often a divisive force as much as a cohesive one and very often religious convictions can lead to anti-social or disruptive attitudes and behaviour. Yinger is well aware that religion may not always be integrative but argues that there are circumstances in which it is unable to perform its essential integrative role. He list six such circumstances but considers these factors to be things which reduce the integrative power of religion. He simply does not consider the possibility that religion may itself be a factor promoting disintegration. Religion is still seen as essentially integrative; it is just that in certain circumstances it is inhibited from performing its role.

The evidence suggests, however, that to the extent that religion does have value for the individual, this may well be in conflict with any alleged socially integrative role. As Betty Scharf has put it, 'it is not clear why a religion which meets the personal need for ultimate meaning in the face of death and frustration should also constitute a "refusal to allow hostility to tear apart one's human associations"' (1970, p. 75). We only have to remember, she reminds us, how certain religious sects have tended to withdraw from and even express hostility to the wider society and prevailing social order to see this. In fact, most religious innovations have been reactions to prevailing social conditions and have sought not to integrate and make cohesive a society which is seen as unsatisfactory but to change that society.

The contradiction in Yinger's theory, Scharf argues, derives from his desire to hold on to the view of religion as a response to ultimate questions transcending the everyday life and goals of particular groups. But in doing so he shows how the social function of religion, which he considers basic, may not in fact be fulfilled. He postulates an individual and social need for religion but fails to systematically relate the one to the other.

There is a second contradiction in Yinger's approach, which is related to his characterisation of the social function of religion in terms of its power to justify deprivation and injustice by providing non-competitive and non-scarce goals, such as salvation, which make exploitation and inequality in this life seem relatively unimportant. The contradiction here is the reverse of the one that Scharf mentions. It is not just that the function of religion for the individual may prevent it from fulfilling its function for society but conversely that its social function may prevent it fulfilling any need for the individual.

If religion, for example, promises salvation in the next life but makes it conditional upon quiescent acceptance of injustice in this life, then one might argue that while it may provide some sort of answer to the question of why injustice exists it nevertheless does a disservice to the individual if it prevents action to bring about change and a more just society. This would, of course, be the sort of criticism of Yinger that a Marxist would make. As Giddens (1978) points out, the functionalist approach deriving from Durkheimian tradition neglects the ideological dimension of religion which aids the legitimation of domination of one group by another.

Yinger, however, anticipates this criticism to some extent. In claiming that religion integrates society he is not claiming that that is necessarily a good or desirable thing, simply that as a matter of fact this is what religion does. It may integrate a just or an unjust society. The functionalist approach makes no value judgements about the desirability of integration of any particular social order but merely points to the objective role of religion.

This does not, however, really answer the point that in fulfilling its function for society religion may be dysfunctional for the individual. Second, it is somewhat misleading to imply that the integration of a just society and an unjust society are the same sorts of process. Two rather distinct senses of the term 'integration' are implied by Yinger's claim. Integration may involve the resolution of conflicts through a process of persuasion, mutual adjustment and compromise or it may involve manipulation, deception, and so on. Religion may, whether consciously, unconsciously or at least in effect, play the second kind of role. The problem with Yinger's approach is that it makes these rather different processes seem to be the same kind of thing. In any case, as Turner (1991) points out, too great an emphasis is placed by the functionalist and Durkheimian approaches upon collective beliefs and values expressed traditionally in religious forms as the primary integrating force in society. There are many other processes by which social cohesion is generated including economic interdependency, force, habit and pragmatic accommodation and acquiescence. Societies, also, can often function perfectly well despite relatively high levels of conflict, disaffection, disagreement over or indifference to prevailing norms and values.

The final example of this tendency to fuse psychological and sociological approaches in order to overcome the difficulties of functionalism that we shall examine is the work of O'Dea (1966). The essence of religion according to O'Dea is that it transcends everyday experience and we need this transcendental reference because existence is characterised by three things – contingency, powerlessness and scarcity. By contingency he means the fact that existence is full of uncertainty, danger and vulnerability. Life, safety and welfare are precarious. By powerlessness he means the fact that we cannot do very much to remove uncertainty from existence and by scarcity he refers to the fact that because wants seem to be almost unlimited goals and values are differentially distributed in society.

These characteristics of human life produce frustration and deprivation, adjustment to which is made possible by religion. Religion helps adjustment to what O'Dea calls the 'breaking points' of daily existence. It provides answers to basic problems such as death and suffering by giving meaning to distressing experiences. This is very necessary according to O'Dea. 'If they are found to be without meaning the value of institutionalised goals and norms is undermined' (1966, p. 6). Religion provides a 'larger view' which makes misfortune and frustration seem relatively unimportant. Life in the ordinary and everyday world is fitted into this larger view which includes the super-empirical. Without it there would seem no need or reason to conform to norms of social life.

O'Dea lists six functions of religion for the individual and the society.

1 It provides support and consolation and thereby helps support established values and goals.
2 Through cult and ceremony it provides emotional security and identity and a fixed point of reference amid conflicts of ideas and opinions. This is the priestly function of religion and involves teaching doctrines and performance

of ceremonies. It gives stability to the social order and often helps maintain the status quo.

3 It sacralises norms and promotes group goals above individual goals. It legitimises the social order.

4 It also provides standards which can be a basis for criticisms of existing social patterns. This is its prophetic function and can form a basis for social protest.

5 It aids the individual in understanding him or her self and provides a sense of identity.

6 It is important in the process of maturation, in aiding the individual at the crises of life and point of transition from one status to another and is, consequently, part of the educational process.

Unlike Yinger, O'Dea does not think that these functions are always fulfilled by religion. It is not, therefore, an inevitable feature of society. Nevertheless, it has, O'Dea points out, been practically universal in known social systems. He also admits that the functionalist approach is partial and incomplete in that it fails to raise or answer significant questions and tends to overemphasise the conservative functions of religion. It neglects the creative and sometimes revolutionary character of religion. He further concedes that the functionalist approach tends to neglect the process of secularisation and admits that claims that secularisation cannot proceed to the point where religion will disappear cannot be supported. Finally, he admits that religion may have actual dysfunctions and again lists six of these which correspond to its positive functions.

1 It may inhibit protest against injustice by reconciling the oppressed.

2 Its priestly function of sacralising norms and values may inhibit progress in knowledge.

3 It may prevent adaptation to changing circumstances through its conservatism.

4 Its prophetic function can lead to utopianism and unrealistic hopes for change and, consequently, inhibit practical action to this end.

5 It can attach individuals to groups to the point where conflict with other groups is promoted and adjustment prevented.

6 It can create dependence on religious institutions and leaders thereby preventing maturity.

After such a battery of qualifications to the functionalist approach one might well ask if there is anything much left of it. Once one admits, as O'Dea does, that religion is not a functional necessity then the functional approach to understanding it seems vacuous. We are still faced with the problem of why a religious solution to problems occurs in certain situations but not in others and with understanding in what circumstances the religious response does occur. In short we are still left with the major questions. To say that the religious response to difficulties may sometimes be of positive value individually and socially but at other times may be dysfunctional, is to say nothing very significant. The same is probably true of any institution or pattern of behaviour. It certainly does not explain anything. Religion, we are told, may integrate society or inhibit change, give consolation or promote conflict, provide stability or hinder progress – a whole variety of effects which are good, bad and indifferent. None of them explains the occurrence of the religious response or religious sentiments and actions.

Recent functionalist approaches, then, although going some way towards the development of a synthesis of earlier insights have been somewhat limited in their achievements. Meaning theories, which we examine in Chapter twelve, go much further towards a satisfactory synthesis. Before examining them, however, examples of applications of the functionalist approach, specifically to aspects of religions studied by anthropologists working in tribal societies, will be discussed.

11 Taboos and rituals

Functionalism dominated social anthropology for several decades, particularly in Britain and the Commonwealth countries in which Malinowski and Radcliffe-Brown's ideas were so influential. The work of anthropologists in tribal societies shows this influence very clearly and in this chapter some of this work will be outlined and discussed and contrasted against alternative perspectives in order to get as clear a picture as possible of how functionalist ideas have been applied. Just two themes among the many that the anthropological literature covers, namely taboo and certain types of ritual, specifically communal rituals and *rites de passage* are considered. Alongside functionalist accounts of these sets of belief and behaviour we shall examine also various alternative interpretations.

TABOO AND RITUAL AVOIDANCE: THE FUNCTIONALIST PERSPECTIVE

Misfortune in many societies may be attributed to a variety of supernatural or supramundane causes including the actions of gods, spirits, demons, ancestors or witches. It may also be considered to be the automatic consequence of a breach of taboo regulations. A taboo is generally defined as a ritual prohibition and the word derives originally from the Polynesian word *tapu*. The notion of taboo is extremely widespread in human cultures and religious systems including the 'higher' or world religions where it is often associated with ideas of sacredness or holiness as well as with ideas of profanity and pollution. The latter are particularly strong in Hinduism and Judaism.

An early theory of taboo, that of Robertson Smith (1889), argued that in its aspect of impurity, contagion, or danger, taboo represented the survival of primitive superstition. The notions of holiness and sacredness of the higher religions, in contrast, he thought to be quite distinct. In fact it is impossible to separate these elements in the notion of taboo. No real distinction is made between what is sacred and what is polluting in the conceptions of taboo in many cultures.

Also, as Steiner (1967) points out, taboos and ritual avoidances, even where they embody an element of contagion or pollution, are being created continuously right up to the present and are by no means primitive survivals. Robertson Smith's own Victorian society was taboo-ridden. Many ordinary things could not be mentioned in polite conversation, such as trousers, which had to be referred to by the euphemism of 'unmentionables'. One might question the implication that such avoidances are ritual in character but in this broad sense contemporary society may be said also to have its taboos, although they are perhaps less extensive.

Another major difference between such prohibitions in modern industrial societies and in traditional societies is, of course, that in the former there is no belief that breach of taboo regulations will result in some kind of misfortune whereas there is such a belief in the latter. Radcliffe-Brown emphasises this aspect of taboo in tribal societies. He offered a functionalist interpretation of taboo or, as he preferred to call it, ritual prohibition, which he defined as 'a rule of behaviour which is associated with a belief that an infraction will result in an undesirable change in the ritual status of the person who fails to keep the rule' (1952b, pp. 134–5). It is this change in ritual status which places the person in a situation of vulnerability and danger.

The rules of behaviour generally concern things that must be avoided, in which case Radcliffe-Brown speaks of them having ritual value. Anything which is the object of ritual avoidance has ritual value and this may include people, places, objects, words, or names. Radcliffe-Brown considered that these ritual values are also social values or, in other words, things of common concern or significance which bind two or more persons together. He thought that the key to understanding taboos lay in this relationship between things which have ritual value of a positive or negative kind and things which have social value. The object is to uncover the social functions of ritual prohibitions.

Such ritual actions, Radcliffe-Brown said, establish certain fundamental social values and in doing so enable an orderly society to maintain itself in existence. The ritual behaviour does this because it symbolically expresses the social value of a thing, occasion or event. He illustrates with an example from his own fieldwork among the Andaman Islanders, namely the set of ritual avoidances surrounding childbirth. The parents of a girl who is about to give birth are forbidden to eat certain foods and their friends are forbidden to use the names of the parents. Because of these avoidances the event acquires a social value. Radcliffe-Brown takes, then, the opposite view to those, such as Malinowski, who see such ritual behaviour as a means of generating confidence in a situation of anxiety and uncertainty. If anything, in Radcliffe-Brown's view, the ritual behaviour creates anxiety and ensures a concern with the event and outcome which might not otherwise have existed.

It is largely in this process of generating a common concern, by the sharing of hopes and fears, that human beings are linked together in association. As Radcliffe-Brown puts it:

> By this theory the Andamanese taboos relating to childbirth are the obligatory recognition in the standardized symbolic form of the significance and importance of the events to the parents and to the community at large. They thus serve to fix the social value of occasions of this kind.

> (1952b, pp. 150–1)

As for the things to which ritual prohibitions are attached, they are chosen because they are themselves objects of important common interest or because they are symbolically representative of such things. The notion that some misfortune will befall those who do not keep the taboo is a rationalisation, according to Radcliffe-Brown.

The functionalism of Radcliffe-Brown's approach to the analysis of taboo and ritual avoidance is clearly problematic and suffers from the sort of difficulty discussed in the general treatment of functionalist approaches in Chapter ten. The essential points are that the behaviour is said to occur because of the necessary social effects that it has. But the need that these effects be produced does not guarantee that they will be and thus cannot be the explanation of the behaviour. Neither do those who observe the taboos do so in order to bring about the alleged effects, of which they are in any case probably unaware. Their reason for observing the taboos, apart from socialisation and custom, is that failure to do so will bring misfortune. It will not do to dismiss this as a mere rationalisation.

FREUD ON TABOO

Freud likened taboo behaviour to that of obsessional neurotics on the grounds that both involve an apparent absence of any motive for the prohibition, both derive from an inner compulsion, both involve the idea of contagion, and both give rise to injunctions which require some ritual performance, usually purification, to be undertaken if the taboo is breached. A central element in taboo behaviour for Freud is ambivalence towards the object which is taboo. There is a desire to touch it or come into contact with it which is repressed as well as a horror or fear of touching it. Such ambivalence derives from the fact that the institution of taboo represents the repressed desire to touch the genitals and at the same time a horror of doing so.

As Steiner (1967) points out, Freud's characterisation of taboo is incorrect in a number of respects. First, the feeling that the taboo must be observed is quite unlike the compulsion that the obsessional neurotic feels and derives from custom not from inner drives. Second, the actions that the obsessional neurotic performs are not at all like the rituals that are involved in taboo behaviour which, again, are not private but a matter of custom.

Even more importantly, the characterisation of taboo in terms of ambivalence could not successfully be applied to the whole range of taboos found in various societies. The taboos surrounding menstrual blood, Steiner argues, surely involve no repressed desire to come into contact with it. Also, there seems no more reason to believe that taboos reflect anxieties (as well as desires) than there is to accept Radcliffe-Brown's claim that taboos may serve to generate anxiety.

RECENT APPROACHES

More recent interpretations of taboo behaviour have drawn, as Steiner (1967) points out, on the work of Van Gennep's *Les Rites de Passage* (1960 [1908]). Van

Gennep pointed out that taboo behaviour is nearly always an important element in transition rituals and is related to the belief that a transition from one status or condition to another is inherently dangerous. This has provided an important clue, Steiner argues, to the nature of taboos. They seem to be very much associated with transitions, boundaries, ambiguities, anomalies and so on – in other words, things which are at the margins of established categories, the transitions from one category to another, or things which do not quite fit into established categories.

Such is the view developed by Mary Douglas (1966). Douglas also considers that contemporary industrial society is as taboo-ridden as any traditional society. Our ideas of cleanliness and dirt are not just a question of hygiene. We tend to think of the ritual avoidances of other peoples as being entirely ritual in character and as having nothing to do with hygiene. There have been attempts to explain them in terms of a concern with hygiene but while there may be something in these ideas they have, on the whole, not very successfully explained ritual avoidances. Douglas suggests that neither traditional nor contemporary avoidance behaviour is entirely or primarily a matter of hygiene: 'our ideas of dirt also express symbolic systems' and 'the difference between pollution behaviour in one part of the world and another is a matter of detail' (1966, p. 35).

This concept of dirt is not really a product of fear of infection or of transmission of germs or diseases, according to Douglas. The idea of dirt is much older than our knowledge of the causes of disease and the mechanisms of their transmission. Ideas of dirt have, in fact, to do with notions of order and disorder.

> If we can abstract pathogenicity and hygiene from our notion of dirt, we are left with the old definition of dirt as matter out of place . . . . Where there is dirt there is a system. Dirt is the by-product of a systematic ordering and classification of matter in so far as ordering involves rejecting inappropriate elements . . . . our pollution behaviour is the reaction which condemns any object or idea likely to confuse or contradict cherished classifications.
>
> (Douglas, 1966, p. 35)

This interpretation, Douglas claims, would allow us to comprehend the essential nature of taboo in both its aspects. Anomalous things are dangerous and must be avoided; they have a kind of power. Consequently, they come to be classed along with the sacred, which is also dangerous and powerful.

Douglas looks at a wide range of things from this point of view in order to show how her interpretation fits. For example, in a chapter entitled 'The Abominations of Leviticus' she interprets the dietary restrictions of Judaism in terms of the Israelite system of animal classification. Animals which do not quite fit the major categories are tabooed and cannot be eaten. A major category is that of animals that chew the cud and have cloven hooves. The pig does not chew the cud but does have a cloven hoof; it is an anomaly not belonging to any category in this system of classification and so must be avoided.

The widespread taboos which relate to the orifices of the human body and its products are also interpreted by Douglas in this way. Bodily products which cross a threshold are both of the body and yet are rejected by it and become something external to it. They are neither one thing nor the other and become the object of avoidance behaviour.

Taboos relating to bodily emissions, however, have a great deal more to them than this, according to Douglas who sees them as reflecting certain aspects of social order and threats to it. She claims that the body is almost universally used as a symbol for society such that every aspect of the body expresses some social aspect. Rituals often revolve around bodily functions. As Douglas says;

> We cannot possibly interpret rituals concerning excreta, breast-milk, saliva, and the rest unless we are prepared to see in the body a symbol of society, and to see the powers and dangers credited to social structure reproduced in small on the human body.
>
> (1966, p. 115)

For example, she considers ideas of pollution associated with sex and with females to be reflections of a certain kind of social situation, especially one where men's relations with women are for some reason problematic. This might be because there is a conflict of interests between them, because for one reason or another women are able to frustrate the plans of men or resist their control, or where there is a conflict of structural principles.

An example of the latter situation would be that of matrilineally organised societies where there is often a conflict between, on the one hand, the fact that men have authority over their kinswomen who are to a large extent dependent on them, while on the other the residence pattern may be uxorilocal (that is, a man goes to live in the village of his wife on marriage) and men are thus separated from their kinswomen.

Also, Douglas examines the relationship between taboos and morality and the role of taboos in upholding the system of morality and in social control. An excellent example of the use of taboo in social control is given by Firth (1939) who describes how Polynesian chiefs on the island of Tikopia can place a ban on the consumption of certain crops. Normally this is done during times of scarcity to ensure that reserves will not be depleted and that there will be sufficient seed for planting later. The chief will place a sign near the crop which indicates that it is tabooed and anyone breaking the ban is thought likely to suffer a very unpleasant misfortune such as contracting a disease, breaking out in boils, and so on.

In the above example taboos are used for the common good. Douglas points out that they may also have an ideological and political use in situations of conflict. They are not just symbolic expressions of conflicting principles or interests but are sometimes weapons used in the pursuit of those interests.

For example, Douglas interprets the taboos relating to menstruation and menstrual blood, which are very widespread, as being very often essentially manipulative devices for controlling women. By their use men are able to do the following.

1 Assert male superiority by contrasting females as unclean and polluting as opposed to male purity.

2 Designate separate male and female spheres and thereby exclude women from male spheres in order to control strategic resources such as food, tools, etc.
3 Blame failures on breaches of the rules of segregation by women.
4 Attack people and blame them for sickness and misfortune caused by breach of taboo regulations, possibly extracting compensation from them.

An example of taboos relating to menstruation which illustrates how they may be used to manipulate situations is that of the Hadza, an African hunting and gathering people. In this society, men and women are to a very great extent separated. Also women are very largely independent of men. In this situation men show great concern and anxiety about sexual access to women. Marriage is fragile and unstable and divorce frequent. When a woman is menstruating it is taboo for her husband to go hunting or gathering honey along with his fellow men. To do so would bring bad luck on the venture. He has to stay at home. The husband and wife, consequently, are conspicuously set apart from others during this time and there is a periodic reaffirmation and statement of the link between them. Their marital status is publicly demonstrated as a means of retaining an always precarious claim on the wife.

This is, of course, a rather functionalist explanation, and perhaps does not fully explain the existence of the taboo. The same problem exists for all of the ways in which Douglas shows how taboos may be used manipulatively but she does give us, perhaps, some insight into how taboo behaviour of this kind, whatever the reasons for its original appearance, can be put to manipulative uses once it exists.

The idea that tabooed things are things that confound the system of categories has been challenged by later writers on the grounds that it oversimplifies and fails to explain the pattern of taboos found either in Leviticus or in societies in which they have carried out fieldwork. Carroll (1978) broadly supports the basic contention that it is anomalous things which are taboo but argues that the relevant anomaly in the case of Leviticus is that which derives from a fundamental distinction between nature and culture. Human beings (culture) can eat meat but animals (nature) should eat only vegetable matter. Carnivores are therefore anomalous and taboo. The pig eats carrion. Carroll argues that this accounts for many more of the things mentioned in Leviticus than Douglas's theory. Vermin, mould and mildew, for example, belong to nature but invade the world of man and of culture. It also accounts for more than just the dietary regulations, he claims, including regulations relating to leprosy.

But even Carroll's theory cannot account for all the taboo proscriptions of Leviticus as he himself admits. Other critics of Douglas (Bulmer, 1967; Tambiah, 1969) argue that it is not possible to account for taboos in entirely taxonomic terms. While polluting things may be things out of place, there are many different ways in which things can be out of place. Taxonomic systems relating to animals, for example, are closely linked to social classifications and come to be charged as a result with a variety of affective connotations.

Douglas, in later work, has recognised the force of some of these criticisms and has modified her analysis of the Jewish dietary laws (1975). The Jews maintained, she argues, very strict social boundaries. Marriage with outsiders of certain categories was strictly forbidden. Conversely, marriage within the group between fairly close relatives, such as first parallel cousins, was allowed. The ban on eating the pig was not simply the consequence of the way it confounded categories but also because pigs were reared as food by outsiders, i.e. non-Israelites. This dietary rule also celebrates the theme of purity versus impurity – the pig eats carrion. Among the Lele, an African people whom Douglas studied early in her career (see Douglas, 1963), the reverse situation can be found. Here boundaries are weak and the crossing and confounding of boundaries considered a good thing. The pangolin, an animal that does not fit anywhere in the system of categories of the Lele, is sacred to them and not polluting. In short, the *social* situation has a profound influence upon how anomalous things are treated.

It has to be said that such analyses, while insightful and promising, are based on very few instances and must be treated as highly speculative. Much more systematic comparative work needs to be done on the subject of taboo before we can claim to have much understanding of it.

COMMUNAL RITUALS AND RITES DE PASSAGE

Communal rituals are those which involve a kinship group, tribe, village, neighbourhood, community or even sometimes a whole nation. The rituals may be conducted for a variety of purposes such as veneration of gods, prosperity, protection against danger, commemoration of birth, marriage and death. Such rituals have usually been interpreted by anthropologists as means by which a society, community or group upholds central moral values and principles and preserves the moral order. This may involve the recognition of divisions and conflicts and disharmonies which are inherent in the society and may be seen, it is argued by these theorists, as a means of coping with and defusing them. According to this view, many rituals arise as a response to situations in which there is a conflict between the general moral order and the interests which lead to individuals and groups competing with one another. It is supported by frequent observations that many rituals involve and demonstrate an open exhibition of strife and antagonism as well as cohesion and cooperation.

A leading exponent of such an approach is Max Gluckman (1963). He interprets, for example, the great Swazi national first fruits ceremony, the *incwala*, as a symbolic representation of the underlying conflicts within the nation as well as its fundamental unity and cohesion (Gluckman, 1963). In this latter respect Gluckman presents a revised functionalist account of them. In the ritual the political divisions of the Swazi nation are clearly visible. Different groups play different parts in it. Those who stand in a potentially hostile relationship to the royal clan will ritually abuse and criticise the king. The whole ceremony dramatises the potential antagonisms centring on kingship and it symbolises the eventual triumph of the king over his enemies and the ultimate unity of the nation.

Gluckman points out that an ambivalent attitude exists towards the Swazi king. The *incwala* ceremony expresses this ambivalence; 'symbolic acting of social relations in their ambivalence is believed to achieve unity and prosperity' (Gluckman, 1963, p. 126). In other words, accompanying the ritual expression of ambivalent attitudes is the idea that doing so somehow removes the stresses which are seen to prevent the society from realising its aims. We find here a connection in the ideas of these people between the moral order and events in the natural world, a belief that reflects structural contradictions which lie at the root of such ritual expressions, a point which Turner also makes in a meticulous analysis of Ndembu ritual (1968). If the society embodies stresses and antagonisms which become bottled up and are not released in some harmless ritual way then the society will not prosper. The *incwala* ceremony, as a first-fruits ceremony, is closely bound up with the productive cycle in the Swazi economy. Ritual, then, can once again be seen to be about moral relationships and a means of claiming that people depend upon one another for their welfare but in an exaggerated way to the extent that prosperity is only possible if moral conditions are good.

Gluckman also interprets the rites of reversal that used to occur among the Zulu and other people in terms of ambivalence and conflict. In these rites, on a certain day in the year women would throw off all the normal restraints on their behaviour. They would behave aggressively and more like men. They would abuse men and shout obscenities at them, but all in a ritualised manner. Gluckman sees this kind of thing as an instituted form of protest on the part of a subordinate section of the society which gives expression to animosities and frustrations, thereby releasing tensions and repressed feelings. It was believed to increase the harvest and promote prosperity in general. It was the ritual expression, according to Gluckman, of ambivalent attitudes which renewed the unity of the system.

Gluckman's interpretation of such rituals has been criticised by Norbeck (1963) for not taking into account the meaning that the rituals have for the participants. Also, from a survey of similar rituals throughout Africa, Norbeck is led to question the claim that these rituals are forms of protest or rebellion. Gluckman's approach, for example, would not explain the frequent indulgence in transvestism by men in such rituals nor the fact that they often involve the expression of animosity towards women. Rather than being specifically a form of protest or rebellion, Norbeck suggests, they are instances of a much wider range of customs which may be interpreted as the expression of generalised tensions and which may indeed be cathartic. In some cases, far from being protests they may be seen as a form of humour and amusement. Humour, of course, can be a way of expressing and dealing with tension and conflict.

More significantly, Beidelman (1966), through a detailed analysis of Swazi cosmology and certain aspects of the symbolism of the *incwala* ceremony overlooked by Gluckman, comes to quite a different conclusion. It is not the symbolic expression of hostility to the king nor a form of symbolic rebellion but the expression of the separation of the king from the various groups in Swazi society so that he may be free from allegiance to any specific group in order to take on the supernatural powers of his office. Beidelman also takes Gluckman to task for ignoring the actors' own understanding of what they are doing. This can to some extent be recovered from a thorough understanding of their cosmological system which reveals much of the symbolism in the rituals. Gluckman's neglect of this stems from the lingering functionalism of his approach which seeks to find social value and solidarity-generating capacity in rituals even where conflict seems to be involved. Gluckman also neglects, in Beidelman's view, the psychological aspects of ritual – the mechanisms which give it its cathartic effect. The efficacy of symbols is essentially a psychological question, he suggests.

Gluckman's approach emphasises the expressive aspect of ritual. Other theorists place even more emphasis on this aspect as we have seen in discussing the symbolic functionalists such as Beattie who applies his ideas as much to rituals of the kind we are concerned with here as he does to magical rituals. Such writers see rituals as a kind of dramatic performance. Barth (1975) has applied this approach in a study of initiation rituals among the Baktaman of New Guinea. The symbols involved are essentially metaphorical and expressive, he argues. This means they are complex and rich but often also vague and contradictory. But such rituals are not simply drama. They are a distinct genre or form of human activity in their own right and in some ways quite unlike any other. They say things which cannot be said in any other way and provide a meaningful world view which informs daily life and tasks. In this he adopts an approach rather like Beattie, but also like that of Phillips (1970), to religion in general which was discussed in Chapter one.

This interpretation of ritual as expression has been challenged by a number of writers not as being wrong so much as incomplete. Dramatic expression is an aspect of ritual but it is also much more than this in that it attempts to do or to change something. It also has its instrumental side (Bloch, 1974; Lewis, 1980; Rappaport, 1967; Skorupski, 1976). Skorupski in particular reminds us that much of what occurs in ritual is like the formal interaction that takes place between a commoner and a chief. Supplication, for example, is not merely expressive but, since the god is conceived to stand in relation to the supplicant as a chief does to a commoner, it is a form of social interaction on exactly the same pattern as interaction as certain types of human interaction. Many rituals take the form of operative acts. They say something but also do something by saying something.

Bloch (1974) goes further in questioning whether ritual is essentially expressive at all, stressing instead its uses as a means of exercising power and authority, an approach which Douglas (1966) has developed more specifically in relation to taboo, as we have seen above.

The role of ritual in regulating relationships of power and conflict is stressed by Rappaport who sets this in an ecological context. His study of the Tsembaga of New Guinea shows, he claims, that whatever the expressive role of ritual at least sometimes it can play a very material and practical role. The ritual cycle of this people helps to regulate their relationship to the immediate environment and to other surrounding groups. Rappaport shows how the ritual cycle maintains the ecosystem, balances the relationship between people and land and limits the frequency of inter-group conflict. It plays a central part in the mobilisation of allies at times of warfare which is linked to the way in which it also provides a mechanism for redistributing surpluses, especially of pigs in the form of pork, over a wide area at a time when people most need high quality protein.

Finally, on the question of ritual as expressive Lewis (1980), while acknowledging the insights that the approach to ritual as a form of expression gives us, warns of taking it to distorting lengths. Ritual is not exactly like a form of communication but in some ways more like a form of stimulation. It is not performed simply to communicate but to resolve or alter a situation. To emphasise its communicative aspect is to indulge in a contrived intellectualisation of ritual which carries the danger that social scientists will claim to know better what the practitioners are really doing than they do themselves.

The psychological aspects of ritual to which Beidelman (1966) refers remain unaddressed by the interpretation of ritual as expressive. *Rites de passage,* and particularly initiation rituals, even more than such rituals as the *incwala* might seem to demand a psychological interpretation. Initiation rituals commonly involve the humiliation, infliction of pain upon and often the mutilation of the initiates. One way of interpreting this would be to see this as expressing the ambivalent attitudes of adults towards the new generation which is making the transition from childhood to adulthood and the members of which are therefore becoming to some extent rivals of the older generation. One day they will replace them in positions of authority and their relationship of dependence will be reversed as their parents age.

A Freudian interpretation suggests itself here, especially when the alleged aggression takes the form of mutilation of the genitals as in the case of circumcision. There may be a link with Oedipal emotions here since the younger generation are becoming also sexual rivals.

Tempting as such an interpretation is, it would be wrong, however, to overstress this aspect. There are many more aspects to initiation rituals than apparent aggression on the part of one generation towards another. There is also a danger of ethnocentricism here. As Cohen (1964) and Young (1962) have pointed out while it may seem aggressive in the eyes of members of Western societies it may not be legitimate to assume that it is associated with aggressive motives on the part of those who inflict the pain and mutilation. Neither could we explain the pattern of occurrence of initiation rituals of this kind by this approach. If it were true we should expect to find such rituals in all societies.

Initiation rituals have also been commonly characterised as having what we might call an 'educational' function. The initiates are taught to think and act like adults and learn what is involved in taking on an adult role in the community. To some extent the infliction of pain might be seen as a form of shock tactic designed to induce a psychological disposition to behave in an adult manner – a means of driving home the message dramatically and quickly and of making it take root in a firm and fixed manner. The young are stunned into acceptance and understanding of their new role and status and a complete break is made with their previous mode of life which is now put behind them forever. The ordeals may serve, also, as a test and proof of capacity for adult responsibility.

This is not necessarily incompatible with a Freudian type of approach as Whiting *et al.*'s (1958) interpretation shows. They argue that such rituals will be found where sons are potentially likely to feel hostility towards fathers and tend to be highly dependent upon their mothers. Initiation controls these potentially hostile feelings, breaks dependence upon the mother and ensures identification with other males and male roles. It also prevents open and violent revolt of the younger generation against those who exercise authority over them and who are sexual rivals at a time when this is otherwise likely to occur. Young (1962) strenuously disagrees with the more Freudian aspects of this interpretation but also stresses the role of initiation rites in promoting male solidarity. It is the varying importance of this that explains the incidence of such rituals in tribal societies, rather than, as Whiting *et al.* argue, the degree of dependence of the child upon the mother and the degree of potential hostility between son and father. All these theorists, however, emphasise the role of initiation in radically breaking identifications, dependencies and habits of mind and creating new allegiances and orientations by the use of dramatic and traumatic means.

The common experience of suffering and pain by the initiates also serves, as Cohen (1964) observes, to create a bond between them. This is important, he argues, because it is emotional dependence upon their nuclear families that must be broken in the initiates. In societies in which the individual identifies with a kin group wider than that of the nuclear family – in societies in which there are strong unilinear descent groups, for example – it is necessary to reorient the individual's emotional ties away from the nuclear family as he or she reaches adulthood and towards the wider kin group. Initiation rituals are particularly effective in producing this change since they demonstrate to the initiates that they can no longer look to their nuclear families as their sole protector and source of security. It is significant that the rituals are usually carried out by older members of the initiate's descent group and that parents are excluded from them. Cohen shows that initiation rituals of this kind are almost entirely absent from societies in which emotional attachment is solely to the nuclear family and where there are no important kin groups above this level, while a high proportion of societies where the unilinear descent or similar group is of structural importance have such rituals. Not all have them, however, and Cohen admits that this is a necessary but not sufficient condition for the occurrence of such rituals. Why some societies of this kind have them and others do not is something he is unable to answer.

It is not just the passage from childhood to adulthood that is marked by a transition ritual in tribal societies. Most transitions are so ritualised. This is something that Van Gennep (1960 [1908]) emphasised. It was Van Gennep, as we have seen in discussing taboo above, who showed that being situated between two statuses or positions is often considered to be dangerous. Those who go from one status to another pass through a phase of vulnerability in which they are neither one thing nor the other. This condition he termed marginal or *liminaire* and it lies between two phases of most rituals of transition. First, there is a rite of separation in which the subject of the ritual performance is removed from his or her old status. This may involve actual physical removal and segregation from the wider society for a period of time, as in the case of many initiation rituals. After this period of marginality or liminality the subject is integrated into a new status through a rite of aggregation. This often involves a symbolic rebirth of some kind such as passing through a short tunnel or passage, under an arch, or moving through an aperture of some kind.

Transitions from one status to another are, of course, usually marked by some form of ritual in every society but the ritual marking of roles and statuses and movement between them is something which is particularly prevalent in and characteristic of tribal societies. According to Gluckman (1962) this is the consequence of the multiplex structure of these societies in contrast to the simplex structures of modern industrial societies. In multiplex structures the multiplicity of roles in which any two individuals may interact requires that some means of demarcating and signalling these different roles is required. This is done by means of special observations and avoidances, that is, by rituals. In general there is an exaggerated emphasis on custom, which includes ritual, in such societies: 'I suggest that the effect of this relatively "exaggerated" development of custom is to mark off and segregate roles in social groups where they may be confounded' (1962, p. 25.).

The dense interlocking network of relationships in such multiplex structures is one in which moral implications are embedded. How a person fulfils obligations within a given role will have a whole series of effects on other roles and relationships. All of a person's actions are morally significant in any given role because they will have implications for others in a whole variety of ways. Gluckman believes that this is why rituals are associated with changes of activity in most tribal societies. In societies in which roles are largely segregated moral judgements tend also to be segregated. Failure to fulfil the obligations of a particular role does not have moral implications in all or most other spheres of activity. Failure in one role does not necessarily disturb other areas of interaction. Ritualisation, then, isolates and demarcates roles in circumstances where there is a strong tendency for them to be confused and conflated. It ritualises them by exaggerating the prescribed behaviour associated with each role.

The approaches we have been considering – ritual as the expression of ambivalence and as a means of demarcating roles – are concerned with the broad connections between ritual and types of social situation. Other anthropologists have been more concerned with the actual process by which rituals achieve their effects – for example, the catharsis of which Gluckman speaks. Generally this involves the careful analysis of the complex symbolism involved in ritual and of the power of symbolism in achieving various effects.

Turner (1964, 1965), for example, emphasises the way in which the symbols involved in ritual have many different levels of meaning associated with them. They may range between two sets of associations which are at opposite poles to one another. At one pole the symbols refer to the social order, the normative order. At the other pole they refer to natural and physiological processes. These poles he calls respectively either ideological or normative and sensory or orectic.

The meanings associated with the sensory or orectic pole tend to arouse strong emotions. Such emotions tend to be transferred to the other meanings of the symbols, namely the normative or ideological aspects. There is an exchange of qualities which takes place in the psyches of those who participate in or observe the rituals. The normative or ideological order becomes saturated with emotion while at the same time the baser emotions and drives in human nature are enobled through contact with social values. Turner clearly draws, then, on Freudian ideas, in referring to psychological processes of this kind. Presumably the emotional response to certain meanings in the symbols associated with physiological processes – bodily functions, human drives, and so on – is due to the ambivalent attitudes we have to these things resulting from the repressions involved.

Turner's ideas seem promising but as yet remain rather speculative and tentative. Equally so is the work of Mary Douglas. We have seen in the discussion of taboo how she attempts to show that ritual symbolism controls, creates and modifies experience and that she considers that the human body is frequently used as a symbol of the society (1966). This theme is developed further in later work (1973) where she is concerned with 'systems in which the image of the body is used in different ways to reflect and enhance each person's experience of society' (p. 16). Different systems of symbols relating to the body are, she argues, reflections of particular types of social situation. Societies with a particular character will have a different attitude to the body and different norms and customs which regulate bodily activity. They will also have different styles of ritual and religion. In this way she attempts to relate anthropological material to the subject matter of the religious systems of advanced and complex societies.

To take one example, in a social system in which there is an emphasis on subordination to authority we tend to find that all behaviour is regulated by norms. In this type of society ritualism will be high and there will be many taboos. Societal characteristics will be reflected in and through the body and attitudes towards it. Social interaction takes place as if people were spirits without bodies at all. Bodily and organic functions and processes will be closely regulated. Interaction will be highly formal. Posture will tend to be rigid and upright. There will be many standards for politeness and refined behaviour. People will not behave in a physically demonstrative manner. This type of society will have its own religious style which will emphasise formal, ordered and controlled ritualism.

In the opposite type of society, where authority structures are more diffuse and weak, where the individual is less subject to control, the religious style will not emphasise formal ritual but enthusiasm, spontaneity, excitement and effervescence.

Douglas's approach might be criticised for being over-reductionist and indeed at times rather vague and even obscure but her use of anthropological material to develop understanding of wider religious patterns is stimulating and thought-provoking.

In conclusion, it is clear that ritual is an extremely complex and varied form of human behaviour with many different aspects and dimensions and manifesting considerable ambiguity. It is expressive yet instrumental, dramatic yet practical, social yet embodying meanings with psychological import at the individual level, akin to other forms of activity yet perhaps a distinct type of human activity in its own right.

12 Religion and rationality: Max Weber

In modifying the functionalist approach writers like Davis, Yinger and O'Dea introduced the idea that religion is, among other things, a provider of meaning in the face of what threatens to be a meaningless world. Even more than in these contributions the key claim of other recent analyses of religion has, in fact, usually been that the essence of religion is to be found in the fact that it is a response to the threat of meaninglessness in human life, and is an attempt to see the world as a meaningfully ordered reality. In Chapter fourteen we shall look at the ideas of the most prominent of such theorists. However, among earlier theorists, Max Weber to a considerable extent anticipated and laid the groundwork for such an approach and for the synthesis of the various strands from which the religious life is woven.

Weber did not directly confront the broad question of the sources of the religious mentality or the causes of religious belief and behaviour. He was less concerned with the explanation of religion *per se* than with connections between different types of religion and specific social groups and the impact of different types of religious outlook upon other aspects of social life and particularly economic behaviour. However, Weber did briefly develop a general approach to religion as a social phenomenon and attempts to assess its nature and the type of human concern and motivation which underlie it at a number of points in his work.[1]

Perhaps the most explicit discussion of this occurs in his 'The social psychology of the world religions' (1970c). Here Weber set out what is essentially a psychological approach to religion but one which recognises both the intellectual and emotional basis of it and which is so closely integrated with social factors that it has to be considered an eminently sociological account also.

He is careful, however, to dispel any idea that in linking religion to social factors one need adopt a reductionist position. The sociological approach cannot fully account for religion, he states. He rejects the thesis that religious ideas are mere reflections of the material position and interests of social groups. 'However incisive the social influences . . . may have been upon a religious ethic in a particular case, it receives its stamp primarily from religious sources, and, first of all, from the content of its annunciation and its promise' (1970a, p. 270).

He also rejects theories of religion which see it as basically a response to deprivation and, consequently, motivated by resentment, a reference to Nietzsche, although in saying this he acknowledges that there is a very close connection between religion and suffering. In his discussion of this relationship he gives the clearest indication of his fundamental assumptions about the nature of religion and the sources from which it springs.

Those who suffer misfortune, he observes, are, in many religious traditions, thought to have angered the gods who are punishing them, or to be possessed by demons, again often because they are guilty of some action which has made them vulnerable. In accounting for suffering in this way religion has met a very deep and general need. Whatever fortune befalls a person, whether it be good or bad, it cannot be accepted as mere chance. It must be explained and thereby justified in some way. Those who are fortunate need to know that their good fortune is not just luck, the consequence of pure arbitrariness, but deserved. Above all when the fortunate compare themselves to the less fortunate they feel a strong need to justify the difference in terms of desert and justice. Hence the tendency to account for misfortune in terms of guilt and supernatural punishment. Similarly, the less fortunate and those who suffer feel an overwhelming need to account for it in terms which deny its arbitrariness and which see it as part of a meaningful pattern and a just order, whether this entails acceptance of guilt and punishment, the expectation of ultimate compensation, or some other interpretation.

Here we have, then, the root source of religious attitudes, in Weber's view. Religion is fundamentally a response to the difficulties and injustices of life which attempts to make sense of them and thereby enables people to cope with them and feel more confident when faced by them. Religious conceptions arise as a result of the fact that life is fundamentally precarious and uncertain. Uncertainty implies that human beings desire certain things but find their desires are not always fulfilled. There is always a discrepancy between what we think ought to be and what actually is. It is the tension generated by this discrepancy which is the source of the religious outlook.

The discrepancy exists at a number of levels. At the most basic it is simply that between material desires and actual conditions and at another level it is that between normative expectations and actual circumstances. The good and the just do not always prosper while the wicked often do. Religion is an attempt to cope with such facts and by its mediation with the supernatural world it is believed that material desires can be satisfied. Through its doctrines the apparent injustices of the world can be made to seem only apparent.

Religion can thus make the apparently arbitrary world seem meaningful and ordered. The fortunate deserve their good fortune if the wider religious view is taken into account while the unfortunate deserve their fate or are only unfortunate temporarily in this material world and will enjoy their rewards in the hereafter. In this way religion provides what Weber calls a 'theodicy' of good or ill fortune.

Those who enjoy good or bad fortune, however, generally or frequently do so because they occupy positions in society which determine to a large extent their life-chances, their prestige, and so on. Inequalities are not random but part of a patterned structure. Consequently, religious attitudes tend to be associated with particular groups in society. Different groups have somewhat different religious outlooks since they experience the problems that discrepancies between expect-ations and experience create to differing degrees and in different ways. As a consequence, the sociology of religion is, for Weber, fundamentally the study of the relationships between religious ideas and the particular social groups that are the 'carriers' of those ideas and of the consequences for history and society of such religious orientations and their impact upon styles of life, attitudes and behaviour.

In his section on religion in *Economy and Society* (1978), translated and published separately as *The Sociology of Religion* (1965), Weber begins his analysis by looking at what he considers to be the most elementary forms of religious belief and behaviour, namely the religions of tribal societies. In such societies, he observes, religious behaviour is largely motivated by the desire to survive and prosper in this material life. Religious and magical thought and behaviour are not set apart from everyday purposes and are oriented primarily towards economic ends. Questionable as it may be, in tribal societies, Weber believed, people are too immersed in the immediate problems of everyday life and survival to give attention to anything but magical and manipulative means of realising material goals.

It is significant that Weber always speaks of religious and magical behaviour, implying that they are somewhat different, if related. He tends to distinguish them on the basis that magic is largely manipulative and attempts to coerce gods and spirits whereas religion involves the worship of them. Magic, also, conceives of gods and spirits as part of this world or at least immanent in everyday objects and entities whereas religion has a more transcendental conception of deities. 'Primitive' religion, then, tends towards the magical and Weber starts to trace a development from more magical to more religious conceptions and practices in the evolution of human society.

In the earliest stages magic centres on the experience of extraordinary charac-teristics or powers that seem to be inherent in certain objects, actions or persons. In many tribal societies there have been specific terms for such character- istics or powers, for example, *mana* in Polynesia, *orenda* among some North American Indian tribes and *maga* in ancient Persia from which our own word magic derives. Weber chose to use the term 'charisma' to refer to such powers or extraordinary qualities. Magic begins to develop into religion when this charisma is attributed less to the objects themselves than to something behind the object which determines its powers – in other words to a spirit, soul, demon or similar conception.

Once charisma is located outside the material world and in a sense beyond it, the way is open for ethical rationalisation to begin to dominate religious attitudes. The spirits become further and further removed from this world. Man has to rely more and more upon his own skills and techniques to survive and prosper in this world and life. Gods become more and more bound up with ethical con-siderations. They begin to make demands upon men that they should live in accordance with certain moral and ethical principles. Values and principles are increasingly emphasised above narrow self-interest. Weber, in fact, tends to equate religion with the appearance of ethical rationalisation and he tends to see religious developments in terms of development in ethical rationalisation. Once begun the process seems to lead in certain definite directions.

Weber associates ethical rationalisation in religion with the appearance of a priesthood. Previously, the only specialists that had existed within the religious or magical sphere were magicians concerned with achieving concrete material results for clients. The concern of priests is with intellectual matters and with the elaboration of doctrine which generally involves the development of ethical thought.

Weber links the emergence of a priesthood and the development of ethical rationalisation with increasing social complexity. This increases interdependence among human beings because they no longer live in small face-to-face groups in which mutual control and adjustment can be secured by informal and customary means. In complex social situations greater reliance must be placed on law and formal rules and procedures.

In such circumstances there is a need to formulate ethical principles, to propagate them, to iron out contradictions and ambiguities and to deal with new situations and contingencies. This requires specialists in the ethical code and hence a priesthood which tends to develop a professional and vested interest in carrying the whole process still further.

If in the development of human society we can discern a certain pattern of religious development, then, according to Weber, not all groups in society develop religious sentiments to the same degree or with the same intensity. Peasants, for example, like the members of primitive societies, are inclined towards magic rather than religion. Being bound closely to nature and dependent upon elemental forces they tend to be concerned primarily with immediate control of such forces. Their concern is largely with how the world can be manipulated by magical means.

Neither do warrior nor noble classes develop much interest in religious ideas of an ethical kind nor do they spontaneously have much feel for religion. They are inclined, for example, to consider subservience to a deity to be dishonourable. Their religiosity tends to be confined to a concern with warding off evil and defeat, with enlisting divine assistance in battle and in war and with ensuring entry into a warriors' paradise on death. Only when the warrior comes to be convinced that he is fighting in the name of a god or a religion does he really fall under the influence of ethical ideas, as was the case with Islam.

Officials and bureaucrats are also, generally speaking, little inclined towards religion. They are mainly interested in the maintenance of order, discipline and security and religion is regarded by them as a useful instrument for achieving these goals. Typical in this respect was the Confucian, educated administrative class in China, the literati. Weber comments, 'The distinctive attitude of a bureaucracy to religious matters has been classically formulated in Confucianism. Its hallmark is an absolute lack of feeling of a need for salvation or for any transcendental anchorage for ethics' (1965, p. 90). In fact Weber hesitates to classify Confucianism as a religion at all. Neither do wealthy merchants, financiers and so on show any intensity of religious conviction or concern with ethical salvation religion. Their concern with mundane things, their pursuit of worldly material goals and their overall satisfaction with their lot usually prevents them from developing otherworldly, spiritual or ethical concerns. Weber comments that 'everywhere, scepticism or indifference to religion are and have been the widely diffused attitudes of large-scale traders and financiers' (1965, p. 92).

The attitudes to religion of the classes mentioned so far, that is to say the privileged classes, is, then, most often one which seeks legitimation of their position of privilege. They require, Weber believed, only psychological reassurance of the justice of their position and of the worthiness of their mode of life. They are not entirely irreligious but are relatively so and their religious sentiments and aspirations tend not to be towards systematic ethical rationalisation, towards salvation or towards otherworldly aims.

It is the middle and lower classes who have been the real carriers of ethical religions and especially the lower middle class of the urban areas. The lowest classes tend not to develop distinct religious ideas but are highly susceptible to the missionary endeavours of lower middle-class religious leaders, innovators and preachers.

The final major social category that Weber discusses from the point of view of religious orientation is that of intellectuals. Intellectuals may come from a variety of backgrounds, either relatively privileged or middle class, and their contribution to religious thought and ideas varies accordingly. In general, however, intellectuals have been of great importance in the development and elaboration of religious conceptions. Weber believed that all the great oriental religions were largely the product of intellectual speculation on the part of relatively privileged strata. Perhaps even more significant, however, have been intellectuals coming from relatively less privileged groups and especially those who for one reason or another stood outside the main traditional class structure. Such religious thinkers have tended to develop highly ethical and radical religious conceptions which Weber saw as having had great importance and impact upon the development of the societies in which they occurred in contrast to the rather conservative and elitist religious intellectualism of privileged strata.

Highly important in such developments is the role of the charismatic prophet. Much religious change and development, Weber argued, has tended to take the form of rather sudden innovation brought about by exceptional charismatic leaders or prophets. Charisma, as we have seen, may be possessed by things and by people. Charisma may also be inherent or it may be acquired. When acquired by a human being it is usually the result of indulgence in practices which are extraordinary or by undergoing some extraordinary experience. It may, for example, be acquired through rigorous ascetic practices or long hours spent in mystical contemplation or through strange states of mind such as trance, or possession by spirits. Those who indulge in such practices or undergo such experiences are often thought to have extraordinary or exceptional powers.

Charisma, then, represents the extraordinary, the non-routine, aspects of life and reality. It is thus something which can transcend established ideas and the established order. It tends to be radical and revolutionary and opposed to tradition. The charismatic prophet was for Weber one of the most important figures in religious history. The prophet is the agent of religious change and of the development of new and more complete solutions to the problem of salvation. His or her message is one which is accepted out of regard for the personal qualities and gifts of the charismatic leader. Prophecy is fundamentally founded not upon reason or intellectual analysis but upon insight and revelation.

In contrast to the prophet the priest stands for tradition, established authority and conservatism. The priest is a full-time professional attached to a cult and its ceremonies and often administering divine grace as part of an established religious tradition.

Weber distinguished two types of prophet – the emissary or ethical prophet and the exemplary prophet. The latter sets an example to others through his or her own behaviour and not simply or primarily by preaching and advocating a particular way of life or pattern of conduct. The exemplary prophet provides a model which others may follow if they wish and if they are wise enough to do so. An example of the exemplary prophet is that of the Buddha. The emissary prophet, in contrast, preaches a way of life to others claiming that they have a duty or obligation to conform to it on pain of damnation. The emissary prophet typically says, as Jesus did, 'do as I say not as I do'. Exemplary prophecy tends to be elitist. The mass of the population are unable to emulate the prophet very closely if at all and salvation is, therefore, denied to them as an immediate possibility. For the ordinary lay follower it is typically, as in the case of Buddhism, only a distant goal.

Whether provided by prophet or priest the psychological reassurance that religion gives can take a variety of forms but always the aim is, Weber argues, to make sense of the world and this entails making sense of the particular position and typical life–fate of given social groups. Speaking of the variety of religious conceptions Weber says in 'The social psychology of the world religions':

> Behind them all always lies a stand towards something in the actual world which is experienced as specifically 'senseless'. Thus, the demand has been implied: that the world order in its totality is, could, and should somehow be a meaningful 'cosmos'.

(1970c, p. 281)

Weber refers to the needs which give rise to such religious ideas as ideal interests, as opposed to material interests. His conception of the relationship between material and ideal interests and between both of these and religious ideas, and his characterisation of the role of material and ideal interests in social change, is a complex one. It is most clearly and succinctly stated by Weber in another passage in 'The social psychology of the world religions':

> Not ideas, but material and ideal interests, directly govern men's conduct. Yet

very frequently the 'world images' that have been created by 'ideas' have, like switchmen, determined the tracks along which action has been pushed by the dynamic of interest. 'From what' and 'for what' one wished to be redeemed, and let us not forget, 'could be' redeemed, depended upon one's image of the world.

(1970c, p. 280)

So it is not ideas themselves which stimulate change, it is interests. Yet 'world images' can determine which way action in the pursuit of interests will go. This of course implies that one can realise interests in different ways. Faced with a problem there is usually more than one way one can solve it. How it is solved will depend upon one's world picture.

Also, world pictures are, Weber, says, created by ideas. Here Weber would allow for the particular and unique insights of creative individuals and religious innovators such as prophets. The visions and revelations of such people have often contributed to the world images of groups and even whole civilisations.

It is also important to note that interests are of two kinds, material and ideal. Marx would probably have argued that these so-called ideal interests were not inherent but themselves socially determined and therefore ultimately to be accounted for by material conditions of existence. For Weber, however, as we have seen, they are a fundamental aspect of the human condition.

Finally, Weber suggests in this passage that world images, which are created by ideas, determine to some extent ideal interests. The need for redemption or salvation is shaped by the picture of the world the believer has which is in turn shaped by ideas.

It is then a fairly complex relationship that Weber traces between ideas and interests and one which can work out in a variety of ways in different circumstances. Broadly speaking, however, we can say that no set of ideas will have any impact, according to Weber, unless it somehow matches the interests of a significant social group. It does not follow that it will serve their material interests specifically. It might serve their ideal interests. For the most part it will not appeal if it is too much at variance with material interests but it is certainly possible that in certain circumstances individuals will espouse a set of ideas which meets their ideal interests but which actually conflicts with their material interests to some degree.

Ideas for Weber, then, are never simply or merely ideological statements or reflections of the interests of a specific stratum or group. Yet ideas embody certain basic assumptions which have been determined to a considerable extent by the particular circumstances and situation of that stratum or group and the social and psychological forces which have formed its particular outlook and conception of its own interests.

These basic assumptions or presuppositions are at the root of religious conceptions and Weber considers them to be in the last analysis fundamentally non-rational. The way in which religious systems develop on the basis of such presuppositions Weber looks at in terms of rationality. From the basic presuppositions religious ideas can take various directions which are more or less rational.

The concept of rationality is a fundamental one in Weber's sociology but one which has caused a great deal of difficulty and confusion. The problem is that Weber used the term in a variety of different ways. In 'The social psychology of the world religions' he speaks of 'rationalism' as involving 'an increasing theoretical mastery of reality by means of increasingly precise and abstract concepts' but points out that it can also mean 'the methodical attainment of a definitely given and practical end by means of an increasingly precise calculation of adequate means' or simply 'systematic arrangement' (1970c, p. 293). Rationalism in these senses is used by Weber to characterise the particular way in which Western culture and civilisation as opposed to Eastern have developed. The West, Weber believed, was more rational in its approach to all spheres of life and endeavour. Often he seems to be thinking largely of the development of the scientific outlook, the systematic pursuit of scientific knowledge and its application through technology. Along with this goes rational bureaucratic organisation of administration and production. Even in spheres such as music, however, the West developed a more rational approach. All of this promoted greater production but Weber was not necessarily implying that the West is thereby superior. No necessary value judgement is intended by Weber in his use of the term rational to characterise the West. This is shown in his contrast between formal and substantive rationality. The systematic pursuit of profit in capitalism by careful calculation of costs in relation to return, optimal use of resources, elimination of waste, and so on, may be highly rational in the formal sense but it does not necessarily produce substantive rationality in the sense of meeting human goals and needs or the needs of a society as a whole. Formal rationality has nothing to do with values; substantive rationality involves value positions. Whether something is rational in the substantive sense depends upon the values one holds and what is rational in this sense from one point of view may not be so from another. Much of Weber's work is oriented to the understanding of why the West has placed so much emphasis, in Weber's view, upon formal rationality.

In the sphere of religion, rationality for Weber meant the elimination of magical aspects and the removal of contradictions and ambiguities in the solutions to the problem of salvation. There are various directions which this process can take, according to Weber. The directions they do take are in part dependent upon the position in the society of the stratum which is the carrier of the religious ideas. On the other hand, religious ideas may have inherent tendencies to develop in certain ways. As a result they may have a significant independent influence upon the conduct of life of the stratum which is their carrier and indeed upon a whole society and civilisation. Weber was particularly concerned with the practical implications of systems of religious ideas; that is to say their impact upon economic activity. The whole of his work in the sociology of religion is inspired by this definite interest and purpose and it has always to be remembered, therefore, that his work is informed by a specific standpoint and perspective.

Weber outlines in 'The social psychology of the world religions' some of the major directions that religious ideas may take. Where there is a genteel stratum of intellectuals the tendency is towards an image of the world as being governed by impersonal rules. Salvation is an affair of the individual *per se* and can be achieved only by a purely cognitive comprehension of the world and of its meaning. This was the case in India where contemplation became the supreme religious value.

Where there existed a professional class preoccupied with cult ceremonies and myth, or anywhere where there existed a hierocracy, this has sought to monopolise religious values. They have taught that salvation is impossible by one's own efforts but can only be attained through the mediation of priests who dispense sacramental grace. Political officials have tended to develop religion in a ritualistic direction because ritual implies rules and regulation. Chivalrous warriors have employed notions such as fate and destiny and have pictured gods as heroes.

The religious tendencies of artisans and traders are much more variable, according to Weber, but it is among these classes that one gets a tendency towards active asceticism, i.e. the work ethic combined with a dislike of self-indulgence and, therefore, regulation of private consumption. It is, of course, this particular combination of ideas that Weber thought to be of enormous significance for social change and to be an important contributory factor in the development of capitalism.

This active asceticism is only one direction that salvation-type religion may take. There are, in fact, a great variety of forms but within this diversity a number of fundamental types can be discerned which are derived, by Weber, from the basic possibilities inherent in all solutions to the problem of salvation. If the events and facts of this life and world seem to threaten the meaning of a person's existence, that is if they provide a motive for seeking some kind of salvation, the individual can either attempt to escape from the world or he can attempt to find a mode of adjusting to it and of accepting it. Escape from the world is referred to by Weber as an other-worldly orientation and adjustment to the world as an inner-worldly orientation. Having adopted one or other approach there are essentially two paths the individual seeking salvation can take. Whether escape from the world or adjustment to it is sought, it can either be pursued through resignation or through self-mastery. The latter Weber calls asceticism and the former mysticism.

These two sets of alternatives generate four fundamental possibilities.[2] First, salvation may take the form of inner-worldly or active asceticism mentioned above. This involves the total devotion of all worldly activity to the sole end of serving god. Salvation is achieved through activity and hard work in this life and world combined with a renunciation of indulgence in the fruits of that hard work and emphasis upon abstemiousness.

The opposite of inner-worldly asceticism is other-worldly mysticism. Here the goal of salvation cannot be achieved, it is believed, except by rejection of this life and world and this means, ideally, rejection of all worldly desires, pursuits, responsibilities and involvements. The other-worldly mystic preaches indifference to the world and to material pleasures and desires as irrelevant, illusory and transitory. It is an attitude characteristic of Buddhism. It is commonly monastic and, therefore, a way of life which only the religious virtuoso can fully lead and one denied to the ordinary masses.

The inner-worldly approach can be combined with mysticism and this combination is characteristic of religions such as Taoism which have emphasised acceptance of this world and life but which have taught minimisation of the interference of worldly responsibilities with the ultimate goal of mystical contemplation and enlightenment or union with the divine. The Taoists valued earthly existence and sought longevity, even material immortality, but only in order to pursue and to continue in contemplation of mystical truth.

Finally, other-worldy asceticism has sought to achieve salvation through complete mastery and overcoming of all worldly desires which draw the believer back into involvement with the world. The ascetic is not indifferent to desire but rather seeks to conquer it. It is characteristic of monastic Christianity.

Weber's approach to religion, then, is rich and complex. At its root is a psychological approach which emphasises the pursuit of meaning. This is no mere intellectual quest, however, but springs from deeply rooted emotional sources, from the desire for a theodicy of good or bad fortune and out of ideal interests which have to do with a sense of worth, legitimacy and rightful place in the scheme of things. The way in which these needs are met varies according to social position, and the generation of solutions to the problem of salvation is thus very much a social process, influenced by social forces and meeting social exigencies. The individual innovative prophet nevertheless often plays a crucial role in the process and it is a role based upon personal charisma of an unpredictable and, in social or psychological terms, of an ultimately inexplicable kind.

13 The Protestant ethic debate

At first sight it is perhaps puzzling why Weber's *Protestant Ethic* essay has stimulated so much debate in sociology. It was of course a bold claim that he made, namely that the development of that type of economic system which he called rational capitalism which has come to dominate by far the greater part of the globe and which has stimulated such a remarkable growth in technology and production is rooted partly in religious developments at the time of the Reformation. But the intensity of the debate probably has much to do with the fact that, in the eyes of many, Weber seemed to be providing a counter to the materialist conception of history and thereby to Marx in emphasising a religious factor in the process of historical development and change. Many would argue that such an assumption is false on the grounds that Marx's understanding of the materialist conception of history is not of the crude form that Weber took it to be. Such disputes in the history of ideas cannot be resolved here but Marshall (1982) has shown that if Weber had anyone in mind that he was concerned to refute, it was not Marx but Sombart who had argued that capitalism owed its development to the Jews.

Weber, then, was by no means taking up the opposite position to that of the Marxists on the question of the role of ideas in history nor did he deny 'the influence of economic development on the fate of religious ideas' and was concerned to show how while 'religious ideas themselves simply cannot be deduced from economic circumstances . . . a mutual adaptation of the two took place' (Weber, 1930, p. 277–8).[1] He does not offer an idealist explanation of the origins of modern capitalism:

> we have no intention whatever of maintaining such a foolish and doctrinaire thesis as that the spirit of capitalism could only have arisen as the result of certain effects of the Reformation, or even that capitalism as an economic system is a creation of the Reformation . . . . On the contrary, we only wish to ascertain whether and to what extent religious forces have taken part in the qualitative formation and the quantitative expansion of that spirit over the world . . . . In view of the tremendous confusion of interdependent influences between the material basis, the forms of social and political organisation, and the ideas current in the time of the Reformation, we can only proceed by investigating whether and at what points certain correlations between forms

of religious belief and practical ethics can be worked out. At the same time we shall as far as possible clarify the manner and the general *direction* in which, by virtue of those relationships, the religious movements have influenced the development of modern culture.

(Weber, 1930, p. 91).

His argument, then, is a very tentative one. It is that one important factor in the process by which a specifically rational and distinctively European form of capitalism developed was a religious factor. It was a necessary but not a sufficient condition. Many other factors of a material kind were involved. Even this, in fact, probably overstates Weber's case. The religious factor may have been a necessary condition only for the vigour of rational capitalism in certain parts of Europe, not its appearance. There was a close affinity, Weber argues, between the spirit of modern capitalism and the Protestant ethic. Ascetic Protestantism created an ethos which was compatible with modern rational capitalism and did not stand in conflict with capitalist business methods and practices. The capitalist could engage in his work with an easy conscience and indeed with that much greater vigour and enthusiasm in the knowledge that what he did was not only not morally suspect but was in fact the carrying out of God's purposes for him in this life (Fischoff, 1944). The spirit of capitalism which had its roots in ascetic Protestantism stimulated and promoted a distinctively European type of economic development. The motivation and orientation to life that constituted this spirit of capitalism were derived from Calvinist teaching and were characteristic of the outlook of Calvinist and Calvinistic Protestants.

Weber makes it very clear at the outset that what he is concerned with is *rational* capitalism or 'the rational capitalistic organisation of (formally) free labour' (1930, p. 21). He distinguishes this from other forms of capitalism such as adventure capitalism and political capitalism. These have existed throughout history and in many cultures. Rational capitalism is something which has flourished only in recent times beginning in Northern Europe.

Weber begins by noting how frequently certain religious affiliations are associated with success in business and with ownership of capital resources. Those who have enjoyed such success, he points out, seem at certain times to have been overwhelmingly Protestant. This is *prima facie* evidence that there may be some connection. Also rational capitalism and economic development were to be found earlier and to a greater extent in Protestant than in Catholic countries and regions.

Weber goes on to characterise the spirit of capitalism. It is important always to remember that he is speaking of an attitude or orientation and not actual behaviour when he speaks of the 'spirit of modern capitalism'. It can most clearly be seen in the passages that Weber quotes from the works of Benjamin Franklin which best exemplify, in his view, this spirit in its purest, that is to say, ideal–typical form. It is significant that Franklin was not himself a Puritan of any description and expounded the capitalist spirit in a country which was still largely agrarian since this allows Weber to suggest that the spirit of capitalism as an ethos could exist independently of capitalism as an economic system and thereby be a causal factor in its emergence.

The modern entrepreneur characteristically seeks to maximise profit through continuous rational and optimal use of resources not simply because it is prudent to do so but as a duty. This primacy of the profit motive entailed the pursuit of ever renewed profit through reinvestment of the maximum available resources above modest and customary levels of consumption. In other forms of capitalism profits were often dissipated in the form of conspicuous or extravagant consumption. Weber's capitalists tended to regard such consumption and dissipation of capital as morally reprehensible. Money spent on luxuries was lost many times over, Franklin said, because once spent it could not be reinvested and thus multiplied.

The spirit of capitalism involved the work ethic which meant that any time not devoted to the end of making money was considered to have been wasted. As Franklin put it, time is money. That not earned during half a day idling, though no money be spent, is lost many times over. It could not have been necessary for consumption otherwise the half day could not have been spent in idleness. The money could therefore have been invested and multiplied.

The pursuit of profit for its own sake by the most systematically rational means stressed that all waste had to be eliminated, costs cut wherever possible and no resources left underutilised. Careful calculation of cost in relation to returns and accurate book-keeping were essential to this. But this was not just a matter of good business sense and practice. These principles were not simply useful standards for success but a true ethic or ethos peculiar to Western capitalism. 'The earning of money within the modern economic order, is, so long as it is done legally, the result and the expression of virtue and proficiency in a calling' (Weber, 1930, pp. 53–4).

This ethos was not one which came naturally to human beings. The desire to make money was natural enough but not the particular ethos which emphasised the careful and systematic pursuit of money through such rational means, accompanied by an emphasis upon restraint in its use in consumption. It is this which has produced the tremendous pace of economic development in the West. In fact, Weber says, the desire to make money when divorced from such an ethic is correlated with an absence of rational capitalist development. 'The universal reign of absolute unscrupulousness in the pursuit of selfish interests by the making of money has been a specific characteristic of precisely those countries where bourgeois-capitalistic development, measured according to Occidental standards, has remained backward' (Weber, 1930, p. 57).

The most important force which has impeded the emergence of such a spirit Weber terms traditionalism. Characteristic of this attitude is the tendency only to work for as long as is necessary to earn enough to satisfy customary demands and needs or expectations. Weber said that no man by nature wished to earn more and more for its own sake; men for the most part wish simply to live to a customary standard. This was very much the attitude of labour in the pre-capitalist era and in parts of the Third World today where if enough can be earned in three days to satisfy customary needs people will tend only to work for three days.

The spirit of capitalism for Weber, then, was something new and distinctive and characteristic of the rising stratum of the lower industrial middle class. It was such groups who, Weber argued, upheld the ideal of the expression of virtue and proficiency in a calling. It was an ideal which had its roots in religious sources and Weber attributes considerable importance to it.

The notion of the calling was essentially a product of the Reformation, Weber argues. It was not entirely new in itself but certain aspects and emphases of the Protestant interpretation were distinctive in his view; 'the valuation of the fulfilment of duty in worldly affairs as the highest form which the moral activity of the individual could assume' (Weber, 1930, p. 80). This imparted a religious significance to everyday activity which Weber contrasts with that of Catholicism. For the ascetic Protestant the only acceptable way of life from a religious point of view was one which did not seek to go beyond this world but to live in accordance with the obligations imposed by one's existence in this world. This was in complete contrast to both Catholic and Lutheran attitudes.

> The typical antipathy of Catholic ethics, and following that the Lutheran, to every capitalistic tendency, rests essentially on the repugnance of the impersonality of relations within a capitalist economy. It is this fact of impersonal relations which places certain human affairs outside the church and its influence, and prevents the latter from penetrating them and transforming them along ethical lines.
>
> (Weber, 1961, p. 262)

The idea of the calling did not always lead to the rational capitalistic stereotype of business activity which Weber believed was fostered by the spirit of capitalism. It depended upon how it was interpreted. The idea had been developed by Luther but his interpretation was on the whole one which had rather conservative and traditionalistic implications. According to Luther 'the individual should remain once and for all in the station and calling in which God had placed him and should restrain his worldly activity within the limits imposed by his established station in life' (Weber, 1930, p. 85). The Lutherans preached obedience to authority and acceptance of the way things were and did not contribute in any direct way to the development of the spirit of capitalism, according to Weber.

Calvin's interpretation of the idea of the calling was in contrast radical in its implications and promoted the spirit of capitalism among Calvinists and Calvinistically oriented groups, even though there was no intention on Calvin's part that it should have any such consequences. They were entirely unforeseen, Weber argues. In addition to the Calvinists certain other groups with strong Calvinistic influences in their theologies were significant in promoting this radical idea of the calling, namely Pietists and the Baptist sects. Weber also mentions Methodism in this respect but probably incorrectly.

It was the specifically Calvinist doctrine of the elect or predestination which combined with the idea of the calling gave it its radical impact. According to the doctrine of predestination, a certain part of humanity, the elect, will be saved and the rest eternally damned. No one can earn their salvation because this would be to bind and to obligate God who cannot be so obligated. God may save the worst sinner if he so chooses. Who is to be saved and who not is entirely a matter of God's will and is predetermined since God is omniscient and must therefore know already whom he will save.

For the individual this helplessness and uncertainty of fate were psychologically intolerable. Some way had to be found of knowing that one was to be saved. It was not sufficient simply to trust in God as Calvin himself had taught. Calvinist preachers taught that the devout could seek some sign of being among the elect. Everyone had a duty to regard themselves as saved and the sign they might be given was that of worldly success in their calling. Also, they could attempt to attain a state of self-confidence in their elect status by engaging in intense worldly activity. The consequences, Weber claims, were that God was seen to help those who helped themselves by regulating their life conduct in an ascetic and rational way. In effect, Calvinists came to believe that they had to prove themselves before God, not as a means of earning their salvation but rather as a means of assuring themselves of it. This and the belief that God had not placed us in this world for our own benefit and pleasure but to be his instruments, to carry out his commandments and to glorify him, led to a total rationalisation of life conduct. 'The moral conduct of the average man was thus deprived of its planless and unsystematic character and subjected to a consistent method for conduct as a whole' (Weber, 1930, p. 117).

In striking contrast to Catholic teaching, then, the ascetic Protestant could not fall back upon ideas of atonement and remission of sin through confession and penance, good works or giving to the church. The necessity of proof before God for Calvinists meant unceasing devotion to one's worldly calling which neither Catholic nor Lutheran interpretations of duty entailed. The organisation, also, of many of the Protestant sects influenced by Calvinism produced a similar devotion to worldly duty in that one had an obligation to prove oneself not only before God but also before other members. This was a theme which Weber developed further in a slightly later essay on the Protestant sects.[2]

Such an ethic would have provided a basis for life highly appropriate to the conduct of business in a rational capitalist economic system and would have fitted in extremely well with the practical concerns of lower middle-class artisans, traders and businessmen. It was an ethic which when adopted by workers overcame their traditionalism rendering them diligent, responsive and adaptable.

The consequences of ascetic Protestantism, then, were that the religious life was no longer something to be lived apart from the everyday world but within it. In the Middle Ages Christian asceticism had retreated from the everyday world into the monasteries. 'Now it strode into the market place and slammed the monastery door behind it' (Weber, 1930, p. 154). And in a later series of lectures Weber was to say that 'Such a powerful, unconsciously refined organisation for the production of capitalistic individuals has never existed in any other church or religion, and in comparison with it what the Renaissance did for capitalism shrinks into insignificance' (1961, p. 270).

Ascetic Protestantism was not opposed to the accumulation of wealth as such;

it was opposed to the enjoyment of it. The consequences of consuming wealth were, inevitably, idleness and temptation. Puritanism believed sensual indulgence to be both sinful and irrational since it was not devoted to the sole end of glorifying God and fulfilling his commandments.

The work ethic, the systematic pursuit of profit and the emphasis on abstemiousness naturally led to surpluses which could only be reinvested, in short, to the accumulation of capital. Capital accumulation and deferred consumption were the key to the enormous economic dynamism of modern capitalism and to the breakthrough to continuous growth as a normal feature of modern societies.

> When the limitation of consumption is combined with this release of acquisitive activity, the inevitable practical result is obvious: accumulation of capital through ascetic compulsion to save. The restraints which were imposed upon the consumption of wealth served to increase it by making possible the productive investment of capital.
>
> (Weber, 1930, p. 172)

> when asceticism was carried out of monastic cells into everyday life, and began to dominate worldly morality, it did its part in building the tremendous cosmos of the modern economic order.
>
> (Weber, 1930, p. 181)

Once on its way, the modern economic system was able to support itself without the need of the religious ethic of ascetic Protestantism which in many ways could not help but sow the seeds of secularisation in modern society by its own promotion of worldly activity and consequent expansion of wealth and material well-being. Calvinistic Protestantism was its own gravedigger.

CRITICISM AND DEFENCE, COUNTER-CRITICISM AND COUNTER-DEFENCE

Weber's thesis has inspired a flood of words and many criticisms. Many of Weber's critics have failed to understand his point and have criticised him for or have cited evidence against things he did not claim. Samuelsson (1961), for example, points out that while the first capitalist countries may have been Protestant, not all Protestant countries were capitalist. There is no simple relationship between Protestantism and capitalism nor any clear pattern in the relationship between them. The Protestant countries show considerable variation in the extent of their development and not all Puritan communities were economically advanced. These points ignore Weber's quite explicit and clear statement that he did not think that it was only Calvinistic Protestantism that was important for the development of rational capitalism but that many other factors were important, variations in which would account for variations in the strength and pattern of development of capitalism. Weber was quite aware that it was possible to find capitalism without Calvinism and *vice versa*. Both Samuelsson and Tawney (1938) referred to a spirit of enterprise and innovation associated with economic enterprise and advance, most clearly seen in Renaissance Italy or the Hanseatic towns, which predated the Reformation. But this is no refutation of Weber. Samuelsson also mentions Calvinistic Scotland where capitalism did not develop until relatively late. But this, again, ignores the fact that Weber states that many other conditions are required for capitalism to emerge and flourish not just the appropriate motivations stimulated by ascetic Protestantism.

On the face of it Weber's thesis has plausibility. But plausibility is not the same as verification. This plausibility might in any case, it has been argued, be an artificial one which results from Weber's methods and in particular his use of ideal types (Robertson, 1970, pp. 172–3). The spirit of capitalism and the Protestant ethic are pure types, distillations of essences which are not claimed to have existed in this pure form in reality. Reality is complex and the method which uses ideal types is a way of removing all factors not strictly relevant to the hypothesis in question. The relationship between these ideal types will also hold in reality to the extent that reality approaches these types. Whatever the merits of this method, however, a danger might be that in defining the types in the first place a selection of elements is unconsciously made which makes them effectively the same thing. This gives plausibility to the thesis but at the expense of tautology. The spirit of capitalism *is* the Protestant ethic (Marshall, 1982).

This does not necessarily invalidate Weber, however. If the spirit of capitalism was nothing other than the Protestant ethic expressed in the context of practical business activity, this could still have provided an important stimulus to the development of rational capitalism as a system of action. The essence of Weber's argument is that A (the Protestant ethic) produces B (the spirit of capitalism) which affects C (rational capitalist action). There may be problems with the link between A and B such that it is difficult to disentangle one from the other but the really central question is whether C is actually significantly affected by A/B in the way Weber suggests.

On this point it is crucial to note that Weber nowhere offers any evidence. One of the central weaknesses of his essay is that it lacks any empirical validation of his thesis. It is also a remarkable fact, despite so much having been written about it, that there has been almost no attempt to verify or refute it empirically. One of the few attempts to do this is that of Marshall (1980). What Weber would have needed to show to establish his claims empirically was that:

1 Calvinistic and ascetic Protestants did in general behave in accordance with the Protestant ethic.
2 Non-Protestants behaved differently.
3 Early capitalistic entrepreneurs were predominantly Calvinistic Protestants.
4 Such people were indeed imbued with the spirit of capitalism.
5 This spirit did indeed derive from ascetic Protestantism.
6 They did in fact conduct their businesses in accordance with the spirit of capitalism.

Weber does none of these things. Marshall attempts to do some of them in the context of sixteenth- and seventeenth-century Scotland. He finds that Calvinist pastoral teaching during this period in Scotland was very much as Weber had portrayed it. Scots capitalists also seem to have conducted their business much in accordance with the spirit of capitalism. Marshall was able to uncover some evidence, though not sufficient to firmly establish the point since the evidence is sparse and difficult to come by, that their attitudes to the conduct of business were derived from their Calvinism. Marshall considers that in the Scottish case, then, there are fairly good grounds for supporting the general thrust of Weber's thesis as far as the business class in concerned. The same could not be said for the attitudes and conduct of the labouring classes for which little evidence is available.

In a later work, Marshall (1982) stresses that Weber himself provided very little empirical evidence of the sort that his study of Scotland seeks to do. He argues that the central weakness of Weber's procedure is that it assumes that certain motives and understandings underlie the actions of rational capitalist businessmen and infers these motives from an examination of those actions. Weber produces no direct evidence of the motives of early capitalists – no evidence independent of their observed actions. Without such evidence there is no way of knowing that something like the Protestant ethic or the spirit of capitalism informed their behaviour rather than the exigencies of the situation they faced. Conversely we can assume nothing about the traditionalism of medieval businessmen from the way they behaved (Marshall, 1982, pp. 108–19). Their conspicuous consumption and accumulation of luxurious possessions, rather than testifying to relatively less rational recklessness and desire for status and aggrandisement could simply have been the most sensible way to use wealth in certain market and political conditions. Investment in luxury goods – gold, jewellery, fine houses, and so on may have been the best way to preserve wealth in an uncertain world in which opportunities for other forms of investment were limited. In the prevailing circumstances this may well have been the most rational strategy for preserving property and those who followed it, therefore, were no less imbued with a spirit of enterprise than the most abstemious and hard-working Calvinist Protestant.

The same point concerning the relationship between action and motivation may be made about the alleged 'traditionalism' of labour in pre-capitalist economies (Marshall, 1982, pp. 126–31) whereby the time spent working is limited to that which is necessary to earn sufficient for a customary standard of living. Again motives are imputed on the basis of observed behaviour. It may, however, be that in a situation of limited supply of consumer goods, for example, there is little point earning more than money can buy. There may be a whole set of circumstances, knowledge of which reveals the behaviour in question to be perfectly rational, or motivated by quite different values and beliefs than those it appears to be motivated by given the assumptions and the theoretical expectations of the observer.

Weber, then, Marshall (1982) concludes, merely asserts and does not show that capitalists thought in a certain way. His thesis rests on no sound empirical basis. Nor has subsequent work, apart from Marshall's study of Scotland, placed it on any firmer empirical ground. On the other hand nor has it disproved it.

A similar criticism of Weber is made by Walzer (1963) who argues that the values of Protestantism, as he sees them, were characterised by a need to bring passions and desires under rigid control at a time of change and disorder and motivated by anxiety and fear of chaos; quite unlike those that Weber attributes to Protestantism and not at all conducive to rational capitalistic behaviour or accumulation of capital. These were not the attitudes of the entrepreneur. If businessmen often preferred to do business with Protestant sectarians as Weber said was the case (Weber, 1970b), it was because they were always being watched. Puritan congregations were characterised by constant suspicion and distrust of one another and collective vigilance against any individual member falling prey to temptation. This tended to make them narrow and conservative in their views. The emphasis on control of passions and desires was not the consequence of a determination to live daily life in accordance with God's intentions but of fear and insecurity.

Walzer's criticisms of Weber perhaps miss the point to some extent. Perhaps the values of Protestantism that Walzer emphasises are only the other side of the coin of those that Weber emphasises and not incompatible with the thrust Weber believed they had. Insecurity and anxiety are not necessarily inhibitive of hard work in the pursuit of a calling; quite the contrary in fact. After all, Weber acknowledges the psychological insecurity that the doctrine of predestination induced in those who accepted it and was explicit in emphasising that hard work in the pursuit of one's calling was the way Calvinistic Protestant preachers recommended for the removal of that anxiety and for attaining some reassurance of salvation.

A further criticism of Weber that is often made is that it was not so much Protestantism as a set of religious doctrines that contributed to the development of rational capitalism so much as the position of certain Protestants who were minorities in their societies (Tawney, 1938; Trevor-Roper, 1973). The marginal position of Protestant minorities, and Calvinistic Protestants were often in a minority position, it is argued, encouraged innovation and individualism – values which were congruent with rational capitalist activity. Exclusion from traditional occupations forced them, also, into new types of economic activity. Against this view is the fact, which Weber himself had pointed out, that Catholic minorities did not succeed in business or acquire the values of the spirit of capitalism.

Luethy (1964) has countered this apparently incompatible evidence with the claim that Catholic minorities were not actually in dissent against a long established and dominant tradition as were Protestants despite their minority position. It was the dissenting nature of Protestantism and especially where it remained a minority faith that gave it its dynamism, not any specific set of religious or theological views. Protestants were often successful in many spheres of life, not just in commerce. But it was not the Protestant Reformation *per se* that generated this dynamism, innovative capacity and new outlook upon life according to Luethy. These developments and changes predate the Reformation and can be found in many parts of Europe, some of which remained Catholic. What extinguished this new spirit in some parts of Europe was the Catholic Counter

Reformation whereas the Protestant Reformation in some circumstances fostered their development. In fact, before the Counter Reformation some of the most progressive and dynamic areas of Europe, such as northern Italy, were those which later on were to stagnate under the restrictive regime of the Counter Reformation which stifled initiative and enthusiasm. Luethy contrasts the northern Protestant Netherlands or Holland with the Spanish Netherlands which became Belgium. There was nothing in particular which favoured Holland economically but there rational capitalistic enterprise and industry flourished while in the Spanish Netherlands it was destroyed.

If Calvinistic Protestantism was particularly associated with the bourgeoisie it was because, Luethy argues, only they had the independence necessary to stick to a faith while the state and the princes adopted compromises or retained Catholicism. An example is that of the Huguenots in France. This independence accompanied by a minority position made such people a great force for change. 'The significance of Calvinism in world history lies in the fact that it failed to win political power and thereby remained almost free of political–opportunistic considerations and princely usurpations' (Luethy, 1964, pp. 102–3). The Calvinist–Puritan did indeed have a new mentality. He answered only to God and his conscience and was therefore free and responsible. The Calvinist community bowed to no human authority. Such men were a 'yeast in the Western world, the most active agents of the development towards a modern Western society in which "capitalism" is but one strand among many' (Luethy, 1964, p. 103).

14 Religion and meaning

Max Weber, as we have seen, saw religion as essentially providing theodicies of good and bad fortune. While this is in many respects more of a psychological than sociological approach, Weber's integration of this insight which in itself integrates both intellectualist and emotionalist elements, with an eminently sociological analysis of the interrelationships between beliefs and social groups makes him one of the forerunners of those who have attempted to synthesise the insights of previous theoretical approaches. Among these one of the most influential has been Peter Berger who, like Weber, finds in religion the main source from which people have through the ages sought to construct a sense of meaning in their existence. A slightly earlier and important contribution, however, which similarly emphasises meaning, is that of Clifford Geertz.

CLIFFORD GEERTZ

The main source of Geertz's theoretical ideas on religion is his article 'Religion as a cultural system' (1966) where he approaches the subject from what he calls the cultural dimension of analysis. This means looking at religion as a part of a cultural system. By culture he meant 'an historically transmitted pattern of meanings embodied in symbols, a system of inherited conceptions expressed in symbolic forms' (p. 3). As part of culture religion deals in sacred symbols and what sacred symbols do, Geertz says, is

> to synthesise a people's ethos – the tone, character and quality of their life, its moral and aesthetic style and mood – and their world view – the picture they have of the way things in sheer reality are, their most comprehensive ideas of order.
>
> (p. 3)

Geertz, then, distinguishes two basic elements – a people's ethos and their world view. Sacred symbols or, in other words religion, play an important role in creating a world picture and in relating it to the ethos. Sacred symbols make the ethos intellectually reasonable by showing it to be a way of life ideally adapted to the state of affairs that the world view expresses. On the other hand, the world view is made convincing because it is constructed in such a way that it fits the actual way of life.

Ethos and world view, then, are mutually supportive. 'Religious symbols formulate a basic congruence between a particular style of life and a specific metaphysic, and in doing so sustain each with the borrowed authority of the other' (p. 4). From such considerations Geertz arrives at a definition of religion and this definition is perhaps better seen as a condensed theory of religion. We saw in Chapter one that definitions often conceal theoretical predilections. In Geertz's case the theoretical element is quite conscious and deliberate. Religion, he says, is:

> a system of symbols which acts to establish powerful, persuasive, and long-lasting moods and motivations in men by formulating conceptions of a general order of existence and clothing these conceptions with such an aura of fac-tuality that the moods and motivations seem uniquely realistic.
>
> (p. 4)

Geertz goes on to unpack this 'definition' and to explicate further its various parts. In doing so he sets out in detail his theory of religion.

His first point is that religion is a set of symbols. A symbol, he points out, can either stand for something, represent or express something or it can act as a sort of blueprint or instruction for what to do. We might illustrate this idea with an example which Geertz does not use himself but which expresses the point quite well, namely that of a set of traffic lights. The red light tell us something about the situation we are coming up to – that we are approaching potential danger from traffic crossing our path. But it also predisposes us to act in a certain way; it gives an instruction and indicates a course of action that should be adopted. It both represents a situation and at the same time acts upon the world to bring about certain behaviour. In the same way religious symbols express the world and at the same time shape it. They shape the social world by inducing dispositions to behave in certain ways by inducing certain moods. For example, they may make worshippers solemn, reverential, and so on. Or they may produce exultation, joy or excitement.

Religion does these things, Geertz goes on to say, by formulating concepts of a general order of existence. People need such concepts, he argues. They need to see the world as meaningful and ordered. They cannot tolerate the view that it is fundamentally chaotic, governed by chance and without meaning or significance for them. Three types of experience threaten to reduce the world to a meaningless chaos. Geertz calls them bafflement, suffering and evil.

Bafflement is the experience which comes about when unusual or dramatic events occur which none of the normal means of explanation are competent to deal with. Religion provides an ultimate answer as it explains the otherwise inexplicable. Geertz sees religious beliefs as attempts to bring anomalous events and experiences within the sphere of the, at least potentially, explicable. In this category of anomalous events and experiences he would include such things as death, dreams and natural disasters.

This sounds on the surface very intellectualist and somewhat Tylorean but Geertz sees this need for explanation as also an emotional need. He says, for example 'any chronic failure of one's explanatory apparatus . . . to explain things' which cry out for explanation tends to lead to a deep disquiet' (p. 15).

Geertz focuses upon unusual or anomalous events and puzzling phenomena. Without denying the force that such events are particularly likely to have, one might also acknowledge that the very daily, mundane, humdrum routines of life might, for some people at least, also come to be questioned in respect of the meaning of such routine. The very ordinariness of much of daily existence may threaten at times to appear without significance precisely because of its ordinariness and routine character. Religion may thus be not just an attempt to deal with odd aspects of the world but also to make life significant in a broader context in the face of the sheer routineness of existence.

To return to the experiences which Geertz feels most threaten our view of the world as a meaningful order, the second he mentions is that of suffering. Geertz is opposed to the view that religion helps people to endure situations of emotional stress by helping them to alleviate it or escape from it. He specifically mentions Malinowski's views in this respect as being inadequate. He describes Malinowski's theory, in Nadel's words, as the 'theology of optimism'. The problem of religion, as Geertz sees it, is not how to avoid suffering but how to accept it, how to make it sufferable. Most of the world's religious traditions affirm the proposition that life entails suffering and some even glorify it.

Whereas the religious response to bafflement is primarily an intellectual one, the religious response to suffering is largely an emotional or affective one. In its intellectual aspects religion affirms the ultimate explicability of experience. In its affective aspects it affirms the ultimate sufferableness of existence. It does this by providing symbolic means for expressing emotion. It attempts to cope with suffering by placing it in a meaningful context, by providing modes of action through which it can be expressed and thus understood. To be able to understand it is to be able to accept it and endure it.

The third type of meaning–threatening experience is that of evil. What is central here is the common feeling that there is a gap between things as they are and things as they ought to be. This feeling is important when it takes the form of an awareness of a discrepancy between moral behaviour and material rewards. The good often suffer and the wicked prosper. Geertz, of course, echoes Weber and many of the functionalists in this. As he puts it, 'the enigmatic unaccountability of gross iniquity raises the uncomfortable suspicion that perhaps the world and man's life in the world have no genuine order at all' (p. 23).

Religion attempts to make moral sense of experience, of inequality and of injustice. It attempts to show that these things are only apparently the case and that if one takes a wider view they do fit into a meaningful pattern. A very common way in which this is done is of course to claim that injustices in this life are compensated for in the next.

To sum up, religion tackles the problems of bafflement, suffering and evil by recognising them and by denying that they are fundamentally characteristic of the world as a whole – by relating them to a wider sphere of reality within which they become meaningful.

But why do people accept such beliefs at all? How do they come to acquire convictions of this kind? It is to such questions that that part of Geertz's definition which speaks about clothing conceptions of a general order of existence with an aura of factuality is addressed.

Geertz is opposed to psychological explanations of why people accept religious conceptions. Although bafflement, suffering and evil drive people towards belief in gods, spirits, and demons, this is not the real basis upon which the beliefs actually rest. The real basis of particular beliefs lies either in authority or tradition, according to Geertz. Religion is only one perspective on the world among others. The problem thus boils down to first, what is distinctive about the religious perspective in contrast to others and second, how do people come to adopt it?

What is distinctive about the religious perspective, Geertz claims, is that it is characterised by faith. The scientific perspective is essentially sceptical; it is always putting its ideas to the test. The religious perspective does the opposite; it tries to establish its ideas as being true beyond doubt or beyond evidence.

The mechanism which generates faith is ritual, according to Geertz. It is in ritual that religious conviction is generated. For example, he says 'the acceptance of authority that underlies the religious perspective that the ritual embodies flows from the ritual itself' (p. 34). Ritual is both the formulation of a general religious conception and the authoritative experience which justifies and even compels its acceptance.

One point of criticism might be made here. If religious conviction arises from participation in rituals, then why do people participate in rituals in the first place? This is the same problem that plagues the theories of all those who see ritual as primary and belief as secondary, including, as we have seen, Robertson Smith, Durkheim and Radcliffe-Brown.

In the last part of his definition Geertz refers to the moods and motivations created by religion being made uniquely realistic. The operative word here is 'uniquely'. Geertz is saying that religious perspectives are each unique ways of approaching the world – ones which seem uniquely realistic to those who espouse them and eminently practical and sensible. It is this imperviousness of religion to doubt that religious perspectives seem to acquire that gives them their power to affect society so profoundly, according to Geertz. The fact that believers within each religious perspective regard their own perspective as obviously and self-evidently the most sensible and realistic one gives such perspectives great potency.

Since each perspective is unique, any attempt to assess the social value or function of religion *per se* becomes impossible. Questions about whether religion in general is functional or dysfunctional cannot be answered, Geertz argues. They can only be addressed to particular religions. We can only sensibly ask whether this or that particular instance is functional in its circumstances and it may well be that any given religion or religious movement is not functional or integrative for the society in which it occurs.

Thus Geertz departs from the functionalism of many theories that appear on the surface to be similar to his own and despite his definition of religion being cast in functional-sounding terms. We might ask on this point whether the definition is inclusive to the extent of covering systems of ideas such as nationalism, communism and so on. It would, like many functionalist definitions, seem to do so. And although his analysis admits of the possibility of dysfunctions it retains a lingering functionalism in many respects and lacks a dynamic aspect which would allow us to understand the role that religion plays in social change and social conflict. To put it another way, it overlooks the issue of power and authority in relation to religion (Asad, 1983). There is no analysis in Geertz's essay of the processes by which symbols induce the moods and motivations they are alleged to. Here we must attend, Asad argues, to the social process involving authoritative practices, disciplines and discourses which give force to religious ideas and symbols. Geertz's account relies upon an assumed efficacy implied to lie inherently in the symbols themselves and in culture and upon mental states produced by such symbols and by rituals.

Clearly, Geertz's approach is one which is influenced by and attempts to synthesise many of the insights of previous approaches including intellectualism and emotionalism. Similar in this respect is the approach of Peter Berger.

PETER BERGER

In his major theoretical contribution to the sociology of religion Berger (1973) argues that society is a dialectical phenomenon in that it is at one and the same time a human product and an external reality that acts back upon its human creators. The process by which we create our own social world through mental and physical activity, experience this social world as an external and independent reality and find ourselves shaped by it is one in which a meaningful order is imposed upon experience. Such a meaningful order Berger terms a *nomos*. 'Men are congenitally compelled to impose a meaningful order upon reality' (1973, p. 31).

The nomos is a social product; it is socially constructed. Isolation from society undermines a sense of order and those who become so isolated tend to lose their footing in reality. Their experience becomes disordered; it becomes *anomic*. The nomos, then, is a shield against the terror that ensues when the world threatens to appear to be without order and meaning. Experiences such as death are a severe threat to the sense of order. Death is not simply a disruption of the continuity of relationships, it threatens the basic assumptions upon which the social order rests.

The nomos is usually seen as being 'in the nature of things', a taken-for-granted, obviously true picture of reality as it actually is. Although humanly constructed it is seen as a natural phenomenon and part of a world beyond and transcending human will, capacities and history. It is religion which upholds this sense of the sheer reality and naturalness of the humanly constructed nomos. The nomos is, through religion, given a sacred character and becomes a sacred *cosmos*. It is sacred because it is seen as mysterious and vastly powerful. 'Religion is the human enterprise by which a sacred cosmos is established'

(1973, p. 34); 'it is the audacious attempt to conceive the entire universe as humanly significant' (1973, p. 37).

Berger goes on to show how religion brings human society into relation with this sacred cosmos, how it locates human society in a wider cosmic picture and in the process legitimates the social order. Such legitimation may take a variety of forms but always the precarious and transitory constructions of human activity are given the semblance of ultimate security and permanence.

The relationship between religion and society is important in another way. Religious conceptions of the world are underpinned and maintained as credible by a specific set of social processes which constitute what Berger calls a 'plausibility structure'. These are the social processes by which religious views are promoted, disseminated, defended, or assumed. If this plausibility structure is undermined or weakened religious convictions can easily lose their hold on the mind.

Because human social arrangements, roles, obligations and institutions are so precarious we need to be constantly reminded of what we must do and of the meanings embodied in our culture and institutions. It is ritual that does this reminding. In ritual the continuity between the present and the societal tradition is ensured; the experience of the individual is placed in the context of a history.

Religion does not simply legitimate and make sense of the social order. It makes sense of experiences which might otherwise be disruptive and disordering. It legitimates marginal situations and experiences – those which are at the limits of everyday ordinary experience. Included here are such things as sleep and dreams, death, catastrophes, war, social upheaval, the taking of life, suffering and evil. Religious explanations of such things Berger calls, following Weber, a theodicy. It is the role of theodicy to combat anomie. Religion 'has been one of the most effective bulwarks against anomie throughout human history' (1973, p. 94).

Because of its very power to overcome anomie, however, it is also one of the most powerful forces of alienation in human life. That view which sees the world as external to the individual and which determines human beings and which forgets that they also change and determine their world, in short, an alienated world view, is precisely the view which serves to maintain an ordered and meaningful view of reality and which prevents anomie. It is the alienating power of religion which gives it its power to ensure stability and continuity of the tenuous formations of social reality.

> The humanly made world is explained in terms that deny its human production . . . . Whatever may be the 'ultimate' merits of religious explanations of the universe at large, their empirical tendency has been to falsify man's consciousness of that part of the universe shaped by his own activity, namely the socio-cultural world.
>
> (1973, p. 96)

Berger, however, warns against a one-sided approach on this point. Because of the dialectical relationship between man and society it is possible that religion can be not just a force which alienates but also a force which may de-alienate and which can legitimate de-alienation; 'religious perspectives may withdraw the status of sanctity from institutions that were previously assigned this status by means of religious legitimation . . . . One may say therefore, that religion appears in history both as a world-maintaining and as a world-shaking force' (1973, pp. 105 and 106).

Berger's approach is clearly an ingenious synthesis of Durkheimian, Weberian and Marxist insights. There are two main criticisms that might be made of it. First, it does not confront the possibility that the need for meaning might be the product of a specific type of social situation or relationship to nature as a Marxist approach would maintain. In other words it assumes this as an inherent and universal human need which is independent of specific social or other conditions. It does not, therefore, tell us much about why a religious outlook occurs in some situations and in some individuals but not in others. It also means that Berger's approach retains a lingering functionalism in its emphasis upon the order-promoting role which, despite the qualifications, remains predominant in the approach.

Second, it does not address the question of whether modern society can continue effectively while an alienated world view prevails. One might argue that a modern society can only progress and can only prevent anomie by *overcoming* an alienated world view.

THOMAS LUCKMANN

A close associate of Berger, Luckmann's approach to religion also emphasises meaning. Religion, for Luckmann, is coextensive with social life itself. The modern Western trend towards secularisation is interpreted by him as merely a decline in *traditional* religious forms and institutions not in religion *per se*. Certain fundamental questions and problems still confront and always will confront human beings which relate to what he calls the dominant, overarching values, their social-structural basis and the functioning of these values in the life of the individual.

Luckmann sets out in *The Invisible Religion* (1967) to determine the 'anthropological conditions' of religion by which he means those conditions which underlie all religion, conditions which are universal aspects of human beings and of human life. These underlying conditions give rise to a whole variety of specific religious manifestations, that is to say particular religions and religious institutions, the specificity of which is related to prevailing circumstances in each case. But Luckmann is concerned with the religious impulse before it assumes its varied historical forms each of which is just one way in which a fundamental process in human life becomes institutionalised into a concrete form. Each is just one institutionalisation of the general process by which a 'symbolic universe' is socially constructed and related to the world of everyday life.

Symbolic universes are systems of meaning by which everyday life is brought into relation with a transcendent reality. They are meaningful systems because they are socially constructed and supported. The process by which this comes about is possible only for beings which transcend their biological nature; in other words, it is possible only for human beings because they are self-aware and capable of reflecting on their experience. They are thus because they are social creatures who must interact with others in ways which require that they take the part of the other in order to anticipate the other's reactions to their own actions and thereby shape their own actions accordingly. This allows them to see themselves as others see them and in the process they acquire a sense of self.

Luckmann sees this process of the acquisition of a sense of self as essentially a religious process. It is coextensive with socialisation of the child and in the process of socialisation the child is also presented with a picture of reality, a world view, which embodies the symbolic universe that gives meaning to reality and to the existence of the individual, locating the self within this symbolic universe. In short, in past societies this has generally been accomplished through a religious system in the traditional understanding of the term. In present society it is achieved through ideas such as self-realisation, self-expression, and individual autonomy which are not generally thought of as constituting religious values but which are religious in a wider and fundamental sense.

The central problem with Luckmann's approach is that it is not clear why we should accept that the transcendence of biological nature is fundamentally a religious process. What is religious about it? Religion and socialisation are, of course, closely interwoven in most traditional societies but it does not follow that socialisation is inherently religious in character. Religion need not enter into the process. Even if Luckmann is right that what is distinctively human is the transcendence of biological nature and of self and that this is what makes it possible for human beings to be moral creatures and to develop universalistic values, it does not follow that this makes human life *inherently* religious except by simply calling all this 'religion'.

15 Secularisation

For meaning theorists the process of secularisation in modern industrial societies is problematic as it is for all theories that locate the source of religion in the human condition. In Berger's case, if religion provides *the* bulwark against alienation, how is secularisation possible? Many theorists including Luckmann have simply attempted to deny that secularisation is taking place at all. It is an illusion generated by the decline of traditional forms of religion. In place of these forms, however, new forms are growing up continuously, these theorists argue. Berger, however, does not deny the facts of secularisation and is in fact one of the leading theorists of this phenomenon. Before examining his view, however, some background discussion is necessary. In this chapter, also, other views on the process of secularisation will be contrasted with those of Berger.

The demise of religion in modern society has been predicted by many theorists, especially those writing in the nineteenth century. Tylor, Frazer, Marx, and later Freud, all expected, as we have seen, religion to fade away as science came to dominate the way of thinking of contemporary society. Others, who thought of religion in more functional terms, foresaw the disappearance of religion in the familiar and traditional forms to be replaced by something based upon non-supernaturalistic and non-transcendental foundations. Comte invented a new religion based upon the rational and scientific foundations of the new science of sociology to fill the vacuum. Durkheim saw the beginnings of a new functional equivalent to religion emerging in the values of the French Revolution.

Many more recent theorists have rejected such ideas, holding that religion is as much a part of modern society as it has been of any society in the past, while often acknowledging that its specific forms may indeed change. Bellah (1971), for example, has argued that the notion of secularisation forms part of a theory of modern society stemming originally from the Enlightenment reaction to the Christian religious tradition characterised by a strong cognitive bias and emphasis on orthodox belief. The theory of progressive secularisation functions to some extent, Bellah argues, as a myth which creates an emotionally coherent picture of reality. In this sense it is itself for Bellah a religious doctrine rather than a scientific one. Since religion performs essential social functions it will again move into the centre of our cultural preoccupations, he believes. Many other theorists, particularly in recent years in the face of the rise of many new religious movements and of fundamentalism have come to similar conclusions (Crippen, 1988; Douglas, 1983; Glasner, 1977; Glock and Bellah, 1976; Greeley, 1973; Hadden, 1987; Luckmann, 1967, 1990; Martin, 1969, 1991; Stark and Bainbridge, 1985; Wuthnow, 1976a, 1976b). For some theorists of this persuasion, also, religion will not lose its transcendental character, despite the rationalism and scientific and technological basis of modern society.

On the other hand the secularisation thesis continues to receive just as much support and the arguments of its opponents have been equally subjected to criticism even if some of this acknowledges that secularisation may not be an inevitable or uniform process (Berger, 1973; Dobbelaere, 1981, 1987; Lechner, 1991; Wilson, 1966, 1982). Others see the process as complex identifying both secularising and resistant or even anti-secularising forces (Campbell, 1972, 1982; Fenn, 1972, 1978, 1981; Martin, 1978; Sharot, 1989).

Whether modern society is secularised or undergoing a process of secularisation depends very much on what one means by religion. Much of the dispute on the question of secularisation stems from the fact that there are radically different conceptions of what religion is among theorists. Wilson (1982) points out that those who use functionalist definitions tend to reject the secularisation thesis while those using substantive definitions are more likely to support it. Some have defined religion in such inclusive terms, as we saw in Chapter one, that there would always be something which would count as religion. For such writers secularisation is an impossibility. It is ruled out almost by definition. Such inclusive definitions, however, are, as we have seen, highly problematic.

Even when one defines religion in a more restrictive way, disagreement remains on the question of secularisation. Much of it stems from the question (which is closely related to that of the definition of religion) of what one means by secularisation. The term has been used in a number of different ways. A useful survey is provided by Shiner (1966). Shiner distinguishes six meanings or uses of the term. The first refers to the decline of religion whereby previously accepted religious symbols, doctrines and institutions lose their prestige and significance culminating in a society without religion. The second refers to greater conformity with 'this world' in which attention is turned away from the supernatural and towards the exigencies of this life and its problems. Religious concerns and groups become indistinguishable from social concerns and non-religious groups. Third, secularisation may mean the disengagement of society from religion. Here religion withdraws to its own separate sphere and becomes a matter for private life, acquires a wholly inward character and ceases to influence any aspect of social life outside of religion itself. Fourth, religion may undergo a transposition of religious beliefs and institutions into non-religious forms. This involves the transformation of knowledge, behaviour and institutions that were once thought to be grounded in divine power into phenomena of purely human creation and responsibility – a kind of anthropologised religion. The fifth meaning is that of desacralisation of the world. The world loses its sacred character as man and nature become the object of rational–causal explanation and manipulation in which the supernatural plays no part. Finally, secularisation may mean simply movement from a 'sacred' to a 'secular' society in the sense of an abandonment of any commitment to traditional values and practices, the acceptance of change and the founding of all decisions and actions on a rational and utilitarian basis. Clearly this usage is far wider than any which refer only to an altered position of religion in society.

Clearly, these meanings are by no means mutually exclusive. The diversity, however, is linked to the diversity of meanings of religion and leads Shiner, echoing Martin (1965b), to say that the appropriate conclusion to come to is that the term should be dropped entirely. This seems somewhat premature. The core meaning of the term would seem to be the decline, and perhaps ultimate dis-appearance, of specifically religious beliefs and institutions which seems to encompass Shiner's first, second, fourth and fifth meanings. The processes involved might be different, and would each require empirical investigation, but the end result would seem to be much the same. Secularisation in this sense may or may not be occurring and may or may not be a permanent process. If it is not, what may be occurring is something like Shiner's second meaning – privatisation of religion. Or this may simply be an aspect or a phase of the first set of processes.

In any case, there seems no need to abandon the term or the concept. Much confusion has been caused by those who have sought to define secularisation out of consideration (Martin, 1965b)[1] sometimes on the grounds that the term is a weapon used by those opposed to religion to undermine it. This is no more necessarily true than it would be to say that obfuscation of the question has been the weapon of those who find the very idea of the secularisation of contemporary society an uncongenial one to contemplate.

This is not, of course, to say that the notion is a simple or straightforward one or that for more precise consideration of its various aspects other concepts or terms are not required. Thus, Dobbelaere (1981) uses the term 'laicisation' to refer to the complementary processes of desacralisation, differentiation and transposition and has subsequently distinguished between secularisation on the level of the individual, of the society and within religion itself (1985, 1987).

Disagreement on the question of secularisation is not, however, only a matter of terms and concepts. There is much dispute about whether contemporary society is less religious than past societies, whatever one understands by religion. It is sometimes argued that we have a false view of the religious nature of past societies and that there was as much irreligion in the past as there is today. The notion of an 'age of faith' is an illusion created partly as a result of concentrating on the religious beliefs and attitudes of the elite, of which we have more abundant information, and failing to look at those of the ordinary people (Goodridge, 1975; Douglas, 1983). Against this, writers like Wilson (1982) have rejoindered that such a view tends to be founded on the assumption that secularisation is the same thing as dechristianisation. The claim that the past was just as secular as the present, and therefore the present just as religious as the past, actually amounts to the claim that the past was no more Christian than the present and the present, therefore, no less religious than the past. But the survival of paganism and 'folk religion' in ostensibly Christian societies testifies to their more religious character than contemporary society. It will hardly do, either, to dismiss the paganism, folk religion and magical beliefs and practices of the past as not being true religion as Turner (1991) does. To do so would, by implication, exclude the belief systems of most tribal societies from the category of 'religion' and restrict it unduly solely to the world religions such as Christianity, Buddhism and Islam. Even then there would be serious problems in dealing with folk and popular interpretations of these.

Turner, however, does not take a straightforward anti-secularisation stance. Both the secularisation and anti-secularisation theorists are right up to a point, he argues. In the feudal era Catholic Christianity was very much the ethos of the upper class or nobility but remained weak among the peasants. There was and was not a golden age of religiosity against which one can contrast the present situation. This was the golden age of elite religiosity which functioned largely to provide an ideological prop for the system of property rights and inheritance. It aided the land-owning class in controlling sexuality, especially of women, in such a way as to bolster the property distribution system based upon primo-geniture which was designed to maintain the concentration of land ownership in the hands of the nobility. The landless peasantry found little to attract them in Catholicism and remained often indifferent or even hostile to it and wedded to pagan or folk practices of a superstitious or magical kind (see also Abercrombie *et al.*, 1980).

While acknowledging very probable differences between elite and peasant belief and practice one can hardly consider this a very strong argument against the secularisation thesis for the reason already stated. It is, in any case, somewhat dubious to argue that the influence of Catholic Christianity in the feudal era was based primarily on considerations of property transference. While it may have been put to this use by the land-owning class and while this may have entailed a certain interpretation of Christian teaching, it is misleading and a one-sided analysis to claim that this is the essential role of medieval Christianity. We have only to think of the cult of the Virgin Mary and of the saints to see that it had great significance as a popular form of belief and practice which addressed the concerns of ordinary peasants as it continues to do in many rural peasant communities today, especially in the Third World and developing countries. And just as it may often flourish alongside indigenous pagan and folk beliefs and practices in these regions so it probably coexisted similarly with pagan and folk religion in the feudal era in Europe.

Another argument that those opposed to the secularisation thesis tend to stress is the alleged prevalence of many private and individual practices in modern society outside the context of organised religion – from private prayer to super-stition, from listening to religious broadcasts on the radio to an interest in astrology and reading one's stars in magazines. Again the question of the definition of religion arises here. There is a tendency to favour extremely inclusive definitions on the part of some of those who deny that secularisation is a particular feature of contemporary society.

A second problem with this argument, as Wilson (1976) has pointed out, is that if the alleged religiosity underlying such private activities does not find expression in any institutionalised or collective form that in itself testifies to the precarious position of religion in contemporary society. Wilson acknowledges that many individuals may, in fact, retain some form of private religious belief or practice in a largely secularised society. For him secularisation is the 'process by which religious institutions, actions and consciousness lose their social significance' (1966, p. 14). Loss of social significance, however, may be a stage on the way to the demise even of private religiosity.

The extent to which religion has lost or is losing its social significance is, of course, an empirical question but it is very difficult to find reliable means of measuring this. It is even more difficult to measure the extent of personal and private religiosity. Figures for Church attendance and affiliation are notoriously unreliable as indicators of religious convictions or of the significance of religion in the lives of those who attend. In the United States, for example, Church attendance is far higher than in Britain and most European countries but this may be so because in the United States attendance at Church indicates membership of the community, adherence to the values of the society and nation, and respectability, much more so than it does in Britain (Herberg, 1956; Wilson, 1966, 1982). To some extent the American Churches and denominations have been internally secularised (Luckmann, 1967, p. 36). On the other hand attempts to directly ascertain beliefs through surveys can yield equally misleading results. If they ask about belief in God, for example, replies may indicate as much about the way the respondent thinks it appropriate to reply or how he or she has learned to respond to such questions as it does about inner personal convictions.

Bearing in mind such problems, the evidence would appear to be in favour of the view that religion, in general terms, is in decline in most Western industrial societies, at least in so far as they are Christian. Acquaviva (1979) concludes from a survey of the data relating to Latin America as well as the United States and Europe, in short, the whole Christian world, that 'everywhere and in all departments, the dynamic of religious practice reveals a weakening of ecclesial religiosity and, within certain limits, of every type of religious belief, including the belief in God' (p. 83).

The general pattern of this weakening is that it is more marked in the Protestant countries of Northern Europe than in Catholic countries of the Mediterranean region. Britain falls somewhere in the middle. Holland and Belgium, however, show a somewhat less marked trend, at least until recently, and the United States perhaps the least marked but this on the basis of Church attendance and similar indicators subject to the qualifications made about them above. The countryside and rural areas tend to be more religious than urban areas. Women tend to be more religious than men and, significantly, housewives more so than working women. The young and the old are more religious than the middle aged and the middle classes more than the working classes. Industrial workers are the least religious of all social groups or categories. Decline in religious beliefs and practices tends to be higher among Protestants and Jews than it is among Catholics although the latter seem to be catching up.

Turning to theories and explanations, firstly of the overall trend towards secularity, the process is clearly linked to the degree of industrialisation and urbanisation but in no clear or simple way. The correlation between industrialisation and secularisation is by no means perfect. The United States, for example, is one of the most industrialised nations but it is not necessarily the most secularised. Secularisation is a consequence of the complex social changes that have occurred as a result of, which are associated with, or, indeed, which have contributed to, the process of industrialisation and urbanisation. For this reason, to understand why secularisation has occurred we have to take a very broad historical and comparative perspective.

Explanations of the process will naturally depend upon the type of theory of the role of religion in society one favours. The explanation for the weakening or disappearance of religion depends upon one's account of why it was present in the first place. If religion is explained as the result of or reaction to deprivation and oppression then the explanation of secularisation will refer to the growth of affluence and democracy. If it is the result of lack of understanding then secularisation is the consequence of the growth of science. If it is the product of fear and uncertainty secularisation is the result of our growing ability to explain and control the natural world. If it is a neurotic response to life's circumstances on a collective scale, then secularisation is the consequence of the fact that we have as a species reached a mature stage of development. If it is what holds society together, then secularisation is the result of the fact that some more appropriate set of values is required in modern circumstances. If religion was the way in which men and women gave meaning to their existence, then secularisation may be the consequence of a crisis of meaning or the process by which new ways of providing such meaning, more appropriate to prevailing conditions, are sought.

It follows, finally, that if we do not have an entirely satisfactory theory of religion then we shall not have a fully satisfactory theory of secularisation either. On the other hand, if we could understand what it is about contemporary society that tends to weaken religion, we may gain a better understanding of the presence and strength of religion in past and other societies. The question of secularisation is, then, of crucial theoretical significance.

Secularisation, although linked to industrialisation and urbanisation, as noted above, must be seen in terms of the more fundamental and broad social change that has both promoted and resulted from these developments. Perhaps the dominant view, stemming from Weber, is that it is the growth of rationality in the West which is the key to the process of secularisation. This would explain the fact that it is Protestant countries that have been the most affected. There are two aspects to this approach each of which is somewhat differently emphasised by various theorists. First, there are those factors which are internal to Christianity which, in Weber's view, culminated in Protestantism and especially Calvinistic Protestantism. Second, there are those factors external to Christianity and which are associated with the growth and development of modes of thought and ways of viewing the world which are an alternative to Christianity or indeed religion in general.

The set of factors internal to the Christian tradition are stressed by Berger in his influential analysis (1973). Berger is concerned with the 'the question of the extent to which the Western religious tradition may have carried the seeds of secularisation within it' (p. 116). This does not mean that he thinks that Christianity has an automatic inherent tendency to develop in the direction of secularisation. He acknowledges that there must be many factors involved which are external to the religious tradition, that is, social and economic factors. In his view, however, such factors have their effect not so much upon religion in general but upon Christianity in particular. They bring about and promote tendencies already inherent within the Christian tradition. In a particular kind of social environment Christianity manifests tendencies towards secularisation whereas in the case of other religions such tendencies are absent and these religions are not therefore subject to the secularisation process even when development, modernisation, industrialisation and urbanisation take hold in those societies. In this sense Christianity can be said to be its own gravedigger.

These tendencies within Christianity go back to its very roots, according to Berger, which were, of course, in Judaism. They were 'contained' by Catholicism but unleashed by the Protestant Reformation. The Reformation was associated with a changing class structure and the replacement of feudalism. In its turn it released the forces of secularisation within Christianity.

This thesis is, of course, strongly reminiscent of Max Weber and Berger follows him very closely in his analysis. All one has to do is to substitute 'rationality' for 'secularising forces' and one has Weber's essential thesis on the development of Christianity and of European society.

Berger, then, emphasises the tendency associated with increased rationality which Weber termed the 'disenchantment of the world'. Judaism had rejected magic, mysticism and so on and this was taken over by Christianity as was the ethical rationality of Judaism. The early Christian Church, in Berger's view, took a retrogressive step. It watered down the monotheism of Judaism. It re-established a degree of mysticism and re-introduced sacramental and magical elements. But the forces promoting rationality were too strong to be wholly eliminated. The inner-worldly ethic was retained and preserved in the tradition. Also, the radical nature of Christianity, its tendency to seek to transform the world, was preserved through the Middle Ages by those groups who found in it inspiration, hope and justification for rebellion. The ethical nature of early Christianity, and its concern for justice, were never forgotten.

The rationalising tendencies of Christianity were to culminate in Protestantism and in particular Calvinism, the most rational form of religion to emerge in human history, according to Weber – at least in terms of formal rationality. It is this very rationalism of Protestantism that lies behind secularisation in Berger's view. Protestantism was, therefore, the prelude to secularisation. 'Protestantism may be described in terms of an immense shrinkage in the scope of the sacred in reality, as compared with its Catholic adversary' (Berger, 1973, p. 117).

Protestantism disposed of the sacramental and ritual aspects of Catholicism to a large extent. It divested itself of mystery, miracle and magic. Its conception of

God was of an absolutely transcendental being who, although he had created the world, remained wholly separate from it. Berger argues that this radical separation of the sacred and profane spheres in Protestantism was of great significance. Protestantism reduced the relationship and contact between God and man to such an extent that it did not take very much to sever the tenuous link entirely. This tendency goes right back to the very earliest developments in the Judeo-Christian tradition: 'the roots of secularisation are to be found in the earliest available sources for the religion of ancient Israel' (p. 119). Para-doxically, however, it was the great religious revival and intensification of religion which we know as the Reformation which sowed the seeds for the demise of religion.

Another crucial factor central to the Christian tradition is the type of religious organisation that it developed, namely the Church. If Berger is right about this it is somewhat ironic since it was this aspect of Christianity which Kautsky (1925) emphasised as accounting for the tremendous success of Christianity in spreading throughout and surviving in the Roman world. The Church type of organisation eventually led in the direction of secularisation, according to Berger, because this type of organisation entailed an inherent potential institutional specialisation of religion. This has not been a common characteristic in the history of religions. Its implications were that other spheres of life could be and were progressively relegated to a separate and profane realm and thereby removed from the juris-diction of the sacred. This meant that these other spheres could more readily become subject to the process of rationalisation and the application of new ideas, knowledge and science. The Church and religion became less and less significant for the conduct of life and less and less convincing as an interpretation of the world.

The loss of the monopoly of religious matters by one organisation, the process of denominationalisation associated again with Protestantism, has also played an important part in promoting secularisation. Wilson (1966) agrees with Berger on this point but considers this not simply to have played an important causal role in promoting secularisation but as being also a consequence of it. In Wilson's view, Methodism was of considerable significance in Britain from the point of view of rationalisation because it attracted the working classes. It promoted, conse-quently, everything associated with ascetic Protestantism among a whole new social stratum. It facilitated the acquisition of an inner discipline in the new social order among this stratum in place of the external discipline of the regulated life of the community that was disappearing as a result of the Industrial Revolution.

Religious pluralism has not, however, only aided the spread of the rational-ising tendency, it has also had a more direct effect in leading many away from religion. The situation where one can choose between one religious interpretation and another, where rival interpretations and organisations compete in the 'market place' of religions as Berger puts it, is likely to result in a devaluation or loss of authority for the religious view generally. The pluralistic situation where one can choose one's religion is also a situation where one can choose no religion at all.

When a single religious doctrine and organisation come to dominate to the exclusion of all others it rarely tolerates the emergence of a non-religious view on the part of whole groups, and often even of individuals, within the society.

We should not forget, however, that religious pluralism has also impeded, to some extent, the process of secularisation in providing a non-establishment religious outlet for the disaffected and the working class. Methodism not only promoted rationality, Wilson acknowledges, but constituted an important religious revival. Nevertheless, in the long run pluralism has promoted secularisation rather than religion. The secularisation process has passed through a phase of religious pluralism and the latter must be seen as an important aspect of the process of secularisation.[2]

Berger's theory of secularisation is persuasive and would fit the fact that it is the Christian world and particularly the Protestant world that has undergone the greatest degree of secularisation. On the other hand, he does perhaps over-emphasise the factors internal to Christianity. The importance of the Church type of organisation and of religious pluralism might be acknowledged but to say that secularisation is the outcome of inherent tendencies only unleashed by certain social changes after more than fifteen hundred years of containment by Catholicism is very difficult to accept. It would seem equally true to say that it is these social changes which are fundamental but that they affect, however, Christian countries and societies much more than others. On the other hand, it may well be that Christianity has itself contributed to or in some way facilitated, perhaps failed to inhibit, these very social developments. In short, the relationship is much more complex than Berger's theory supposes.

Wilson's analysis focuses more upon those factors external to the Christian tradition which underlie the process of secularisation. Again it is the growth of rationality that plays the central role, he believes, but in his analysis, as in that of most writers who emphasise such external factors, it is not inherent tendencies in Christianity that are central but the autonomous growth of scientific knowledge and method. The argument is that this has undermined the credibility of religious interpretations of the world. Particularly important is the application of the scientific method or approach to society, a factor which Berger also stresses in a later work (1971). The promise of religion has been undermined in its millennnial aspects and so has its capacity to legitimate and justify the social order.

Again, the separation and the institutional specialisation of religion are important here. People look to political institutions and processes for justice and for better conditions, not to the Church or to the life hereafter. The state is expected to provide for those in need. The Church has lost its educational role and with it its ability to promote its message and itself. The role of the Church in defining moral standards has declined now that parliaments and politicians increasingly concern themselves with such questions. The Church retains mainly its role in performing the major *rites de passage* and even this is declining steadily.

A further factor stressed by Wilson (1976, 1982) is the decline of community in the modern urban setting and consequent change in the locus and nature of social control. In true communities social control has a moral and religious basis whereas in the modern, rational, technical and bureaucratic world control is impersonal and removed from its former moral and ethical basis. Religion loses its significance in such a setting as do the communal values which traditionally received expression in the form of collective rituals and religious celebrations.

Despite the importance of these arguments there is also one central weakness in this approach. The processes referred to are perhaps only secondary and not fundamental in accounting for secularisation. The growth of alternative inter- pretations of the world of a materialist and scientific kind is itself a part or aspect of the very process of change of which the decline of religion is also a part. It is simply the other side of the coin. The rise of science is no more the cause of the decline of religion than the decline of religion, or at least certain forms of religion, is the facilitating factor allowing the rise of science. The growth of one and the decline of the other are part of the same process. Both are the result of deeply rooted underlying changes.

Of course, it is certainly true that the spread of science has helped to under- mine religion. Once science came to have the prestige that it won and to form the basis of so many aspects of life it could not but help call religious views of the world into question. But this is so not so much because of anything inherently contradictory in a scientific outlook and a religious one. As has been emphasised many times in this book, religion does not necessarily, at least in any fundamental sense, address itself to the same kind of question or problem that science does. Religion does not necessarily ask how things in the natural world are connected or related empirically. It may be solely concerned with the question why things are the way they are, given that they are that way. Science may reveal to us the way the world is constructed but the questions about the meaning of the world and of human existence remain. It has sometimes been said that science does not tell us anything that we *really* want to know. It depends of course on what we do really want to know or think knowable and it does not follow that religion can tell us this either but the point is that they need not necessarily come into conflict with one another (Bellah, 1971; Stark and Bainbridge, 1985).

They need not but in fact they generally have in the Western tradition because religious doctrine has sought to pronounce on empirical matters and on the basis of scripture rather than on the basis of empirical evidence. It was bound to lose in these struggles; that over the position of the earth in the solar system and over evolution being notable examples. And it was bound to be somewhat discredited as a result.

Wilson is well aware of these points but does not draw the appropriate conclusions from them. For him it is simply that religion suffered a loss of prestige. The crucial point, however, is that while this is true, it is not the fundamental process. It is not an inevitable consequence that religion or even Christianity need be undermined by the growth of science. Specific doctrines may indeed be so undermined but not necessarily the religious view of the world if it can adjust and modify its doctrines. Evolution, for example, may still present a mystery which for some requires a religious interpretation as to its meaning.

The essential point is that science does not just appear from nowhere. The critical, open, sceptical attitude which characterises science is a recent phenomenon which seems to have arisen in specific social and historical conditions – the same social and historical conditions that initiated the long road towards secularisation. It was not simply the result of a slow accumulation of knowledge and evidence about the natural world. For hundreds of years little scientific progress was made in Europe which under the domination of medieval Catholicism remained less open to new ideas, less innovative and less original in thought than the ancient Greeks had been. Science quite suddenly burst forth in the early modern era.

Marx and Engels argued that it was the decline of feudalism and the rise of the bourgeoisie which, despite the Reformation, and indeed if Berger is right to some extent also because of it, were the reasons that religious views of the world and legitimations of the social order received a serious blow. The bourgeoisie laid the foundations for materialism even if they retained a religious outlook. Only the final great upheaval of the bourgeois revolution, the French Revolution, managed to cast off the religious outlook completely. But the bourgeois revolutions paved the way for materialism and the rejection of religious modes of thought. It was this which created the *possibility* of science. This period witnessed the growth of the scientific approach to the world and advances in all spheres of knowledge. It was an age in which atheism became possible for some.

In the field of politics it was no longer doctrine and scripture that were seen to legitimate governments and regimes but citizens. The divine right of kings was rejected. The affairs of this mundane world were increasingly seen as having nothing to do with God or religion. The social order was no longer seen as ordained by God but a matter of contract, agreements or decisions made by human beings. In other words the materialist approach develops alongside the decline of religion which both facilitates it and is a consequence of it.

The process of secularisation has not, however, been a smooth and continuous one. Social developments rarely are. There have been religious revivals and declines and the graph of religiosity has its peaks and troughs. Some have detected an overall decline. Others have seen longer-range cycles and regard the secularising trend as having reached its peak and can see signs of the re-emergence of religion. The rise of the New Religious Movements and of Christian fundamentalism are the developments most often pointed to as evidence of this. Nor has the pattern of secularisation been an even or homogeneous one across different societies. The process of secularisation is greatly affected by the surrounding social context, or the religious history of the country.

The author who has paid most attention to the different patterns of secularisation, David Martin (1978), bases his analysis primarily upon the degree of religious pluralism or of religious monopoly present in the society but incorporates, also, a wide range of variables in his account including the strength of religious minorities and their geographical dispersion, the relationship between religious groupings and the dominant elites and the inherent character of the various religious traditions. The main types of situation distinguished by Martin are: first, that of total monopoly where the tradition is Catholic; second, the duopolistic type where a Protestant Church is the major organisation but with a large Catholic minority; third, the still more pluralistic situation exemplified by England with a large state Church and a wide range of dissenting and other groups; fourth, the fully pluralist but Protestant-dominated case such as the United States; and finally those countries that have no Catholic presence including Scandinavia and the Orthodox countries. Martin traces the complex implications of the changing role of religion in society in each of these types and the diverse consequences of this changing role for many aspects of public and private life.[3]

Turning to the question of the permanence of secularisation and alleged religious revival, Stark and Bainbridge (1980a, 1985) have argued that secularisation is a self-limiting process. Neither is it anything new in their view. It is part of the normal cycle of religious development. The process of denominationalisation by which sects progressively lose their sectarian character and move in the direction of becoming Churches is part of the process of secularisation. Ultimately, Churches decline as a result of their tendency to develop ever more extreme worldliness, engendering the emergence of revived religious groups (sects) or new innovative developments (cults). While acknowledging that the rise of science stimulated an unprecedented, rapid and extreme degree of secularisation in contemporary society Stark and Bainbridge argue that science cannot fulfil many central human needs and desires. It cannot remove all suffering and injustice in this life, it cannot offer an escape from individual extinction, it cannot make human existence meaningful. Only God can do these things in peoples' eyes. Religion, then, will not only survive and rise to prominence again, it will be transcendental or supernaturalist in form. It is more likely to be, further, the innovative cult movements rather than the sectarian revivals of established traditions that will flourish since the latter can only come up against, in their turn, the same forces which have brought about a degree of secularisation in the first place. The new cult movements, however, are generally free of the deficiencies of the older traditions which have made them inappropriate to the needs of an altered social situation.

Signs of the continued central importance of religion and its potential reinvigoration are found by Stark and Bainbridge in the fact that those who report no religious affiliation or belief in their surveys are more likely to accept or show interest in some form of unorthodox or fringe supernaturalism such as astrology, yoga and Transcendental Meditation. Americans who have grown up in non-religious homes are more likely to belong to a religious denomination than not to. And although the more secularised American denominations are in decline, the least secularised are not. Finally, recent decades have witnessed the emergence of hundreds of new religious movements.

Stark and Bainbridge reject the charge of Wilson (1976) and Fenn (1978) that the new sects and cults are marginal, insignificant 'consumer items' in the religious supermarket. Such a view fails to see the potential importance of new religions and is rooted in Christian-Judaic parochialism. It also stems from a failure to distinguish between different types of cult. Stark and Bainbridge consider that it is what they call the cult movement that is significant not what they term the audience cult and the client cult. The audience cult has no formal organisation and is a form of consumer activity. Its doctrines and ideas are disseminated and consumed through magazines, books, and the media. An example might be UFO enthusiasts. The client cult is rather more organised but only to the extent that the typical services offered – teachings, therapies, and so on – are offered on the basis of a practitioner–client relationship requiring some degree of organisation on the practitioner's side but none among the clientele. Both of these differ from the fully organised cult movement which differs from the sect only in that it is a new group standing quite outside older and more established religious traditions. Stark and Bainbridge's theories apply only to cult movements. The tendency to conflate cult movements, audience and client cults has led others, Stark and Bainbridge claim, to mistakenly assess all cults, including cult movements, as trivial and marginal phenomena.

Stark and Bainbridge offer empirical verification of their theory in the form of two derivative hypotheses which can be tested using data they have gathered. The first hypothesis holds that cults will abound where conventional churches are weakest because in these areas a greater proportion of the population, free from attachment to established churches, perhaps as a result of geographical mobility, will be able to experiment with new ideas. The second hypothesis holds that there will be a greater incidence of sectarian revival than new cultic experiments where the traditional churches are relatively strong. Stark and Bainbridge find their hypotheses confirmed by their data and conclude that cult and sect formation are not functional alternatives to secularisation but different responses. Secularisation has greatly undermined the traditional churches but it has not produced an irreligious population, only an unchurched one. Even in areas of low church membership belief in the supernatural remains high.

Stark and Bainbridge may be criticised on the ground that whatever the strength of the correlations they find the numbers involved in new cults and sects remains extremely low and insignificant (Bibby and Weaver, 1985; Lechner, 1991; Wallis and Bruce, 1984). Against this Melton (1993) shows that new sects, cults and movements have been founded at an accelerating rate in the United States and, while a few do disappear, most of them continue to survive and to flourish. Melton's argument is based entirely upon the number of new sects and cults. The crucial statistic, however, as Lechner, Wallis and Bruce point out, is the ratio of recruits to the new movements to the loss of membership of the older mainstream denominations and sects. This loss is far greater than the increase in numbers involved in the new movements at least as far as Europe is concerned. Stark and Bainbridge's analysis, even if it applies to the United States, would seem to be somewhat ethnocentric.

Anticipating such a point Stark and Bainbridge are careful to point out that they do not think that the new sects and cults are filling the gap left by the churches only that to the degree that a population is unchurched there will be efforts to fill the void. This still leaves them rather open to the criticism that such efforts will remain precisely that rather than achievements. They also fail to address the question of why it is that audience and client cults have mushroomed in recent decades. It is these, perhaps, rather than cult movements that are coming to typify the modern spiritual scene leading us to question their rejection of Wilson's claim that it is the very marginality of these phenomena which testifies to the degree to which religion finds difficulty retaining any hold in the contemporary situation. Stark and Bainbridge take refuge in the claim that we do not know whether some, or perhaps only one, of these new movements will take off in the future just as new movements have in the past. This is, however, to enter into speculation and cannot in itself support their theory. Also, as Dobbelaere (1987) points out, we should not forget that most of the world religions only took root among the masses with the help of rulers. Since then the structures of society have changed in such a way that it is extremely unlikely that the historical processes that led to state promotion and dissemination of particular religious systems will ever be repeated. And if many efforts continue to be made by individuals and groups to promote new religions none may succeed to any great extent. It may be, to use an analogy from Berger (1971), that the supernatural cannot rise above the status of a rumour. It may be that the contemporary predicament is that people do need and desire the kind of promises that religion has traditionally offered but find all the alternatives, old and new, no longer credible.

Rather similar to Stark and Bainbridge's emphasis on the potential significance of the new cult movements is Campbell's view of the role of the cultic milieu (1972, 1982). Whereas specific cults generally are transitory, the cultic milieu is, he claims, a constant feature of society. It is characterised by seekership and there has been a major shift in contemporary society away from commitment to specific doctrines and dogmas and towards seekership or in other words a valuation of individual intellectual and spiritual growth. This is reminiscent of Wallis's 'epistemological individualism' (Wallis, 1984) (see Chapter seventeen, p. 213). Rationalisation, then, does not, in Campbell's view, promote permanent secularisation but may actually strengthen the superstitious, esoteric, spiritual and mystical tendencies in modern culture. Even those who acknowledge the superiority of science are not usually in a position to judge between orthodox and heterodox claims and are likely to accept beliefs in flying saucers, extra-sensory perception and a whole host of other quasi-scientific beliefs. Sharot (1989) points out that since what characterises science is its acknowledgement that it does not have all the answers and probably never will, it leaves much territory for magical ideas to occupy since these can claim to explain what science cannot. In so far as people may not come to wholly endorse the scientific world view, and it is unlikely that they will, they will be susceptible to all manner of magical and mystical beliefs. Such beliefs are likely to be highly individualistic and fragmentary. This is because, Bibby and Weaver (1985) argue, in contemporary industrialised societies individuals play a variety of specialised roles which are not amenable to legitimation by overarching meaning systems.

Luckmann (1967) has also characterised contemporary societies as having no need for such overarching systems of values because they do not need religious legitimation. Religion becomes an aspect of private life, of individual choice from a variety of alternatives which can be constructed into a personally satisfying system. This leads Luckmann to argue that modern societies are witnessing a profound change not in the location of the religious away from the 'great transcendences' concerned with other-worldly matters, life and death, towards the 'little transcendences' of life which concern self-realisation, self-expression and personal freedoms (1990).

Arguments such as those of Campbell and Luckmann are open to the charge that Wilson makes against those who point to the new sectarian and cultic movements as a source of religious revival, the more so given the fact that these little transcendences are most likely to find their expression in somewhat ephemeral cultic forms which Stark and Bainbridge agree are unlikely to develop into major religious forms due to their reliance on magical elements.

It is this lack of overarching values or the necessity for them in integrating modern social systems that is stressed by Fenn in his extensive discussion of the secularisation process (1972, 1978, 1981). Fenn's work has its roots in a dialogue with the functionalist view of religion as the essential integrating and legitimating force in society. He rejects the assumption that modern societies like the United States must be held together by systems of overarching values in which case there is no necessity for any religious legitimation of the social order. Fenn discusses the process of secularisation in terms of the boundary between the sacred and profane in society. It is a boundary which various groups, collectivities, organisations and individuals seek for their own various purposes to determine. Secularisation, then, is a process of struggle, dispute, conflict, or negotiation, involving social actors who attempt to press their own claims and views of reality and not an automatic or evolutionary process. It is a complex and contradictory process which at each stage is liable to conflicting tendencies. For these reasons it is, therefore, reversible.

Fenn discerns five stages in the process of secularisation. The first is the differentiation of religious roles and institutions which begins very early and of which the emergence of a distinct priesthood is a part but which continues throughout the history of religion. The second stage consists in the demand for clarification of the boundary between religious and secular issues. Secular structures are generally differentiated from religious ones well before the spheres of jurisdiction of these religious and secular institutions have become clear. They may never, in fact, become wholly distinct but remain blurred. This blurring of the distinction between the sacred and profane is itself something that may be promoted by the very process of secularisation itself. The third stage involves the development of generalised religious symbols which transcend the interests of the various components of society. In the American context, Fenn is referring here to the development of what has been called the 'civil religion' (Bellah, 1967). In stage four minority and idiosyncratic 'definitions of the situation' emerge. Political authority is secularised but there is a dispersion of the sacred as many groups seek legitimacy on religious grounds. Finally, in stage five there is a separation of individual from corporate life.

At several stages the contradictory nature of the process can be seen. The emergence of a civil religion is a stage of the process and yet also a form of desecularisation. In attempting to determine definitions of situations the state may seek to curb religious autonomy and restrict the scope of religion, especially sectarian forms and yet at the same time seek to borrow the authority of sacred themes and principles in order to legitimate itself.

Fenn suggests that the form of religious culture which is perhaps most compatible with modernity is that which grants a limited scope to the sacred and which promotes a low degree of integration between corporate and individual value systems. It is occult and esoteric religion which best exemplifies this type of religious culture. It can be practised without coming into conflict with everyday occupational roles since it confines itself to very particular times, places, objects, and issues. It provides an ecstatic and magical form of activity and an opportunity to indulge in the irrational against the enforced rationality of formal and bureaucratically structured organisations and roles of everyday life. Clearly Fenn is close to Campbell in this view and Wallis's 'epistemological individualism' would fit well here. A recent study which exemplifies Fenn's points empirically and insightfully (Luhrmann, 1989) shows how followers of witchcraft and magic in the London and surrounding areas of South Eastern England are for the most part well educated, well-qualified professionals many of whom are scientifically trained and employed in such industries as computers and as research chemists.

Fenn goes further than writers such as Campbell and Wallis, however, in emphasising the difficulties that religious cultures with overarching value systems, which give a very wide scope to the sacred and which require a high degree of congruence between the private and the corporate spheres, can present in contemporary society in which technical rationality dominates and which are not and cannot be integrated by overarching values. A religious culture of this kind generates conflicts and tensions in contemporary society.

For Fenn, then, religion may persist in modern society but with a very different role and character. Secularisation actually produces a distinctive religious style appropriate to modern circumstances (Beckford, 1989, p. 116).

> Secularisation does not drive religion from modern society but rather fosters a type of religion which has no major functions for the *entire* society . . . . The affinity between secular societies and certain types of sectarian religiosity, then, derives from the tendency of both to foster the disengagements of the individual's deepest motivations and highest values from the areas of political and economic action.
>
> (Fenn, 1972, p. 31)

There are many advantages in Fenn's approach particularly his emphasis on secularisation as the boundary between sacred and secular being a matter of social contest and the complex and often contradictory nature of the process. There is a worrying aspect to his work, however, which stems from his very deliberate eschewal of any attempt to define his terms and concepts clearly or to directly address central debates. He considers that any attempt to define too precisely what religion or secularisation mean would fail to reflect the ambiguous and highly contested meanings these terms have in everyday life. He abdicates any responsibility to state as precisely as he can what he means by religion and secularisation by declaring his intention to put such difficulties themselves at the core of his analysis since they provide critical information as to the nature of secularisation which is 'lost by analysts who use only satisfyingly clear concepts with adequate boundaries' (1978, p. 29). A technically adequate vocabulary is of little use, he claims, in interpreting the contradictory aspects of secularisation. There is much confusion in such claims. It may be true that critical information might be overlooked in the desire to fix concepts precisely but it does not follow that one's own vocabulary can be vague, loose and contradictory in confronting the issues. Fenn confuses the contradictory nature of the *process* of secularisation with the contradictory nature of the concepts that have been used to describe it and with the contradictions that exist within and between discussions, debates and theories about it. How could Fenn know that the contradictions and disagreements about the meaning of secularisation can provide useful information about the nature of the process unless he knows what the process in essence is? His conception is, in fact, left to a large extent implicit apart from the characterisation of it as the separation of the sacred from the secular. Such a conception is clearly related to the more inclusive definitions of religion which are associated with Durkheimian and functionalist approaches in which Fenn's roots clearly lie and with which he has not entirely broken despite his criticisms of the functionalist account of religion.

It is this conceptual ambiguity in Fenn's work that may underlie his characterisation of the process of secularisation as contradictory and therefore reversible. For example, the desecularising tendencies of stage three, with the emergence of a civil religion, clearly assume an inclusive conception of religion whereas the secularising aspects of this phase presuppose a more restrictive conception. It is not clear, therefore, if Fenn is showing that the process of secularisation is in reality contradictory and ambivalent or whether he is showing that it can be seen as such when one takes into account the conflicting conceptions of religion that underlie debates about secularisation. We are not sure to what extent he is attempting to further our understanding of the process of secularisation *per se* or our understanding of what has been said about it and debated – a discussion of theories and views of secularisation. It would seem that what he is actually doing is rather the latter than the former. In this respect his work may be enlightening but it is misleading if it pretends to be other than this.

A final point about Fenn's work is that it is largely applicable only to the United States. Indeed most discussions of secularisation are addressed to the Christian Western world. Little has been said on the question of the extent to which non-Christian and non-Western countries are or are not undergoing such a process and why. However, the contributors to a recent collection of papers relating to this question generally cast doubt upon the likelihood of a similar process of secularisation taking place in the non-Western world. Pereira de

Queiroz (1989) argues that in the case of Brazil the rise of the new and often syncretistic sects and in particular Umbanda, which has become almost a new national religion rivalling Catholicism, tells against the thesis that industrialisation and modernisation will bring about a similar decline of religion that the West and the developed world have witnessed. Arjomand (1989) shows that the political ideology of Islamic fundamentalism in its various forms, most of which have rejected Western models of liberalism, nationalism and socialism, is very much a modern development which seems to run counter to earlier expectations of growing secularism and materialism as the forces of development took effect. In Malaysia Islamic fundamentalism is the counterpart of the new religious movements that have affected the west, Regan argues (1989). It has generated a new religious feel to the culture which has come to characterise almost every aspect of modern life. In Africa, according to Jules-Rosette (1989), the reaction to industrial change has often been to seek novel ways to create a sense of religious unity and group identity through the integration of the sacred into everyday life.

Comparing Europe, North America and the Middle East, Martin (1991) concludes that secularisation is largely a European phenomenon and relates this to the struggles between the Churches and secular forces in the history of Europe in the early modern era which discredited religion to an extent not experienced elsewhere. These struggles are, however, now at an end, he claims, leaving religion some space perhaps once again.

While it may be agreed that such evidence from the Third and developing world might lead us to question whether secularisation is the inevitable consequence of modernisation and industrialisation, it is far from conclusive. Many of these societies have hardly yet industrialised to the extent that Britain had when Methodism and other non-Conformist denominations made their great advance among the new industrial working classes. Today Methodism is among the most rapidly declining of denominations. Martin (1991) warns proponents of the secularisation thesis, however, against too much reliance upon this sort of alibi and also against the tendency to dismiss intensified religiosity in Eastern Europe as essentially nationalism and only incidentally religion.

The fact is that we do not yet know if secularisation is a specifically Western or a specifically Christian phenomenon or if it is a phenomenon of industrialisation or of some wider process of modernisation. It is unlikely to be simply the result of industrialisation. Non-Christian and non-Western countries, therefore, may only experience it if their industrialisation is accompanied by westernisation or modernisation along Western lines. If secularisation is specifically a Christian phenomenon they are certainly unlikely to undergo it since westernisation, if it occurs at all, is unlikely to mean Christianisation.

16 Religion as compensation: Stark and Bainbridge

Perhaps the most systematic recent attempt to provide a general theory of religion is that of Stark and Bainbridge (1980b, 1985, 1987).[1] Their approach is not easily classifiable in terms of intellectualist, emotionalist or sociological theories but along with meaning theories it shares many features with all of these approaches and attempts to synthesise the insights of many of them.

Stark and Bainbridge present what they consider to be a deductive theory of religion (1980b, 1987) in that it is derived deductively from a general theory of human nature and action constructed from a small number of basic axioms concerning the fundamental characteristics of individuals and small groups and a larger number of propositions, most of which are either derived from these axioms or from other propositions which are themselves derived from these axioms or from a combination of the two. The theory relies very heavily on exchange theory which is based on the principle that all, or nearly all, human interactions can be treated as a form of exchange. This basic and very general theory is then developed further to account for a wide range of specific forms of religion and in particular is applied to the understanding of the emergence and development of sects and cults. And as we saw in the previous chapter they also apply their ideas extensively to the understanding of the process of secularisation and what they claim is a process of desecularisation in contemporary Western Christian societies. Space does not permit a detailed presentation from first principles of their deductions here. We shall take up the account at the point at which religion enters the picture, referring back to prior propositions as necessary.

Religion, Stark and Bainbridge argue, is essentially an attempt to gratify desires or, as they put it, secure rewards. Rewards are defined as anything which human beings desire and are willing to incur some cost to obtain. Rewards include very specific and limited things as well as the most general things such as solutions to questions of ultimate meaning and even unreal or non-existent things, conditions or states. Costs are anything that people attempt to avoid. Thus it follows that a cost will be accepted in order to secure a reward if the reward is valued more highly than avoidance of the cost. Stark and Bainbridge see rewards and costs as complementary. If a reward is forgone it is equivalent to a cost while if a potential cost is avoided it is equivalent to a reward.

Stark and Bainbridge see religion as the attempt to secure desired rewards in the absence of alternative means. The rewards to which religious belief and behaviour are addressed are those of a very general kind, the pursuit of which involves supernatural assumptions. In order to obtain rewards human beings seek and develop what Stark and Bainbridge call explanations, namely statements about how and why rewards may be obtained and costs incurred. Since explanations tell people how to obtain rewards they are themselves desirable and, therefore, also rewards in themselves. Religion deals in supernatural explanations. By supernatural Stark and Bainbridge mean forces believed to be beyond or outside nature which are able to overrule natural physical forces.

Rewards, however, are not always obtainable, especially since they include things which may not or do not exist. In the absence of the actual reward, explanations may be accepted which posit attainment of the reward in the distant future or in some other non-verifiable context. Such explanations Stark and Bainbridge call 'compensators' in lieu of actual rewards. These compensators are treated as if they were themselves rewards but are, in fact, hopes for future rewards and intangible substitutes for them. There is a tendency, where rewards are strongly desired yet difficult to obtain, to accept compensators which are not readily susceptible to unambiguous verification. Rival explanations which are easier to verify tend to be found false and are rejected, leaving the field to those which are more difficult to verify and therefore to disprove.

Very general compensators, that is those that promise very general rewards of the kind mentioned above, can only be supported by explanations that make reference to the supernatural. That is to say that religion provides a set of beliefs about how very general rewards can be obtained as well as a set of compensators in the face of the impossibility of attaining such rewards here and now. An example used by Stark and Bainbridge is that of the desire for immortality. The uncertainty of attainment of this aim leads to compensators being invented, the validity of which cannot be determined empirically but which must be accepted on faith.

Compensators are not, however, necessarily religious in character. Religion is a system of compensators of a high level of generality based upon supernatural assumptions. Certain goals require explanations and compensators of a supernatural kind – they are simply that kind of desire or question. These are the questions of ultimate meaning and purpose in life and the world. In this respect Stark and Bainbridge are close to the meaning theorists discussed in Chapter fourteen. For this reason they dismiss the idea that their theory is essentially a deprivation theory. Deprivation may play an important role in stimulating religious endeavour but it is by no means the only or the most significant factor. Those who are least deprived still seek answers and solutions to fundamental existential questions; they still seek explanations and compensators of a very high level of generality. Some deprivations are shared by rich and poor alike such as the inevitability of death. And as Weber pointed out, religious commitment may be inspired not only by the hope of overcoming deprivation but may also be an expression and justification of privilege.

More specific desires which cannot be fulfilled and for which compensators are devised are, according to Stark and Bainbridge, magical in nature. The distinction between general and specific compensators allows them to distinguish between magic and religion. Magic does not concern itself with the meaning of the universe but with the manipulation of reality for specific ends. Being so concerned with specific goals it is vulnerable to empirical test in a way in which religious claims are not. It tends to flourish, therefore, in circumstances in which people lack effective and economical means for subjecting claims to empirical test. Magical beliefs are distinguished from scientific beliefs on the basis that their claims are held without regard for empirical evidence of their truth 'and which are found wanting if they are properly evaluated' (1987, p. 41). Magic offers only compensators, then, because it does not provide real rewards but promises of reward which are false. Magic is not based upon compensators which are supernatural in kind: only religion offers this. Stark and Bainbridge are able to identify, therefore, many contemporary forms of magic flourishing in western, rational, technological society which are often based upon scientific-sounding ideas but which are not supported by evidence. They include what Stark and Bainbridge call pseudosciences and pseudotherapies which provide compensators for a wide range of specific desires but do not make reference to the supernatural.

Stark and Bainbridge go on in *A Theory of Religion* to develop the core theory in various ways including derivations of beliefs in gods and spirits and the emergence of religious specialists and organisations. These are derived from a general theory of social structure and culture. We need not set out all of the details of this here but simply note that in the process of the development of social structure and culture, according to Stark and Bainbridge, specific cultural specialisations emerge and evolve into cultural systems, one of which is concerned with religion. Similarly, when societies reach a certain size and level of complexity, specific social organisations emerge including religious organisations.

Early in the development of religious conceptions the idea of gods emerges. Gods are supernatural beings who share with humans the attributes of having consciousness and desires. In seeking certain rewards human beings come to imagine beings such as this who are able to give them the rewards they desire. Since Stark and Bainbridge's theory is based upon exchange theory they naturally present the relationship that worshippers have with their gods in terms of an exchange relationship. They postulate that when humans cannot satisfy their desires themselves they will seek to satisfy them by entering into exchange relationships with other human beings. When other human beings are unable to satisfy them they will tend to invent the compensator that there are supernatural exchange partners who can satisfy these desires. Since humans seek rewards from the gods by exchanging with them it follows that gods must be like other exchange partners in having desires which humans can satisfy. Thus the gods make demands upon people in return for rewards either immediate or eventual. Since many rewards are not in any other way attainable, the gods tend to be seen as powerful in relation to humans who are seen to be dependent upon them.

However, Stark and Bainbridge point out, perceiving themselves to be following Malinowski, people will only enter into exchanges with gods if no cheaper or more efficient alternative for the satisfaction of their desires exists.

With the growth in size and complexity of society religious specialists tend to emerge. In order to understand how and why this is so Stark and Bainbridge utilise a further basic postulate of their system, namely that explanations as to how rewards can be obtained and of the value of compensators must be evaluated before they can be accepted. Explanations vary with respect to how easy or difficult it is to evaluate them and the costs involved in doing so. Very general explanations and compensators which offer very general rewards, and this includes religious explanations and compensators, are the most difficult to evaluate. It becomes impossible for any individual to evaluate all the explanations on offer. People come to rely upon those they trust to carry out such evaluation and will accept explanations evaluated by them. Some come to specialise in certain areas and religion is one area where such specialisation is particularly likely. This is because in most other areas of life explanations and compensators are much more subject to the possibility of empirical testing and assessment. The propositions of religion are very often not so susceptible. In other areas, then, specialisation cannot emerge until sound empirical knowledge has been established. For example, mining and metalworking are fields where specialisation is impossible until sound knowledge and technique have been developed. Religion as a specialisation is not constrained in this way. For this reason, Stark and Bainbridge argue, religion will be one of the first specialisms to emerge in human society.

Once such specialists emerge they will tend to combine in organisations which will seek a religious monopoly. This is because the authority of explanations will be greater to the extent that there are no competing explanations and disagreements about such things. Competition tends to undermine the value of explanations. Such a monopoly generally requires the dominant religious organisation to establish a close alliance with the state since it is the state in such societies that wields sufficient power to enforce a monopoly. At this point Stark and Bainbridge explore relationships between church and state. We shall not go into the details here.

Since Stark and Bainbridge base their approach on exchange theory they speak of religious specialists and organisations as exchanging rewards, explanations and compensators with others. Religious specialists, or priests, claim to mediate between human beings and the gods, communicating to people what it is the gods require of them in return for the rewards and compensators the gods offer. In this way priests and religious organisations come to have considerable power in society and influence over norms and standards of behaviour. Since the rewards of religion are often things which can only be achieved in the long term, even after death, the relationship between priests and religious organisations on the one hand, and worshippers on the other tends to be a permanent and enduring one. Consequently, religious organisations tend to be enduring and relatively permanent. The relationship that worshippers have with them tends to take the form of commitment, and usually life-long commitment, rather than periodic patronage for specific ends as they arise. This makes religious specialists and organisations especially influential, powerful and able to control and set standards for behaviour. They come to play a very central and important social role.

Stark and Bainbridge postulate that the more complex a society becomes the greater the scope of the explanations which make up its culture. This applies to its religious explanations also and it follows from this that gods come to have greater scope the more complex is the society and culture. They come to govern more and more aspects of life and to offer greater rewards and compensators. An aspect of the development of complexity is systematisation. Higher order explanations are developed which subsume and account for lower order explanations. Explanations of more general scope emerge. This, again, applies to religious explanations with the consequence that the gods come to govern wider aspects of reality and life. The result is that increasingly fewer gods of increasingly greater scope are worshipped.

Magic, in contrast to religion, does not tend to throw up specialist organisations. This is because magic offers very specific rather than very general compensators like religion. Specific compensators are highly susceptible to disconfirmation and for this reason long-term exchange relationships between magical specialists and clients cannot develop. If long-term, relatively stable exchange relationships cannot develop then an organisation will not develop. Durkheim was right to characterise religion as having no church. Magic involves individual practitioners each with a fluctuating clientele with whom they exchange for very limited and specific purposes and this differentiates magic from religion.

While early on magic and religion tend to be closely associated, as society becomes more complex they tend to become increasingly differentiated in terms of specialists and organisation. Religion does usually offer specific rewards to some extent but to offer too much of this kind risks religion being discredited through disconfirmation of its specific explanations and compensators. Over time religious specialists will tend to reduce the amount of magic they supply leaving others to specialise in the provision of this type of compensator. The roles of magician and priest, then, tend to become increasingly differentiated as does religious and magical culture generally.

Nevertheless, a variety of relationships between magical and religious culture is possible and in many societies and religious traditions there is a degree of overlap between them. Where religion continues to provide supernaturally-based specific compensators it will tend to oppose supernaturally-based magic outside its own system. On the other hand, if religion has more or less relinquished the provision of supernaturally-based specific compensators it will tolerate their provision by specialists outside its own organisation. The first situation is characteristic of Catholicism and the second of orthodox Buddhism and Taoism.

These latter instances are extreme developments, Stark and Bainbridge argue, in which God has become infinite in scope and one in number and therefore loses all interest in this world. An impersonal principle such as the Tao cannot provide rewards and compensators and cannot act as an exchange partner. People, however, require an active God who can provide compensators for intense desires. Consequently, if a religion evolves to the point where it has only one god of infinite scope and is unable to provide supernatural specific compensators it will have little to offer most people. It can no longer render evil meaningful in human terms. Evil becomes simply a natural feature of the world which people must bear the burden of attempting to vanquish on their own. The depersonalisation and desacralisation of evil in contemporary liberal Protestantism are, significantly, accompanied by a dramatic fall in support.

The greater part of Stark and Bainbridge's *A Theory of Religion* is devoted to a discussion of the way in which religious organisations and traditions tend to divide, that is, to religious schism and to the way in which new rival and alternative religions rise up in opposition to established ones. In short, it is devoted to the study of sectarian and cult movements. This is much more familiar territory for Stark and Bainbridge since much of their previous work has been devoted to these topics. This work and its formal systematisation in *A Theory of Religion* will be examined in the next chapter, however, along with other relevant contributions to the study of sects and cults. First, their general theoretical approach will be discussed and assessed.

Stark and Bainbridge's attempt to set out an extensive, systematic, deductive theory of religion which explains all of its fundamental characteristics and general development is sufficiently ambitious (there are a total of 344 empirical propositions and 104 definitions of concepts) that it is bound, as they themselves fully acknowledge, to contain flaws, inconsistencies and gaps. There are, indeed, many linkages which appear problematic. Examples include the proposition that the most general compensators can be supported only by supernatural explanations of which Stark and Bainbridge say it is self-evidently true. They go on to say that since to seek the purpose of life is to presuppose that it has a purpose and since this implies the existence of intentions and motives and therefore a consciousness, the necessary conclusion is that some conscious agent is at work to which intentions, motives and purposes will be attribued. This is by no means self-evident. To say that people seek a purpose in life or the purpose of life may imply no more than that they seek meaning in it and in doing so they may well arrive at conclusions which do not suppose the existence of some supernatural realm, divinity or principle. Some religious traditions, notably Buddhism, do not place the supernatural at the centre of their systems. It is debatable whether conceptions of the supernatural are part of orthodox Buddhism at all.

This raises the question of Stark and Bainbridge's equation of religion with belief in the supernatural. As we saw in Chapter one there are problems with such a definition. Stark and Bainbridge say very little in justification of their use of such a definition and simply brush aside the issues claiming that the alleged problems they pose, especially in relation to Buddhism have been adequately dealt with by Spiro (1966). But this will not do as a reading of the relevant section of Chapter one above shows. In any case Spiro, as we saw there, is careful not to define religion in terms of the supernatural preferring the term superhuman which is, however, not without its own difficulties.

A second example of breakdown in deductive logic concerns the proposition that human beings will tend to conceptualise supernatural sources of rewards and costs as gods (1987, p. 82). This may or may not be true but is not derived in any clear way by Stark and Bainbridge from their axioms and other propositions but merely asserted. Seeking great and difficult rewards human beings, Stark and Bainbridge assert, simply imagine supernatural exchange partners who can deliver these rewards with no account of why this should be so. The underlying assumption seems to lie in the commitment to the use of the approach of exchange theory. Since all human interaction is some form of exchange, rewards can only be obtained through entering into exchange relationships. If one can enter into exchange relationships to obtain rewards of a general type with certain beings then these beings must have a will and purposes like those of human beings and must, therefore, have the characteristics of gods. None of this is, however, clearly stated. And in any case, while such reasoning might explain why belief in supernatural sources of reward will tend to take the form of gods, it still fails to account for why people come to think that they can get the rewards they desire from supernatural sources in the first place.

There are many other examples of gaps in the chain of reasoning in Stark and Bainbridge's account. Those mentioned above might have been chosen at random. They do concern, however, rather central aspects of the theory and have been focused upon for that reason.

Another weakness of the approach lies in its reliance on exchange theory. This is not the place to undertake a critique of this theoretical approach. We might simply question here whether human interaction can successfully and completely be described solely in terms of the language of exchange and more specifically if it is appropriate for the explanation and understanding of religious beliefs and behaviour.

Perhaps one of the chief difficulties, however, with Stark and Bainbridge's approach, as Wallis and Bruce have pointed out (Wallis and Bruce, 1984; Wallis, 1984, pp. 62–3), concerns the central notion of a compensator. It is not at all clear why many religious beliefs should constitute compensation of some kind. In what sense is belief in immortality a compensation for anything? Such a belief may give comfort in the face of the threat of meaninglessness that death seems to hold for us but this is not the same thing as a compensation for the fact of mortality but a denial of it or of the significance it might otherwise have. Use of the notion of compensation betrays on the part of Stark and Bainbridge, according to Wallis, an assumption that real rewards can only be material and immediate. Non-material and long-term goals become simply compensators for what cannot be attained now rather than things desired for their own sake. This is to imply that what religion offers is essentially unsatisfactory and only acceptable in the face of an inability to obtain what is really desired. The approach illegitimately introduces a substantive atheism into the analysis of religion rather than methodological atheism.

This claim, however, does something of a disservice to Stark and Bainbridge who do not quite say what Wallis accuses them of. What they do say is that such things as the belief that one can achieve immortality stem from desires which cannot be satisfied in the way everyday and mundane desires can. In this sense immortality is a kind of reward. A reward for Stark and Bainbridge is simply anything which is desired and for which something will be sacrificed to obtain. Stark and Bainbridge define a compensator as the postulate of a reward according to explanations which are not readily susceptible to unambiguous evaluation. A compensator is resorted to when a desire cannot be fulfilled. 'Compensator' is, perhaps, an unfortunate choice of term since it tends to be interpreted in the sense of a substitute for what people really want but cannot get. It carries the connotation of consolation prize. Stark and Bainbridge do not, however, use the term in quite this way. They are careful to point out that a compensator is a promise of the reward and not a substitute of something else for it. As with a promise one cannot be sure that it will be kept. Evaluation of it is necessary and not always easy. Religion promises, among other things, very general rewards, one might say of the transcendental kind and these are, of course, extremely difficult to evaluate with any certainty precisely because they are not of a material or mundane nature.

The real problem is to see why it is that compensators will be accepted; why people will accept explanations, as Stark and Bainbridge put it, which promise that the reward can be obtained but which cannot be unambiguously evaluated, if evaluated at all. Contrast Stark and Bainbridge's approach with that of a meaning theorist such as Weber, with whom, in claiming that their approach is not a deprivation theory, Stark and Bainbridge consider that they agree. In the face of gross injustice, of suffering, of inevitable death, life threatens to appear without meaning. Religion places these aspects of life in a context where they make sense. The force of a belief in immortality, remaining with this particular example, is that it makes physical death appear to be part of a world which is not senseless. Another belief which may have such force is that of reincarnation or the extinction of the self in a state of *nirvana*. Of course, the idea of immortality in a heaven or paradise or of *nirvana* may well be thought by believers to be a highly desirable thing but the real force of such ideas may be their capacity to make sense of an otherwise apparently meaningless reality. The language of reward and cost simply does not do justice to these conceptions. For this reason, it is difficult to see why such ideas will be accepted as promises of reward, as compensations. It is difficult to see why people should simply imagine the existence of powerful exchange partners who can, if the terms are right, satisfy all desires. It is easier to see why this belief might come about as a means of making sense of things rather than simply as a means of concretely securing something, although it may well be seen this way at the same time. It is because its primary role is to make sense of things and not to secure rewards that it does not matter too much, if at all, if it is difficult to evaluate unambiguously in the way that accounts of how to achieve mundane goals can be evaluated.

It is in relation to this question of evaluation of religious promises that Wallis and Bruce offer a rather more telling criticism of Stark and Bainbridge. They are guilty of what Wallis and Bruce call explanatory dualism. In distinguishing the rewards that religion offers as opposed to those of mundane techniques or science, Stark and Bainbridge say they are not readily susceptible to unambiguous evaluation. This basis for making such a distinction Wallis and Bruce find problematic. It does not accord with contemporary philosophy of science which holds that conclusive verification of scientific claims is not possible. Even unequivocal falsification of scientific propositions is questionable according to Wallis and Bruce's understanding of philosophy of science. In any case, many scientific propositions whether or not they are verifiable or falisifiable in principle are not so in practice. This does not make them religious propositions. Conversely, there are many religious claims that may be in principle as verifiable as scientific ones.

The difference between science and religion lies not in the ease or difficulty of the empirical verifiability of their respective propositions, according to Stark and Bainbridge, but in the fact that science, at least as a social practice and at the institutional level, encourages empirical testing and disconfirmation while religion seeks to protect its claims from disconfirmation. One might add the point here that many religious claims are, in any case, not the kind of claims for which empirical verification is appropriate. In so far as religious statements are expressions of the meaning of things the question of empirical verification is irrelevant.

Stark and Bainbridge, then, treat scientific propositions as if they were unproblematic with regard to verification and the reasons people have for believing them are similarly unproblematic. They are believed because they are true. Religious beliefs are those which are problematic in this respect and if people espouse them there must be some special reason for this which it is the task of the sociologist to uncover. Because the beliefs do not accord with the sociological observer's view of the world there must be some pathology behind them or some sociological or psychological factor which has impaired the normal propensity to accept only what is clearly true. But it is simply not relevant to an understanding of the beliefs of, say, the Trobriand Islanders or the Azande that they do not accord with those of a Western observer. To place the fact of our own disagreement with them at the centre of our analysis as Stark and Bainbridge do is likely to lead to misunderstanding and distorted accounts of religious systems.

Also, Stark and Bainbridge's discussion of magic and how it differs from religion is very unsatisfactory. Magic deals in specific rather than general compensators. Clearly magic does seek to secure concrete rewards (although it too may be bound up with the attempt to see the world in terms which are meaningful and we should not overlook this aspect of it). However, precisely to the extent that it does seek concrete rewards, the notion of compensation is misapplied to it. Unlike religion, magic does not really offer the reward eventually at some deferred time but offers it now. Those who practise magic do so because they believe that it delivers concrete benefits immediately. They are not in their own minds accepting compensators in the face of a lack of techniques for securing what is desired but using special techniques to actually secure those desires.

The reason that Stark and Bainbridge believe that magic deals in compensators is because they think of magic as false technique. Magic, they say, refers to specific compensators that promise to provide desired rewards without regard for evidence concerning the designated means. Here the criticism that Wallis and Bruce make of their explanatory dualism is equally if not even more pertinent. From the point of view of the practitioners of magic, as was made very clear in Chapter three, there is very good evidence that it actually secures and not simply promises rewards. One might not share their view about the evidence but that is hardly relevant. The relevant question is not why do the practitioners of magic use it in the face of our awareness of an absence of any evidence that it works but on what basis do they believe that there *is* evidence that it works and what processes underlie their conviction that the magical beliefs are acceptable. Evans-Pritchard's classic study of the Azande is addressed very much to this question. Even then, all this, of course, assumes that magic is best conceived as consisting of empirical techniques which are not based upon evidence. If one accepts a position like that of the symbolists discussed in Chapter three, then Stark and Bainbridge's understanding of magic is even more off the mark. Certainly, their account fails to do justice, to even mention, the crucial symbolic dimension of magical behaviour. They seem unaware of the relevant anthropological literature and to have a shaky picture of tribal religion in general.

Finally, on a number of points of evidence Stark and Bainbridge's generalisations seem to be wanting. One example relates again to tribal religion with respect to which they claim that in the more simple cultures the gods are minute and very numerous such that nearly every rock, tree, stream or plant is thought to be inhabited by a supernatural being of limited and local power. This completely ignores or is entirely ignorant of the fact that in some of the most simple societies, the Congo pygmies for example, religious ideas are little developed at all and they are far from the animists that Stark and Bainbridge's proposition would lead us to expect them to be.

At the other end of the scale, their claim that eastern religions such as Buddhism and Taoism which have developed conceptions of an impersonal principle of divinity which is incapable of entering into exchanges with humans who therefore come to have no interest in the religion seems very wide of the mark, especially in the case of Buddhism. Certainly, Buddhism tends to leave magic to magicians, as Stark and Bainbridge rightly point out. Perhaps one could say the same of philosophical Taoism, although the magicians concerned here are very much Taoist magicians. The prediction that would follow from Stark and Bainbridge's claim, however, is that Buddhism should by now be one of the world's weakest and most rapidly declining religions which it clearly is not.

There is much more that could be said about Stark and Bainbridge's rich and extensive contribution to the general theory of religion but it is to their work on sectarian and cult movements that we must now turn in the next chapter.

17 Sects, cults and movements

Religious sects have attracted an enormous amount of interest from sociologists as have the New Religious Movements (NRMs) which have mushroomed in the industrial societies of the West in recent decades. This is not simply because they have been important aspects of religious history in all the great religious traditions of the world or because many of the important religious traditions themselves began as sectarian breakaways or schisms from established traditions but also because sects have a fascination in their own right. Sects are in many ways religious experiments which offer the sociologist an opportunity to study religiosity in its purest forms uncontaminated by the complexities of motive, organisation and doctrine that the long-established Churches and denominations entail. Sects also offer the opportunity to study what are often radically new ideas and beliefs, styles of organisation and life and the background against which and from which they emerge. Since a large proportion of the membership of some of them may be very recent converts they offer an opportunity to study the process of conversion to unorthodox and 'deviant' beliefs and practices and how such 'deviance' is maintained against the pressures of the wider society. They offer, then, insights into religious change and the emergence of new religious traditions. They are, in short, something of a laboratory for the sociologist of religion.

Sectarian movements and schisms have often been bound up with social divisions and conflicts. This is particularly true of the older sectarian movements within Christianity. To this extent the study of sects is also the study of social divisions. It also involves the study of attempts to build ideal societies, free of the imperfections of the dominant surrounding social milieu, which attempt to embody religious ideals, values and principles in some form of concrete social organisation. Sects have often attempted to order human social relationships in new ways and to socialise new generations in their values and patterns of life.

In this chapter we shall focus only on certain aspects of the sociological study of sectarianism and of cult movements, especially the general processes by which sectarian schism occurs and cult movements emerge which have been extensively discussed by Stark and Bainbridge (1985, 1987) as indicated in the previous chapter. Many other aspects of sectarianism, to the understanding of which they and many others have made significant contributions, for example, the process of conversion to sects and cults and the patterns of their internal evolution and development, cannot be examined here. Our focus will be on the most general considerations. Before looking at contemporary work in this area, however, it is necessary to present some background in the history of the sociology of sects since this has greatly influenced the course of subsequent debates.

A pioneer in the sociological study of sectarianism was Ernst Troeltsch who followed his friend Max Weber to a considerable extent in his characterisation of the nature of the sect in relation to the Church. Weber characterised the Church as an institution which administers religious sacraments and as a result has a form of power which enables it to maintain order. The threat of withdrawing sacramental benefits gives it this 'hierocratic power'. The Church is thus like a political association. In theory membership is compulsory and all embracing. At least, no special act of joining or special qualification is required. Members are born into the Church.

The sect, on the other hand, is a voluntary association. It makes no claim to regulate the religious lives and behaviour of those who do not wish to be considered members. Membership is in fact restricted to those who are qualified to be members. This requires some test of religious or ethical eligibility such as proof of religious commitment. Normally members are not born into the sect. The children of existing members usually have to make a positive commitment when old enough to do so.

Weber thought that sects usually tend to develop into Churches. This is related to his notion of the routinisation of charisma. In the sect, charisma is attached to a religious leader whereas in the Church it is attached to an office or offices. The charisma attached to the individual becomes attached to an office as leaders succeed one another over time. As new generations of believers replace older generations a new basis of order thus comes to prevail; charismatic authority is replaced by traditional or legal–rational authority.

Troeltsch accepted this general analysis of Weber but developed and amplified it (1931). Starting from the assumption that different religious outlooks will be realised in different types of social organisation, and working largely in the context of Christianity, he distinguished two broad tendencies in early Christianity which led to two rather different types of religious organisation. One emphasised the free equal community of believers idealistically attempting to realise Christian values such as brotherly love without regard to the rest of society. This attitude tended to play down organisation and hierarchy. The other emphasised the independent organised community which attempted to make use of the surrounding institutions for its own ends. The former was a radical tendency and the latter a more conservative one. While the conservative tendency associated with the Church came to dominate, the radical tendency was far from eradicated within Christianity showing itself in various ways, for example, in monasticism.

These two tendencies underlie Troeltsch's understanding of the distinctions between Church and sect. The former, he said, is an overwhelmingly conservative institution which largely accepts the secular order and seeks to dominate the masses. It is, therefore, in principle at least, universal; 'it desires to cover the whole life of humanity' (1931, p. 331). It utilises the state and the ruling classes and becomes an integral part of the social order. In doing so the Church in many respects becomes dependent on the ruling classes.

The sect is a small grouping which aspires to an inward perfection and aims at direct personal fellowship between its members. It renounces any idea of dominating the world and is either indifferent or hostile to the world, the state and society which is either avoided or will be replaced by an alternative society. Sects spring from the lower classes or those who feel oppressed by the state and by society.

Troeltsch considered that despite the fact that established Churches have branded the sects as departures from true Christianity, they do in fact embrace the early ideals of the Gospels and of primitive Christianity in many ways. This makes them of great significance in the study of the sociological consequences of Christian thought, with which Troeltsch's major study was largely concerned. Their importance is evident in the role they played in the disintegration of the medieval social order.

The main stream of development though has been along the lines of the Church type of organisation which represents the longing for a universal, all-embracing ideal involving leadership of the masses and domination of society and culture. It naturally claimed a monopoly of sacramental grace. To achieve this it had to seek accommodation with the secular order.

Whenever the Church managed to establish its claim as the sole dispenser of sacramental grace to a very great extent, the sectarian impulse in Christianity would come to the fore. The sects repudiated the claims of the Church to control divine grace through the sacraments and emphasised instead the religious value of daily life and personal relationships. The sects attacked the role of the Church in aiding the state and in furthering the interests, as they saw it, of the dominant classes. They tended to attack what they saw as injustice. Thus, Troeltsch saw the sects as largely protest movements.

Out of this clash between Church and sect a third type of religious orientation tended to develop, according to Troeltsch, which he called mysticism. Here doctrine and worship give way to purely personal and inward experience and conviction. He links this mysticism to the growth of individualism in the medieval towns. It is characterised by a free fellowship of believers with little organisation or structure. Emphasis is placed on ideas and not on worship. New ideas and modern views of the world are incorporated into the belief system. The following tends to be middle class and prosperous.

There are obvious limitations and difficulties with Troeltsch's scheme based exclusively as it is on the history of sectarianism within the Christian tradition and during only a certain part of its history. Historically, Christian sectarianism may in some periods have been bound up with and a response to class divisions and tensions. The equation of sect with lower class and Church with middle or dominant class cannot be upheld today or for the religious movements of more recent times. Nor are contemporary or recent sectarian movements breakaways from established Churches. Troeltsch's categories, furthermore, do not exhaust the variety of religious organisations that we observe in contemporary society. The denomination, for example, is clearly not at all like Troeltsch's mysticism but stands somewhere between Church and sect while in certain respects it is unlike either.

The denomination as a further category for classifying types of religious organisation was added to the typology by Niebuhr (1957)[1] who saw the departure from traditional and socially dominant religious doctrines and forms of organisation as a product of changing social and economic circumstances. Sectarianism was for him a product of increased division and differentiation in society. Different social classes or occupational groups adapted religious forms to suit them. In other words, we have a pluralistic situation.

Niebuhr thought, however, that the sect was not capable of surviving for long as an adaptation to a new situation. It would either reconcile itself to prevailing circumstances, at least to some extent, or it would suffer dissolution. Sects, also, tend only to exist for one generation. The second generation become members for very different reasons and out of very different motives to the first. They are born into the sect even if they do have to formally express a desire and intention to affiliate in adult life. The sect, Niebuhr said, becomes in this way a denomination or even a Church.

One factor which aids this process is that sectarian asceticism often makes sect members better off financially and this tends to pull them in the direction of worldly concerns. The religious forms of the poor eventually become middle-class organisations due to the social mobility of their members.

The fundamental characteristic of the denomination in Niebuhr's formulation is that it is not universalistic in the sense of seeking to incorporate the whole population. It is essentially a middle-class and respectable form of religious organisation and style of worship which differs from the sect in that it has a separate ministry. It emphasises individualism as a fundamental value and associated with this is the goal of personal salvation. Its lack of universalism is associated, in contrast to the sect, with tolerance and coexistence with other religious groups rather than antagonism.

Niebuhr's classification of religious organisations has since been much adapted and added to. The concept of the cult corresponding to Troeltsch's mysticism has been added as well as others. In some reformulations of his typology six categories are distinguished and in others seven. The whole debate has become somewhat tedious and sterile. What is more interesting is the discussion of the processes of change in sects and religious organisations as they evolve and develop.

Niebuhr's claim, for example, that the process by which the sect becomes a denomination is primarily one in which the majority of the membership changes its class position, has been challenged. Liston Pope (1942) in a study of a textile area of North Carolina found that denominationalisation had less to do with change in socio-economic status of the membership but simply with success in recruitment and growth in size. As a sect grows it acquires a sense that it can exert more influence in the community and the attractions of this often lead it away from its more sectarian attitudes towards more compromising and accommodating views. It may well attract more well-to-do adherents as a result and so change its social composition this way rather than its original membership achieving affluence and social position. There was little evidence for this in Pope's case study. If anything, those who became more prosperous were likely to leave the sect and to adopt a more socially acceptable religious affiliation. The process of denominationalisation, he argued, is a complex one and he proposed a whole series of criteria by which we may chart the development from sect to denomination.

Wilson (1990) has pointed out that Niebuhr overlooked the fact of the uniqueness of the American context in which there was no established Church, no fixed status hierarchy and where upward mobility of the individual and of religious organisations was very common. Also, Wilson argues, the distinction between first- and second-generation members is somewhat misleading. Sects which are growing make new converts all the time who tend to be more rigorous in maintaining the purity of the sect's ideology and practice than the longer-term or second-generation members and who may act as a force working against denominationalising tendencies.

Pope's ideas have been developed further by Milton Yinger who has in fact proposed several different typologies of religious organisation (1957, 1970)[2]. What is more interesting than these typologies, however, is his discussion of the differing relationship of sect and Church to the world (1946). He argues that both risk losing any possibility of influencing the world and the wider society and thereby undermine their religious goals – the Church by making too great an accommodation to the secular world such that its religious message is lost and the sect by its exclusiveness and radicalism. Whereas the Church may risk debasing its message to the point where it makes no difference to the conduct of life, the sect may risk having too few adherents to have any impact.

The Church must therefore set out to express its religious principles in such a way that those with power in society can be brought under its influence. Yinger finds this to be the case with both Calvinism and Catholicism, for example. The sect, on the other hand, must take on a less sectarian and more Church-like character in order to win a substantial following. It has to become what Yinger call an established sect.

Another major contribution to this debate is that of Bryan Wilson (1970). He characterises the sect as a voluntary association with a strong sense of self-identity. Membership depends upon merit or some kind of qualification such as knowledge or acceptance of doctrine or of conversion evidenced by some form of religious experience. The sect is exclusive and regards itself as an elite in sole possession of the truth. It is separated from the wider society and at odds with prevailing orthodoxy. Certain standards of behaviour are required of members and expulsion may follow any serious or persistent failure to live by them. Regular procedures for expulsion will exist. The commitment of the sectarian is always more total than that of the non-sectarian and he or she is always more distinctly characterised in terms of religious affiliation. The sect has no distinct or professional ministry.

The denomination, while also a voluntary association, has only formal procedures for admission and rarely any procedures for expulsion. It has a less distinct sense of self-awareness and is less exclusive. It admits to being one valid religious movement among others and makes no claim to exclusive possession of the truth. It is not separated from the wider society and its teachings and practices are less distinctive. It has a professional and distinct ministry and is not unduly antagonistic to prevailing orthodoxy.

The key dimensions of Wilson's characterisation centre on the separateness and distinctiveness of the sect and its claim to possess the truth. These have been utilised by Robertson (1970) to derive a fourfold classification of religious organisations. Robertson's classification uses, then, two sets of distinctions to generate four categories: inclusive membership, that is, membership open to anyone, as opposed to exclusive membership where some test or qualification of eligibility is required; and second what Robertson calls the self-conceived basis of legitimacy which takes the form of either a claim to sole possession of truth or where other groups are acknowledged also to possess the essential truth. The four types of organisation may be represented as follows.

| | | Self-conceived basis of legitimacy | |
		Pluralistically legitimate	Uniquely legitimate
Membership principle	Exclusive	Institutionalized sect	Sect
	Inclusive	Denomination	Church

Figure 2 Typology of religious organisations
Source: Robertson, 1970, p. 123

This classification does not imply any linear relationship between the categories or that there is a linear developmental process from one to another (an assumption which has weakened many classificatory schemes). In some ways sects are more like Churches than they are like denominations and in others they are more like denominations. Sects may not always develop into denominations or Churches but may take the form of the established sect. In fact there may be complex trajectories through Robertson's conceptual space.

In fact, the sect-to-denomination pattern may, as Martin has pointed out, be untypical. On the whole, Martin (1962) argues, sects generally do succeed in maintaining their sectarian character while denominations have for the most part never been sects but have possessed their denominational characteristics from the beginning. Typical examples would be the Methodists, Congregationalists and

General Baptists. Perhaps Martin goes slightly too far in claiming the sect-to-denomination pattern is atypical. It might be more fruitful to regard it as one among a number of patterns. Also, the Church-to-denomination pattern is perhaps one which occurs only in a situation of relative religious tolerance and pluralism. Where this is lacking, alternative or rival creeds and organisations are likely to be more sectarian in character.

RELIGIOUS PLURALISM AND SCHISMATIC MOVEMENTS

Previous theories of sectarianism have tended to focus on the internal dynamics of development in religious organisations and have neglected the external environment. Werner Stark (1967) attempted to remedy this to some extent in setting the process of sect emergence in the context of the relationship between Church and state. The essential problem he addresses is why some societies show much greater tendency to sect proliferation than others. Sectarianism, according to Stark, tends to flourish whenever the relationship between Church and state is such that the Church makes extensive compromises with the worldly values of the state. This occurs most often when the boundaries of the jurisdiction of the Church coincide with those of the state, or in other words when the Church is a national Church, an 'established' Church as Stark calls it.

When the Church is wider than any one nation state in its jurisdiction, when it is what Stark calls a 'universal Church', compromise with and accommodation to secular authorities are less likely than in the case of the national Church since the universal Church is not dependent on any one secular authority. Compromise leads to disaffection and this tends to produce a proliferation of sects. In the case of the universal Church, if some degree of compromise with secular authorities is necessary sectarian impulses can more easily be channelled internally into monasticism and various religious orders or groups.

Stark considers that since the Reformation there has only been one genuinely universal Church – the Roman Catholic Church. There has been a much weaker tendency to sectarianism in Catholic countries than in others. Conversely, sectarianism has been most prevalent in Russia and in England where there were firmly established Churches closely allied to the state.

Stark's thesis has been criticised by Scharf (1970) on the grounds that in many Catholic countries the Church has been just as established as the Church was in Tsarist Russia or in England. The Anglican Church, furthermore, was no more established than were the Lutheran Churches in a number of northern European countries during the sixteenth and seventeenth centuries yet sectarianism was not nearly so prevalent in the latter as in the former.

A point one might add is that the repression of rival religious creeds and organisations was much more intense in Catholic countries while in non-Catholic countries a much greater degree of religious freedom prevailed. Also, the tendency of the Catholic Church to accommodate different strands and styles of religiosity within itself is perhaps as much a cause of its survival as a universal Church as it is a consequence of its universality. If there is anything in Stark's thesis it may be that the flexibility of the Catholic Church did result from its relative independence of any particular political regime which allowed it to accommodate a variety of different movements, such as Jansenism, Quietism, or the Jesuits. Finally, the prevalence of sectarianism may have far more to do with social change than with the relationship between Church and state. Catholic countries did not undergo the social, political and economic changes that were associated with the rise of sectarianism in northern Europe.

Some of the above observations cited in criticism of Werner Stark have been made by Stark and Bainbridge (1987) not specifically in criticism of Werner Stark's thesis but in the course of their systematic discussion of the processes of religious schism and sect emergence which is derived from their general theory of religion discussed in the previous chapter. The discussion of their contribution here will of necessity have to be a somewhat simplified one which skirts some of the complexities of their arguments in presenting, hopefully, its essentials.

Stark and Bainbridge deviate from most writers on the subject of sectarianism in the way they define the concept of sect. They are critical of most previous typologies of religious organisations on the grounds that they have generally tended to use a wide range of criteria of which few are essential features of the phenomena in question but which are correlates not found in every instance. The result is confusion, a multiplicity of rival definitions and typologies and the inhibition of sound theorising. Stark and Bainbridge advocate defining concepts in terms of relatively few essential criteria which all instances share. In the case of sects they use, following Johnson (1963), the criteria of deviance and break-away from an established religious organisation. Cults in contrast, while also deviant, are entirely new movements which are not schisms from established religious organisations (Stark and Bainbridge, 1979; 1985; 1987). Both stand in a relationship of tension with the surrounding socio-cultural environment.

The tendency towards sectarian schism is derived by Stark and Bainbridge from the fact that the membership of any religious organisation is bound to be internally differentiated. Especially important in this respect are divisions between the better and worse off and between the more and less powerful both in terms of the rewards they receive within the wider society and within the religious organisation and the positions they hold in such organisations. Thus there is always potential for conflict within organisations, including religious organisations. Sect movements stem from such conflict and occur when certain conditions favour it. Broadly speaking, schismatic sect movements will tend to occur when the relatively deprived members perceive that the potential gains from breaking away outweigh the potential costs. The greater the degree of stratification within religious organisations, the more likely this is to be the case. Sectarianism, therefore, tends to be prominent only in the more stratified societies.

The relatively deprived members of religious groups will tend to place greater emphasis on compensators since they cannot secure as many rewards as the relatively privileged. The latter, in contrast, will tend to play down the provision of compensators by the religious organisation. The relatively deprived members will also tend to be less inclined to conform with general social norms and will tend to seek to promote a greater degree of tension between the religious group and the wider society. The opposite is the case, of course, with the relatively privileged members. A degree of antagonism is the result, leading to an avoidance of relationships between those at either end of the spectrum and rather different patterns of behaviour between them – which Stark and Bainbridge term antagonism, separation and difference. One group of members will find it to their advantage to accommodate to the surrounding social environment while the other will wish to move the group into a greater degree of tension with it.

There are four possible outcomes of the struggle according to Stark and Bainbridge. First, forces will balance one another and the group will maintain unity and cohesion at an equilibrium level of tension with the society. Second, the group may split into two, each section moving in opposite directions, one churchward and one sectward. Third, the relatively powerful may prevail and the group will move churchward – a very common pattern. And lastly, a relatively dissatisfied majority may be successful in moving the group sectward, a relatively rare occurrence requiring rather special circumstances.

Since the third and fourth alternatives are more concerned with sect evolution and development we shall not concern ourselves with them here. Clearly, the chuchward tendency is very reminiscent of the process of denominationalisation emphasised by Troeltsch and Niebuhr. Stark and Bainbridge recognise this and, in fact, claim that many of the findings of work in this and other areas of the study of sects fit well into their theoretical framework which, however, has the advantage of integrating what were a large number of previously 'orphan' propositions into a coherent system.

Remaining with the fundamental process of schism, the fact that tensions exist within religious organisations gives those who are able to lead breakaway movements the opportunity of doing so if the circumstances are right. Those who lead such breakaways are usually those who are likely, as leaders of a smaller organisations, to achieve positions of power and authority more rewarding than those they enjoyed in the parent organisation. As Stark and Bainbridge put it, it may be better to be a bishop of a sect than an assistant pastor of a rural congregation of a large, reputable organisation.

The form of the schismatic movement is likely to be such as to preserve as far as possible the investments in terms of compensators that have previously been made in the parent organisation. Too great a breakaway from the fundamental teachings of the group is likely to threaten those investments. The relatively deprived who tend to be those who break away are particularly unwilling to jeopardise investments. For this reason the sect generally sees itself as preserving the original teachings and principles of the tradition which they see the parent body as having watered down or abandoned.

Whether or not the costs of breaking away outweigh the benefits is determined by many factors, not least the surrounding climate. Where it is tolerant of deviant religious organisations the costs will be less than where it is repressive towards them. In some societies deviant groups have been heavily persecuted. In such circumstances it is not likely that sectarian breakaway movements will emerge very frequently as was the case with Catholic societies during the Middle Ages – the point made above in criticism of Werner Stark.

Similarly, rapid social change may stimulate sectarian schism if it worsens conditions for some members of religious organisations. They may have more to gain by leaving than they had before. Again, the relative stability of Catholic societies compared to Protestant ones was a factor mentioned above in criticism of Werner Stark's thesis concerning the absence of sectarianism in the Catholic countries.

Finally on the question of schism, if the relatively privileged section of a religious organisation finds the organisation to be in a greater state of tension with the surrounding society than they would wish, and feel stigmatised by this, but not strong enough to move the organisation churchward and with the possible consequence that opportunities for rewards through interaction with the surrounding society are inhibited, they may seek to breakaway. Normally they would tend to defect as individuals and join more reputable religious organisations but there may be circumstances which prevent this. One is where their religious affiliation is linked to their identity as an ethnic or racial group. They may not be able to join other more reputable groups because of this. The outcome is likely to be the church movement.

For the most part Stark and Bainbridge's analysis of sectarianism ties in well with other work such as that discussed at the beginning of this chapter. But there are a number of criticisms that might be made of it. One concerns the very definition of the concept of sect itself which might be seen as a rather retrograde step in relation to Robertson's. Of course, this might be considered to be a largely terminological matter and not particularly serious albeit tending to generate confusion. The whole question of terminology and definition of concepts in this area is, however, so confused in any case that Stark and Bainbridge's somewhat idiosyncratic use of the term 'sect' hardly matters. Since they only follow the suggestion of Johnson made some time ago, they are not adding anything new to what is already a confused situation. As long as we remember that Stark and Bainbridge are talking about schismatic movements when they talk about sects rather than the whole range of phenomena that others include under this term, we shall not run into too much difficulty. Whether the conceptual distinction between sects and cults that Stark and Bainbridge make is a fruitful one, and this boils down to the question of whether schismatic and novel movements are best explained differently or in a similar way is a more substantive matter which we shall take up later in this chapter. Other points that might be made about their approach and the relevance of other work to it are best left until after an examination of their account of cult emergence, given that they do treat many types of religious group that others call sects separately under the concept of cult.

The process of sect development, we have seen, is one of schism in the face of social division and stratification for Stark and Bainbridge. The process of emergence of novel religious beliefs and organisations, that is, of cults, is quite different, according to their analysis. They set out three mutually compatible models of the process of cult emergence, the psychopathology, entrepreneur and subculture–evolution models.

The psychopathology model holds that mentally ill persons invent novel compensators and accept them as rewards. Mental illness frees individuals from conventional understandings and can allow considerable creativity. If this seems a bold and somewhat implausible claim it is important to note, however, Stark and Bainbridge's definition of mental illness, namely 'the imputed condition of any human mind that repeatedly fails to conform to the propositions of the prevailing theory of human action' (1987, p. 159). Being an imputed condition it is an explanation of conduct which does not conform to what is normally expected in the society – an explanation which guides interaction with such persons in ways which do not presuppose that their behaviour will be like that of most people. Since this is the case they are relatively free to devise patterns of action and novel ideas.

On the other hand, for most people who might be labelled mentally ill, this is a circumstance which greatly inhibits the social acceptance of what they invent. Furthermore, those who do not conform to the behavioural expectations of the society are not likely to be able to carry out the tasks required to establish any kind of social organisation or group including a cult. Stark and Bainbridge speculate that they may, however, go through a period of illness during which they are highly creative and innovative and during which they create wholly new compensators and religious ideas which they are subsequently able to persuade others to listen to and to embody in a new organisation when they have recovered normality.

The second, entrepreneurial, model recognises that cults are in many respects like businesses. They are created by individuals with entrepreneurial flair because such individuals believe they can profit from doing so. They profit by offering new compensators in return for rewards from their followers. The rewards they receive are in many cases financial but may be intangible things such as prestige, admiration and power. Usually, cult leaders of this kind have had experience of the benefits that cult leadership may bring. Prior involvement in one or more cults also gives them the skills and know-how necessary to establish and run a successful cult. Very often they utilise elements of the belief systems of cults of which they have previous experience, integrating them into a new synthesis and adding perhaps some new elements of their own. Cults, therefore, have a tendency to cluster in lineages such that one can trace the lines of descent and cross-influences. Cult leaders, however, are not always, as this model might lead one to presuppose at first sight, cynical and manipulative in this. Stark and Bainbridge distinguish between honest cult founders who offer only those compensators which they themselves personally accept and dishonest ones who do not accept themselves what they offer to others.

The third model of cult emergence that Stark and Bainbridge offer is that termed the subculture–evolution model. This draws upon sociological work on deviant subcultures including delinquent subcultures. In such groups, which are relatively isolated from the surrounding society in terms of rewarding interactions and exchanges, novel explanations and therefore novel compensators may develop by a process of incremental generation. This is a process by which new compensators are collectively invented and developed through a series of small steps consisting of exchanges. If the process goes on for a long time quite new subcultural types of cult can emerge. Stark and Bainbridge argue that such groups will tend to generate compensators of an increasingly general kind and thus qualify as religious cults.

Religious cults often begin as magical cults. A magical cult is one that offers specific compensators but not of a supernatural kind. The process centres on the the tendency of the members of some subcultural groups to become highly dependent upon one another as a result of their relative isolation from the conventional society. Such a group may experience what Stark and Bainbridge call social implosion by which a high degree of closure is stimulated.

These models of cult formation are clearly somewhat controversial. It stretches credibility somewhat to suggest that many cults are established by the mentally ill, even given Stark and Bainbridge's definition of that condition. They seem to have been influenced in developing this model by work on spirit possession and shamanism in which hysterical-like behaviour is attributed in some societies to invasion of the individual by powerful, demanding spirits. They cite the work of Lewis (1971) in this context and particularly such examples as the Sar or Zar cults of Ethiopia, the Sudan, Somalia and neighbouring areas in which downtrodden and oppressed individuals, usually women, become possessed and some of whom become regular shamans. What they fail to note, however, is that Lewis specifically repudiates the suggestion that possessed persons or shamans are mentally ill. Lewis analyses the Zar cult and those like it in terms of rebellion and what he terms 'oblique redressive strategies' (p. 88). 'We cannot', Lewis says, 'meaningfully reduce shamanism and spirit possession as total cultural phenomena to expressions of private fantasies of psychotic individuals' (1971, p. 186).

Lewis prefers to see spirit possession as a culturally defined initiation ritual for those who feel called to the vocation or profession of shaman – an initiation ritual which testifies to the candidate's ability to contact and deal successfully with dangerous and powerful forces. The crucial thing is that a successful shaman must control his spirits and his behaviour. He is not usually a person whose behaviour is beyond his own control in the way that a mentally disturbed person is. Lewis emphasises that spirit possession and shamanism conform to a culturally defined pattern and are not the idiosyncratic actions of individuals.

Stark and Bainbridge's reasoning in their development of the subcultural–evolution model of cult emergence is somewhat obscure. It is difficult to see why in a subcultural group the members will begin to develop compensators of a very general kind. This is asserted by Stark and Bainbridge rather than derived from their postulates and no evidence is provided for this sort of process. Even more problematic is that they seem to forget in claiming that the generation of general compensators makes such a group religious that by their own definition of religion the compensators have to be supernatural in character. Without this they are only magical cults. It is true that they say religious cults often evolve out of purely magical ones but they do not establish that this is so or make it clear why it is.

Finally, while the entrepreneurial model is perhaps less difficult to accept, one problem that it does throw up concerns the distinction between sects and cults and its relevance for understanding the various types of religious organisation collectively covered by these concepts and the processes which produce religious pluralism. Cults established by entrepreneurs tend to cluster in lineages and have strong family resemblances, Stark and Bainbridge tell us. To the extent that this is true, and it does seem to be true of many cults, we might be led to question the distinction between cult and sect that Stark and Bainbridge make.[3] To the extent that some cults are quite similar to other pre-existing ones they are not novel. Are they not therefore sects? Stark and Bainbridge acknowledge that breakaway groups from a cult are not in fact novel and qualify as sects if they retain much of the original set of ideas. But how novel does a religious group have to be to qualify as a cult? Wallis, Stark and Bainbridge would probably answer this point by saying that their analysis applies to relatively pure types of each and that in reality there will be many mixed types. Their distinction between sect and cult is not necessarily to be taken as a categorical one but as referring to a continuum.

This is fair enough but the point is that their distinction is not in terms of the character of the respective groups concerned but in terms of their origins. The consequence is that cult A and sect B may be very alike while cult C and cult D or sect E and sect F may be very different from one another. Stark and Bainbridge's treatment of them, however, is of very different sorts of phenomena. The sort of group that they see emerging from schismatic tendencies seems very different from that established by mentally ill individuals, entrepreneurs or through subcultural incremental compensator-generation. In reality, religious movements of the kind covered by the terms sect and cult do not seem to fall into this dichotomy. Groups such as the International Society for Krishna Consciousness (ISKCON), otherwise known as the Hare Krishna people, a cult in Stark and Bainbridge's terms since it is not a breakaway group but an imported one and therefore something wholly new in the social context,[4] on the one hand, and the Children of God, subsequently known as the Family, a Christian sect, on the other, share many features in common. If anything it is sects such as the Family that might very well be included in the entrepreneurial model rather than cults such as ISKCON which does not seem to fit any of these models. Other groups such as the Unification Church (Moonies) are again difficult to fit anywhere into the scheme. In many respects it is a Christian group but in others highly novel and it is difficult to see how it could be understood either as a breakaway sect or a cult in Stark and Bainbridge's terms. Again, while highly sectarian by many understandings of this term, since it is rather like groups such as the Watchtower Movement or the Family, it might better be seen in terms of entrepreneurship than sectarian schism.

All this can be seen more clearly when we consider the empirical work that has been carried out on some of the new religious movements that mushroomed in Western societies in the decades after World War II and especially in the late 1960s and 1970s.

THE NEW RELIGIOUS MOVEMENTS

Since World War II and particularly since the late 1960s and early 1970s the Western world has witnessed the emergence of an enormous variety of sects, cults and movements which have often been very controversial and have attracted a great deal of media as well as academic attention. The Moonies, Children of God (now the Family), Jesus People, Divine Light Mission, International Society for Krishna Consciousness, Scientology, Rastafarians, Transcendental Meditation, Rajneeshees, Nichiren Shoshu and The People's Temple are among the better known. Many have looked to or have been derived or imported from eastern societies embodying the mysticism typical of many eastern religions.

Many of them have attracted controversy because of their alleged techniques of recruitment, life-styles and values which have often seemed to run directly counter to those of the wider society. They have been accused of brainwashing, kidnapping, of using hypnosis and other mind-control techniques and drugs. They have been charged with destroying the careers, prospects and lives of young people, of manipulation of the young, of immorality and exploitation. A whole academic industry seems to have grown up concerned with these movements and the issues which surround them. A recent survey described the literature on theories and research relating to them as a 'morass' and that relating to conversion to them as 'formidably vast' (Robbins, 1988).

Many explanations for the rise of these new religious movements (NRMs) have been proferred in recent years. Prominent have been those which have attributed this rise to a crisis in values or norms in modern Western industrial societies and particularly in the United States where the NRMs have flourished most vigorously. Bellah (1976) has argued that the NRMs are a more effective successor movement to the counter-cultural rebellion of the 1960s against the materialist utilitarian individualism of modern consumer society and the technical rationality of a scientifically dominated culture. Glock similarly points to the dominance of scientific and social scientific perspectives which have undermined the emphasis on individualism, personal responsibility and supernaturalism of traditional world views (Glock and Bellah, 1976a). This is to some extent supported by Wuthnow's empirical investigations (1976a) which have discerned a decline in theism and individualism and rise of social scientific perspectives, all of which has allowed greater experimentation in all areas of life including politics and life-styles as well as religion. The result has been a rise in mysticism and a 'consciousness reformation'. This thesis has been criticised by Bainbridge and Stark (1981; see also Stark and Bainbridge, 1985) on the basis of a reworking of the original data and data of their own.

Other writers have placed the emphasis on an alleged normative and moral ambiguity of contemporary culture (Anthony and Robbins, 1982; Bird, 1979) associated with its pluralism and high degree of differentiation which has undermined traditional moral absolutism. A further line of explanation is that which focuses on an alleged decline of civil religion[5], especially in the United States (Anthony and Robbins, 1982; Bellah, 1976). Anthony and Robbins see two strategies for coping with the decline in American civil religion. One, typified by the Unification Church which seeks a 'revitalised synthesis of political and religious values', they refer to as the 'civil religion sects'. The other, more mystical, therapeutically oriented and Human Potential type of movement resists the intrusion of political and civic concerns and values into spiritual life and emphasises individual self-transformation and realisation, a process which entails an underlying monistic unity and order obviating the need for any stress on political unity. Such movements have often attracted the label of 'narcissistic' in consequence.

The decline of community in modern urban industrial and mobile societies is the focus of still other theories of the rise of the NRMs (Anthony and Robbins, 1974; Gordon, 1974; Marx and Ellison, 1975; Robbins and Anthony, 1978). Involvement in the movement and membership in a group may provide this sense of community. For many young people the close bonding, fellowship and sense of community that many of the NRMs provide, especially those which advocate communal living, is deeply attractive. Gordon sees them as to some extent surrogate families. Marx and Ellison argue that the non-communal groups, even the more individualistic and less sectarian human potential groups, serve as part-time quasi-communities expressing a partial utopianism. They can provide the expressive, emotional and indeed ecstatic sort of experience of fellowship that seems to be lacking in the wider society, combining familial with universalistic values. Such experience is often legitimated and understood as an expression of the divine and of spiritual force operating in the lives of the members (Anthony and Robbins, 1974; Petersen and Mauss, 1973; Robbins and Anthony, 1978).

Similar to the quest-for-community approach is that which emphasises the search for identity in the modern impersonal world dominated by bureaucratic structures and characterised by a fragmentation of social roles. Many of the NRMs promote a holistic conception of self. This is particularly true of the therapeutic movements and mystical cults (Anthony *et al.*, 1978; Beckford, 1984, 1985; Westley, 1978, 1983). Implicitly incorporating many of the above approaches, but less specific in identifying any one particular aspect of modern life, is Hunter's (1981) claim that the NRMs, are an 'anthropological protest against modernity' (p. 7).

While all of these approaches outlined seem to make relevant points and to add something to our understanding of the NRMs there are three main difficulties with them. They are generally not well founded empirically, they have difficulty explaining the timing of the upsurge of the NRMs and they tend to overgeneralise from specific instances to what is a very diverse set of movements and groups.

While there is a wealth of empirical studies of specific movements and groups most of the attempts to explain the rise of the NRMs have made little use of them, and have been content to speculate in very broad and general terms about the macro-sociological developments in modern society that they allege account for their rise. As Barker has put it:

> While those who have not read sociological accounts of the new religions might still be at a loss to understand why anyone joins the movements, those who have read some of the sociological literature could well be at a loss to understand why *all* young adults are not members, so all-encompassing are some of the explanations.
>
> (Barker, 1986, p. 338)

Second, the changes in Western industrial societies which have led to this religious outbreak have been in progress for a long time. Why should the religious outbreak of the NRMs have occurred only in the late 1960s and 1970s? Only Glock seems to be aware of this problem (Glock and Bellah, 1976). A head of steam for change in religious and spiritual life was building up, he argues, but it required some trigger event to spark off the process. This was provided by the war in Vietnam which gave rise first to the counter-culture and through this stimulated the growth of the NRMs.

The problem with this is that it is perhaps too great an assumption that the NRMs are all offspring of the counter-cultural rebellion against the Vietnam War (see below). It is, in any case, a dubious claim that the counter-culture can be entirely attributed to the impact of the war. The theory, furthermore, and this would also apply to all of those outlined above, cannot account for the decline of the NRMs during the 1980s since the socio-cultural changes referred to continue.

If it is difficult to account for the timing of the rise of the NRMs it may be because, as some have pointed out, that they are not as new as has been supposed. If this is the case many theorists have been looking for an explanation for something that has not happened. Melton (1987; see also Pritchard, 1976), for example, claims that 'the blossoming of the alternative religions in the 1970s is not so much a new event in Western culture as the continuation of the flowering of occult mysticism and Eastern thought that began in the nineteenth century' (pp. 47–8). Melton admits that there was a very rapid spread of such movements in the late 1960s and early 1970s but explains this in terms of the development of new missionary zeal on the part of many Eastern religions at the time, the spread of information about Eastern religions, the emergence of parapsychology, psychedelic drugs and humanistic psychology. Magnifying and hastening the effect was the rescinding in the United States of the Oriental Exclusion Act which allowed many Eastern religious teachers and leaders to enter the country.

Of course, Melton's arguments could be turned in favour of the crisis-of-modernity theories. If the NRMs are not, in fact, new at all then the problem of explaining the timing of their emergence disappears. They have been growing in Western society alongside the socio-economic changes that ensued during the nineteenth century when Eastern mystical traditions began to receive attention in the West. However, while this may have prepared the ground, as Melton argues, for some of the more mystically-oriented movements that took hold in the late 1960s, by no means are all of the NRMs of oriental provenance and even some of those that are so geographically are not so in terms of doctrine. This is true of one of the most prominent, the Unification Church, which emerged in Korea but which is to a considerable degree Christian in outlook, or at least claims to be. Melton's point is well taken but it tends to overlook the diversity of NRMs.

It is this tendency of crisis-of-modernity theories to overlook diversity which is the third major problem they have. The NRMs might, of course, be seen as different reactions to or strategies for dealing with the problems of modernity as some theories claim, but they fail to tell us why some strategies are adopted by some groups and other strategies by other groups. There are, in any case, more promising approaches which may help us to understand this diversity which focus not so much on the crisis of modern Western society as on its ever increasing pluralism, individualism and market-oriented character.

The diversity of these movements has led to several attempts to classify them in some ordered and systematic manner which will aid understanding. Perhaps the most useful has been that of Wallis (1984) who uses a trichotomous scheme of world-rejecting, world-affirming, and world-accommodating movements.

The world-rejecting type finds the present material world and social order unsatisfactory, corrupt, and unspiritual. It advocates devotion to a god or guru and a denial of self. Such movements often adopt a communal life-style. Groups such as Krishna Consciousness and the Children of God are typical of this type. They are more clearly religious than the world-affirming movements. These are oriented much more to the individual, teaching that personal success, power or fulfilment can be released through the techniques and practices taught by the movement. Essentially this life and world are seen as perfectly acceptable in principle. That which is not satisfactory in the world can be changed by changing individuals not social structures. Usually, such movements involve no or only very loose organisation, collective worship or church. These movements are often little like religions in the conventional sense and often claim not to be religions. Included would be Scientology, Transcendental Meditation and est (Erhard Seminar Training).

Finally, world-accommodating movements are more traditionally-oriented religious movements but which address the individual and the personal interior life rather than the social order. Collective ritual is usually central and there is often an emphasis on personal religious experience of some kind. They are very often protests against a perceived loss of vitality of established traditional religious bodies. Neo-Pentecostalism would be an example. Wallis sees this as not a pure type and says very little more about them in his study. A number of new religious movements, such as the Jesus People and the Divine Light Mission do not fit neatly into these categories but embody elements of more than one type and to differing degrees.

World-rejecting movements have recruited mainly among the young adults of middle-class background. Judah (1974) found that 85 per cent of Krishna Consciousness members in the United States were under 26 and only 3 per cent were over 30. They were mostly of upper middle-class background. Again in the United States, Ellwood (1973) reports that participants in the Jesus Movement were mostly between 14 and 24 and mostly of middle- and upper-class background. Barker (1984) found that in Britain the average age at which recruits joined the Moonies was 23 and that the average age of first generation converts was around 27. About 80 per cent of members were between 19 and 30 and again they were predominantly of middle-class origin.

It is not surprising that there has been much puzzlement as to why the younger generation from comfortable middle-class backgrounds, often well educated or having every opportunity and chance of becoming so and with good prospects in life should give up all this to join communistic and somewhat deviant, even bizarre and outrageous religious cults, some of which require them to spend their time and energies street selling to raise money, or disseminating literature, and which involve suppression of their self-identity in devoting themselves to a guru or leader. It is perhaps not really surprising that these movements were charged with brainwashing, mind-control techniques and the undermining of the converts' independence and will. How else could such obviously irrational behaviour be explained?

The relative youth of converts to the world-rejecting movements suggests that they were, in fact, one manifestation of the experimentalism and rebellion of young people during the late 1960s and early 1970s. Many studies of the NRMs, especially in the United States, have found a strong counter-cultural link in that a high proportion of members in some groups had previously been involved in the hippie, drop-out, drug counter-culture of this period (Downton, 1979; Ellwood, 1973; Judah, 1974). Sects such as the Divine Light Mission, the Children of God and ISKCON are interpreted by these authors respectively as in part embodying a retention of certain counter-cultural values – the rejection of 'straight', respectable society – typical of a large section of youth at the time, but translated into a new idiom which itself rejected the anarchic, ill-disciplined and ultimately self-destructive life-style of the counter-culture. Tipton's comparative study of three groups bring this out particularly strongly (1982).

Tipton compares three very different groups in California: the Living World Fellowship, a fundamentalist Christian group; a Zen meditation group; and est or Erhard Seminar Training, one of the Human Potential therapeutic groups. In order to understand this new and largely middle-class (the Living World Fellowship was not so middle class as the others) form of spirituality (or quasi-spirituality in the case of est) one has to understand, according to Tipton, why youth rebelled against 'straight' society in the 1960s and why its alternative, the counter-culture, was found inadequate as a basis for a new and different life-style.

The rebellion of youth was essentially against the materialism of modern culture, the bureaucratic impersonality of modern life, the lack of community, the lack of authenticity and spontaneity in a world which required much role playing. The timing of the rebellion can be explained in terms of the outcome of a series of developments that had occurred in the preceding decade or two. There had been an enormous increase in educational provision and particularly in higher education. Greatly increased numbers were involved for longer periods. While in

higher education they enjoyed considerable free time and were free from responsibilities. They tended to be idealistic and liberal on social questions and
political matters. Opposition to the war in Vietnam was a factor here. Affluence
had increased after a sustained period of unparalleled growth and there were few
worries about ultimately getting a job or having a career among the young.
Despite this affluence the young in higher education, however, had relatively low
material standards of life which encouraged the rejection of materialism. It was,
nevertheless, possible to live relatively well without a job or career for most of
them, given their freedom from family and personal responsibilities. Finally, the
decline of community and fragmentation of relationships had rapidly intensified
as a result of economic boom and increased mobility. The result was the counter-
culture with its emphasis on spontaneity, love, freedom, permissiveness and
communal life-styles.

The counter-culture, however, led to personal disorganisation, bad experiences with drugs, chaos in and souring of personal relationships, mental illness,
and ultimate isolation, mistrust and loneliness. The final irony was the
thoroughgoing commercialisation and exploitation of the counter-culture and its
degeneration into mere fashion. The sects began to recruit dramatically from this
point on.

They retained much that had characterised the counter-culture. They also
rejected materialism, they often retained its communalism and they rejected
subordination to bureaucratic authority. What was different about them was that
they entailed subordination of the self to a discipline, order or regime, the
acceptance of the *charismatic* authority of a guru or spiritual leader and the
downvaluation of self in relation to the group or movement. The sects turned
counter-cultural values on their head and translated them into a new idiom.
Freedom and spontaneity, they taught, were only real if they involved freely
chosen submission to some order and discipline. Hippie freedom was seen as
illusory and unable to satisfy. It was subordination to authority which claimed it
by right that should be rejected. Subordination to exemplary charismatic
authority was not really subordination but ultimately liberating. Self-fulfilment
is only truly such when it is devoted to the ends of the group not to satisfying the
whims of the individual.

Tipton's analysis, though enlightening and suggestive, is perhaps overstated.
He provides no evidence that the motives of converts for joining were as he says
they were (Wallis, 1984). If a number of the movements did recruit heavily
among ex-participants in the counter-culture this is not so of others (Barker,
1984, Wallis, 1984), while Rochford (1985) found that while early recruits to
ISKCON had been involved, later recruits had no participation in it at all. Nor do
the doctrines of all of these movements embody particularly counter-cultural
values (Wallis, 1984). Tipton rather overstretches the otherwise fruitful thesis
that the NRMs represent a translation of counter-cultural values into a new
idiom. That he is inclined to overgeneralise is shown by his inclusion of a Human
Potential type of movement in his analysis, namely est, which is hardly
anti-materialist. Wallis (1984) finds the roots of this world-affirming type of

movement in the rather different social and personal situation in which many individuals find themselves in contemporary society from those that were attracted to the world-rejecting sects.

Recruits to the world-affirming type of movement are generally older than those to the world-rejecting type (Alfred, 1976; Babbie and Stone, 1977; Ellwood, 1973; Stone, 1976; Wallis, 1984). The average age of participants in Human Potential groups was found by Stone to be 35. Ellwood reports that of the membership of Nichiren Shoshu 17 per cent were under 20, 40 per cent between 21 and 30 and 43 per cent over 30. Babbie and Stone found graduates of est to have a median age of 33 and an average age of 36. Recruits to this type of movement are generally even more predominantly middle class and affluent than those to the world-rejecting movements. Many of them are professionally quali-fied and had generally embarked upon their careers. Unlike recruits to the world-rejecting movements, then, they are certainly not marginal but well integrated into mainstream society, affluent and respectable. It is perhaps even more puzzling why they should become involved in alternative religious and quasi-religious movements.

While studies of such movements have often found recruits to have had personal problems such as illness, financial difficulties or problems with per-sonal relationships, the movements primarily seem to offer, in general terms, self-realisation, fulfilment and self-improvement. Their promise lies in the knowledge, techniques and recipes they offer for 'reducing the gap between aspiration and reality' (Wallis, 1984, p. 51). They offer power, status, self-confidence, personal attractiveness and interpersonal competence to those who feel they lack them in sufficient degree or who want more of them because it is such things that define personal adequacy and give significance to a person's existence in contemporary culture. They offer a means of overcoming feelings of personal inadequacy to those who are relatively successful and privileged – a clear case of relative deprivation. In contrast to world-rejecting movements, the world-affirming movements do not favour subordination of the self but the celebration of the self, spiritual growth and the unleashing of hidden potential. Worldly success is not scorned by such movements which are to a large extent an outgrowth of the achievement orientation of contemporary capitalist society among those who prosper within it and which uphold values largely compatible with it. On the other hand, they seem also to offer something more than mere worldly success. Those who enjoy a fair measure of it may find that it leaves a gap in their lives; they may experience a general sense of malaise. Such move-ments often seek to combine worldly success with the search for meaning. In this they are to some extent a reaction to those same aspects of modern life which the counter-culture and the world-rejecting movements found unsatisfactory – its bureaucratic impersonality, role playing and lack of authenticity, its instrumental values, the lack of community and personal fellowship in a situation of social and geographical mobility and so on – on the part of a section of the population which is, however, to a far greater extent locked into mainstream society and institutions.

To this extent the world-affirming movements may have a better future than the world-rejecting movements. They may be more compatible with the conditions of modern life and the values of contemporary society. They require a much lower level of commitment than the world-rejecting movements, are less stigmatising and may offer, as Marx and Ellison (1975) say of the Human Potential groups, a sense of community and fellowship on a part-time basis rather than the less attractive full-time ventures in utopianism that the world-rejecting movements entail. They do not require subordination to the authority of a leader or of a text or doctrine to the same degree as world-rejecting movements but uphold the much more congenial idea in individualistic modern society of the authority of personal experience (Stone, 1976).

This 'epistemological individualism' (Wallis, 1984, 1985a, 1985b) is associated with a tendency to commodification of what the world-affirming movements have to offer which again is highly compatible with the contemporary situation. In market situations, however, the consumer is sovereign and the result is precariousness in the face of changes in taste and fashion. The reaction to this is product differentiation and eclecticism in order to broaden market appeal and consequent proliferation and tendency towards transitoriness of groups. Commercialisation of the cult market and its consequences are a direct outcome of epistemological individualism, according to Wallis. Heelas (1987), however, questions whether Wallis's market theory applies to some groups.

The world-affirming, spiritual growth, Human Potential movements may well be the religions or quasi-religions of the future. It is questionable whether they are religions or merely use 'the language and trappings of religion' (Zaretsky and Leone, 1974, p. xx). Many, in fact, certainly do not present themselves as such but rather as techniques, therapies, and so on. It might be argued, however, that they have a spiritual dimension. To the extent that they flourish in contemporary society they may give cause to question the assumption that contemporary society is thoroughly secular in character but this raises the complex question of secularisation.

A final question to examine in this section is the controversial methods of recruitment of some of the NRMs and particularly the world-rejecting movements and the charges that have often been made against them that they brainwash converts or use coercive and manipulative methods. The techniques used are certainly seductive. For example, at Moonie workshops potential converts experience effusive protestations of profound liking, constant attention, praise, unceasing expression of warm feeling towards them; what the Moonies refer to as 'love bombing'. The Children of God sanctioned the practice of 'flirty fishing' whereby female members of the group were encouraged to offer sexual favours to potential recruits if by doing so they were reasonably convinced there was a good chance of making the conversion and thereby saving a soul. Whether they go beyond this to use forms of mind control, hypnotism, drugs, social isolation, and physical restraint, as has been alleged, is much more controversial.

One point to note at the outset is that whatever the differences in the recruitment methods of some of the NRMs compared to those of the past, charges of coercive and manipulative conversion are nothing new. They were made against many sectarian movements in the past (Bromley and Shupe, 1981; Hampshire and Beckford, 1983; Miller, 1983). When otherwise perfectly ordinary individuals are attracted to what appear to others to be strange and bizarre sectarian groups, it seems to them this can only be explained in terms of some kind of manipulation or coercive technique which has robbed the convert of mental autonomy and capacity for critical thought and free choice, the modern idiom for which is the charge of brainwashing (Snow and Machalek, 1984). Such charges are also a means of denigrating movements seen as threatening to established institutions according to Richardson and Kilbourne (1983). 'Atrocity stories' of brainwashing and mind control also provide a justification for the use of drastic methods which have been used by families of converts to get them out of the sects including kidnapping and deprogramming (Bromley *et al.*, 1983). In portraying the convert as a brainwashed zombie actions are justified which deny him or her the normal rights of a rational and responsible citizen (Robbins *et al.*, 1983). Often such atrocity stories come from those who have been deprogrammed themselves, providing an alibi for their own seduction (Shupe and Bromley, 1981). Such accounts are frequently the basis for those sociological treatments and even more so a number of psychological analyses which have to some extent supported the coercive conversion hypothesis. They are, of course, not only a rather unreliable basis on which to found such an approach but also subject to the problem of retrospective interpretation of the reasons for their conversion.

Deprogramming has of course attracted the counter-charge from the sects that it is this that is the real brainwashing not the original conversion which was freely entered into. In this way they have often been able, paradoxically, to generate greater solidarity within the organisation and to bind their members to the sect all the more firmly (Barker, 1983).

For the most part sociologists who have studied the NRMs empirically have found no evidence for the brainwashing or coercive conversion charge (Barker, 1984; Bromley and Shupe, 1981; Downton, 1979). Barker's study of the Moonies in particular has delivered the *coup de grâce* to the brainwashing charge. Barker studied those who failed to be converted as well as those who were. If brainwashing were involved one would expect a relatively high rate of conversion among those initially exposed to Moonie influence. What Barker found was that of those who attended Moonie two-day workshops nine out of ten did not join.

Even more striking is the fact that after two years of involvement with and membership in the organisation only about 5 per cent of those initially attracted were still members. Barker found no attempt to coerce them to remain in the movement, to prevent them leaving by physical controls, or to isolate them from the countervailing influences of the surrounding society. Nor were the converts those who might be thought to be most vulnerable – the young, the socially isolated, those not succeeding in their lives. These tended not to join at all or to join only temporarily. Even where the young and socially unanchored do predominate among recruits, this does not support the brainwashing charge since such persons are perhaps easy targets. As Robbins (1985) points out, one might suspect it more if it were middle-aged executives with strong family ties that were prominent among converts.

This is not to say that the recruitment techniques used by the Moonies are not highly active, intensive, persuasive and perhaps even manipulative but the fact that converts may be seduced by the techniques does not mean that they have been coerced. And if some proponents of the coercion thesis mean little more than seductive persuasion by the term 'coercion', this is to broaden the notion so greatly that almost any vigorous set of recruitment practices becomes coercive (Robbins, 1985).

The charge of coercive conversion is by no means the only one that has been made against some of the NRMs. There has often been a very tense relationship between them and the wider society which has shown a generalised hostility to many of them. The nature and strength of social reaction to them have, however, varied from one society to another. The whole question of societal reaction to the sects has itself become the object of sociological enquiry with interesting and important results. As much can be learned through studying our reaction to sectarian movements as can be learned from studying the movements themselves. Such studies seem to be the current trend in this area of the sociology of religion. Space permits only the briefest mention of the subject here but note should be taken of Shupe and Bromley's study of the anti-cult movements in the United States (1980) and particularly of Beckford's (1985) extensive treatment which develops a theoretical framework for the understanding of the relationship between sect and society. The central notion of this framework is the sect's 'mode of insertion into society' that is to say the complex of relationships between the sect and its members on the one hand, between sect and the external society on the other, and interrelationship between these dimensions. The framework facilitates analysis of the sources of tension and conflict which fuel controversies about the sects and enables the author to discern different patterns of conflict including how different sects tend to give rise to different kinds of social concern. One great advantage of Beckford's approach is that it enables him to examine what is distinctive and controversial about some of the contemporary movements' recruitments practices without falling into the trap of necessarily implying coercive or manipulative methods.

18 Conclusion

It is a commonplace in the social sciences to observe that theories are never superseded. New ones and new interpretations of old ones are simply added to the existing stock. This is no less true of the sociology of religion than for any other area of sociology and yet to say this is not to say that no progress has not been made. While none of the theories surveyed in this book can be said to be even close to satisfactory, each has something to contribute. The insights of each approach have largely been retained in the more recent endeavours to provide an overall theory and particularly in meaning theories. This type of approach has the added advantage, also, that it is probably closer to the believer's own understanding of his or her belief, practice and experience. It avoids the rather crude rejection of religious claims as always plainly false that intellectualist theories have often tended to make while at the same time being less dismissive of the believer's own account of his or her belief than sociological and particularly functionalist theories. To say that religion is the way people seek to give meaning to their lives is not something that many believers would disagree with, although in any specific instance they may agree rather less with the sociologist's account of why they seek to provide that meaning and the specific ways they seek to provide it.

Meaning theories in synthesising the insights of intellectualist, emotionalist and sociological approaches have at least in part transcended the problems of each of them. Intellectualist approaches neglect the emotional dimension of religiosity. Emotionalist approaches throw out the baby with the bath water in dispensing with the explanatory role of religious belief. Religion is, among other things, an attempt to understand. But this desire to understand is not, as far as religious belief is concerned, motivated wholly by intellectual puzzlement or curiosity about the world, nor necessarily by a need to manipulate material reality the better to deal with it and to survive and prosper within it. The need to understand stems from emotional sources and may in certain circumstances reach a high degree of intensity. Not to understand is to be bewildered, confused and threatened. The human psyche is such that uncertainty, feelings of unfamiliarity and a sense of the alien are deeply disquieting and discomforting. We do not just seek to understand our world and our place in it out of mere interest; we need to know who and what we are and what place we occupy within the world. Religion seeks answers to existential questions which go to the heart of our sense of identity, worth and purpose. Such things are of vital significance to us. As Berger (1973) states, we are *congenitally* compelled to impose a meaningful order upon reality. Whether we are congenitally so compelled or whether it is possible to live without such a sense of order, it is certainly the case that many or most members of almost all known societies have sought such a sense of order and often with such energy and compulsion that it is difficult to deny that it must stem from emotional drives and needs which seem deeply rooted in the human condition. While it may be admitted that some may not feel the force of this need or feel it to a lesser extent than others, and perhaps this is increasingly the case in contemporary society, many seem unable to live without it being met in some way. Even in contemporary industrial society, one suspects that while the un-acceptability and implausibility of traditional religious messages, not to mention the competing attractions that modern affluent and relative secure existence provides, preclude many people from giving much attention to such questions, they lurk, nevertheless, in the background like unwelcome guests at the party. The however distant but nagging spectre of death, for example, can never be entirely dispelled. The inevitability of death is, of course, something that most theories of religion point to. Death, as we have seen in discussing meaning theories and especially Berger, may not so much be feared because it is the unknown or because it brings an end to the individual but rather because it threatens to make the life the individual does have and live pointless and senseless while living it. To know why we live and why we die is not just intellectually satisfying but allays that potential inner disquiet that otherwise comes from the awful realisation that our individual existence may be quite without any point or purpose. Not that religion is solely about providing meaning, however. We should not forget that as often as it claims to be able to explain and make things seem meaningful it claims also to be able to do things for us. It may, for example, offer us eternal life and, in some sense or other, the vanquishing of death.

In providing meaning religion is often said not simply to address existential questions relating to the individual but also to play a central social role. It provides justification for actions and legitimation of practices, customs and social arrangements. Sociological approaches to religion have usually stressed its role in upholding the social order. It is certainly clear that religious systems have generally been locked into the wider social order. To explain the world in ways that make it meaningful inevitably entails explaining in a meaningful way and thereby legitimating the social order. Thus religion has a social as well as an individual dimension. On the other hand, in the light of the situation of religion in many contemporary industrial societies one might question the extent to which this dimension of religion is fundamental. Turner (1991) has suggested that in modern society it is no longer essential to link systems of belief which provide personal meaning with the institutions of public regulation and legitimation. Religion thus becomes privatised and reduced to a 'range of stylistic options' (p. 240). The sociology of religion has conventionally tended to assume that social cohesion required an interlinking of personal and public orders of meaning. The lesson that can be drawn from the study of the position of religion in modern society is that systems for the maintenance of public order, control and legitimation may follow quite separate paths from those which uphold a personal sense of meaning.

Religion is essentially a social enterprise rather than a purely individual one in another sense. However much they owe to the insights and revelations of innovative individuals, systems of belief which provide personal meaning are collectively developed and socially supported. Those that predominate in a society tend to be those that are supported by the most powerful and influential groups in that society. As Marx said, the ruling ideas are in any age the ideas of its ruling class. Weber shows how each major religious tradition has its social carrier which is in most cases the dominant group in the society. Questions of meaning, furthermore, often stem from a sense of injustice or discrepancy between what is and what ought to be. Since such matters are bound up with patterns of social advantage and disadvantage, religious answers to such questions inevitably address and reflect aspects of the social order.

Each culture and each society, structured diversely as they are, will produce different sorts of answers to questions of meaning. Even within societies and cultures there may be various interpretations of the dominant religious tradition and often quite different sub-cultures with wholly different answers to the relevant questions. Religious diversity across cultures and history is truly remarkable and testimony to the inventiveness of the human mind and imagination. Only a small part of that diversity has been touched upon in this book. The selection of substantive topics was that which best illustrates, in the author's opinion, the application of theories. While other selections could have been made the fact that out of the rich diversity of religious experience this particular selection seemed clearly the most obvious one demonstrates the as yet undeveloped state of theory in the sociology of religion and the little that has so far been done, relatively speaking, in applying theoretical approaches to the understanding of substantive questions. Where theory has been most closely applied, it has been so in a rather narrow field confined largely to Christianity and even then to specific aspects of this tradition. Little has been done in the sphere of the world religions generally, with the monolithic exception of the work of Max Weber, only a small part of which it has been possible to discuss here. It is mainly anthropologists who have examined traditions other than that of Christianity and from the perspective one would expect of anthropology, namely participant observation of the small, usually village community. Few scholars have aspired to match the broad comparative and historical sweep of Weber. The sociology of religion will need to address this deficiency if it is to advance. There can be no substitute for comparative study in any branch of sociology, least of all in the sphere of religion.

Notes

1 INTRODUCTION

1 For a review of the range of stances that are taken and a critical discussion of debates on this issue see Johnson (1977).

2 A radical version of this kind of rejection of the sociological enterprise in relation to religion as it is usually understood is that of relativism. For example, Winch (1964) reprinted in Wilson (1970).

Largely founded upon an interpretation of the philosophy of Wittgenstein, this view denies that it is possible to evaluate the claims of any system of religious thought in terms of universally applicable concepts and categories. If religious or spiritual entities are claimed by the external observer to be unreal, for example, the response of these theorists is to say that the concept of 'reality' used in such a statement is one which takes its sense and meaning from a particular mode of discourse, probably a scientific or at least a secular one, whereas the claims concerning the reality of spiritual entities in particular religious systems each utilise notions of 'reality' which take their sense and meaning within that particular context within which scientific notions of reality have no meaning and are illegitimately applied.

There are many problems with such an attempt to relativise thoroughly all belief systems and render them immune from treatment by a generalising social science but two interrelated ones are particularly serious. Both stem from the exaggeration of the distinctness of different modes of discourse. If there is a fundamental unity among human beings does this not mean that despite great cultural differences we all share certain fundamental and universal cognitive traits such that there are universal conceptions and meanings?

The first type of criticism stemming from such a claim is that if it were not so it would be impossible for us to even understand what other peoples' beliefs actually were or to translate their statements into our own language. This implies the paradox that if Winch *et al.* were correct it would be impossible to know that they were correct. (See the relevant contributions to Wilson (1970) for a fuller discussion along these lines and in particular those of Lukes and Hollis.)

The second type of criticism is that belief systems are not as self-contained and insulated from one another as Winch's view would seem to apply. There is a considerable overlap between different systems of religious belief and between religious belief and other systems of ideas. Even within a particular system of religious belief there are different schools of thought, interpretations and understandings (Hill, 1973, p. 11). The fact that a particular school of thought may well replace and supersede an earlier one poses insurmountable problems for Winch since it entails the rejection by the new of the old. To be consistent, Winch would have to argue that it is just as illegitimate for a religious tradition of thought to reject past beliefs as incorrect or false as it is for social science to do so. But this would be to deny the possibility of change and development in a system of beliefs. Gellner puts it this way:

> either the Christians were wrong or the pagans were; either the Reformation Church was wrong or the Reformers were in supposing *it* to be wrong; either those addicted to superstition were wrong or the rationalists were wrong . . . . One way or another, *someone* must be wrong!
>
> (Gellner, 1974, p. 142)

In other words, it is misleading to postulate the existence of radically distinct modes of discourse with no point of contact between them. In a sense all human discourse constitutes a unity despite the different concerns it may have, the different concepts it may use and the different linguistic conventions and usages which govern it.

3 It might better be termed 'methodological agnosticism' since 'methodological atheism' seems to imply, as Towler (1974, p. 2) has pointed out, that for the purposes of sociological investigation and as a working hypothesis, if not in any absolute sense, religious claims are assumed to be false. 'Methodological agnosticism', on the other hand, would imply that no view need be assumed one way or the other on the matter.

4 Similarly, Turner (1991) accuses Bellah of ducking the issue of the truth claims of religion with his notion of 'symbolic realism' in an attempt to place religion in an inviolable position as a reality *sui generis*. This is, Turner argues, one solution among others to the crisis of religion, rooted back in the nineteenth century, in which religion appeared to be necessary but false.

5 For a recent contribution to the debate over whether Buddhism is or is not theistic see Orru and Wang (1992), who challenge the contention that Buddhism is not theistic since it holds that in order to reach *nirvana* one has to overcome death conceived in the form of *Mara*, the god of death. For this and other reasons, concepts of the supramundane are central to Buddhist teaching according to Orru and Wang. On the other hand, it does not make a very clear distinction between sacred and profane. This basis of Durkheim's definition of religion, then, is not particularly applicable to Buddhism, ironically, and he would have done better to stick to the criterion of belief in the supramundane or supernatural.

4 RELIGION AND EMOTION

1 Otto and those who follow him such as Eliade (1969) claim that experience of the numinous is prior to, more fundamental than and independent of any belief or conceptual understanding of the experience. However this experience is interpreted, according to Otto, and whatever beliefs are derived from it, the experience itself is of something specifically religious which is prior to belief. The problem with this notion is that in order to identify the experience as *religious* one cannot but have reference to some idea of what constitutes the religious, namely some belief or theory. Religious experience is thus constituted by religious concepts and beliefs (Proudfoot, 1985).

2 The anthropologist Vic Turner has adopted this approach in much of his work. See for example 'Symbols in Ndembu Ritual', in Max Gluckman, ed., (1964) and 'Ritual Symbolism among the Ndembu', in Fortes and Dieterlen (1965).

3 Some of the evidence is usefully summarised in Argyle and Beit-Hallahmi (1975, pp. 183–9). See also Harrington and Whiting (1972) and for a cross-cultural study which finds against the Freudian hypothesis, Swanson (1960).

4 See, for example, the references in Spiro (1966).

5 Philp's (1974) useful discussion of Freud's view on religion brings this out.

6 A good general introductory discussion can be found in Storr (1973). For Jung's work on religion see Hostie (1957).

5 BUDDHISM

1 Sanskrit versions of terms are often used by authors rather than the Pali versions. Here the Pali versions are used when the term is first introduced and the Sanskrit version is given in brackets. Thereafter either the Pali or Sanskrit version is used according to context.

2 For similar instances in Sri Lankan Buddhism see Obeyesekere (1968); Gombrich (1971).

7 THE COMING OF THE MILLENNIUM

1 Excluded from the discussion here are millennial sects such as the Seventh Day Adventists which are a somewhat different phenomenon and which do not have the characteristics of the rather more ephemeral and temporary movements which are the concern of this chapter.

2 This accompaniment of military action by millennial expectations is, in fact, quite common in many parts of the world as Wilson's (1973) careful and detailed comparative study shows. The early stages of culture contact and conflict during which military resistance seems feasible are often marked by prophetic and millennial backing of military resistance. When this is seen to have entirely failed then the millennialism tends to become more thoroughly religious and the sole means of deliverance.

8 RELIGION AND SOLIDARITY: EMILE DURKHEIM

1 For an extended discussion see Pickering (1984). Also useful is that of O'Toole (1984).

9 THE BIRTH OF THE GODS

1 See also Swanson (1967) for an application of Durkheim's ideas to the Protestant Reformation.

2 This is what Marx meant by alienation. Swanson, however, lists alienation as a separate cause of the decline of religion. It is not clear what Swanson means by alienation - presumably he is thinking of some kind of exclusion from social groups rather than Marx's use of the term.

10 RELIGION AND SOLIDARITY: THE FUNCTIONALISTS

1 The relevant articles are 'Totemism' and 'Tabu' which, together with the original article on 'Religion and society' are reprinted in Radcliffe-Brown (1952) *Structure and Function in Primitive Society*.

12 RELIGION AND RATIONALITY: MAX WEBER

1 See O'Toole (1984) for a useful discussion of Weber's general approach to religion.
2 For an exposition and development of Weber's conceptual categories see Schluchter (1981, 1987).

13 THE PROTESTANT ETHIC DEBATE

1 The Marxist thesis that Protestantism was a product of capitalism cannot be discussed here nor the critics of Weber's thesis, Marxist or otherwise, who have argued that the causation is the other way round to that claimed by Weber or that given the mutual effects of one upon the other it is the effect of capitalism upon Protestantism that is the more significant. For these points of view see Engels' 'The Peasant War in Germany' (Engels, 1965), 'Ludwig Feuerbach and the End of Classical German Philosophy' and 'Socialism: Utopian and Scientific' (in Marx and Engels, 1957); Kautsky (1988); Tawney (1938); Hill (1961, 1963, 1966). For a discussion and criticism of this approach see Marshall (1980, pp. 254–9).
2 The essay 'The Protestant sects and the spirit of capitalism', in Weber (1970a).

15 SECULARISATION

1 Martin has more recently relinquished this position as the title of his comparative treatise on the question indicates (Martin, 1978).
2 The point has been recently reinforced by Bruce (1990) who also tackles the obvious question that is raised, namely why the United States, noted for its pluralism, shows such vitality in its religious life at least as far as Church and denomination membership and attendance are concerned. Bruce argues that while the United States is pluralist in a very general and abstract sense which refers to the whole society it is not at all pluralistic at the local level. The conservative and Protestant south, for example, cannot be said to be pluralist as far as religion is concerned; far less so than much of Europe. In the United States it has been possible for various groups to create their own, relatively insulated sub-cultures, aided in the modern context by the openness of broadcasting which allows great localism.
3 For an attempt to test some of Martin's more general hypotheses see Giorgi (1992).

16 RELIGION AS COMPENSATION: STARK AND BAINBRIDGE

1 The core theory is presented originally in their article of 1980b. It is much developed and elaborated in their subsequent book of 1987.

17 SECTS, CULTS AND MOVEMENTS

1 For a discussion of Niebhur see Eister (1973).
2 The proliferation of terms and concepts in this area and the resulting confusion has led Beckford (1973) to advocate abandonment altogether of the sect, denomination, church terminology. This seems a little extreme, however.
3 For the main contributions to the question of the definition of the term 'cult' other than those already mentioned see Campbell (1977, 1982); Glock and Stark (1965); Martin (1965a); Nelson (1968); Wallis (1975).
4 Stark and Bainbridge decline to discuss the question of imported groups in their general theoretical treatment (1987) but clearly include such groups as cults in their earlier work (1985).
5 While the notion of a 'civil religion' is one that goes back as far as Rousseau the most influential contemporary formulation of it is that of Bellah (1967). Bellah argued that alongside the mainstream religious traditions in the United States there exists a distinct and well-institutionalised civil religion. In the United States religious pluralism, the absence of any established Church or religious tradition and the consequent relegation of religion to the private sphere meant that the legitimation of

the State and of the political system had to be accomplished by the emergence of this distinct civil religion which, however, draws upon themes common to the major religious traditions present in the society such as belief in God and the importance of God for the destiny of the community. Public ceremonial, respect for the flag, the reverence surrounding certain fundamental 'scriptures' such as the Declaration of Independence and the Gettysburg Address testify to the sacred character of much of public and political life. The civil religion has its own martyrs, sacred places and events, its own solemn rituals and symbols. A particular feature of the American civil religion is that the United States has a God-guided mission in human history.

In the British context a similar argument has been put forward relating to public and state ceremonials such as the coronation of a new monarch, Remembrance Day Service and so on (Shils and Young, 1953).

The clearly Durkheimian thesis of the existence of a civil religion has attracted much debate. For a telling criticism of it see Lukes (1975) who questions its underlying assumption of value consensus and the necessity for this in integrating a society and its neglect of the role of sentiments and practices constituting such a civil religion in upholding a structure of power and privilege. Turner (1991) criticises the thesis on the grounds that it conflates prevalence with cultural dominance and confuses frequency with social effects. One cannot assume from the prominence and visibility of the symbols and rituals of the so-called civil religion that it necessarily fulfils central social functions rather than having only somewhat trivial social effects.

Bibliography

Abercrombie, N., Hill, S. and Turner, B. S. (1980) *The Dominant Ideology Thesis.*
London: Allen and Unwin.

Acquaviva, S. S. (1979) *The Decline of the Sacred in Industrial Society.* Oxford:
Blackwell.

Ahern, E. M. (1981) *Chinese Ritual and Politics.* Cambridge: Cambridge University
Press.

Alfred, H. R. (1976) 'The Church of Satan' in C. Y. Glock and R. N. Bellah (eds) *The New
Religious Consciousness.* Berkeley: University of California Press.

Ames, M. (1964a) 'Buddha and the dancing goblins: a theory of magic and religion',
American Anthropologist 66, 75–82.

Ames, M. (1964b) 'Sinhalese magical animism and Theravada Buddhism', in E. B.
Harper (ed.) *Religion in South Asia.* Seattle: University of Washington Press.

Anthony, D. and Robbins, T. (1974) 'The Meher Baba movement', in I. Zaretsky and M.
Leone (eds) *Religious Movements in Contemporary America.* Princeton, NJ: Princeton
University Press.

Anthony, D. and Robbins, T. (1982) 'Spiritual innovation and the crisis of American civil
religion', in M. Douglas and S. Tipton (eds) *Religion and America: Spirituality in a
Secular Age.* Boston: Beacon Press.

Anthony, D., Robbins, T., Doucas, M. and Curtis, T. (1978) 'Patients and pilgrims:
changing attitudes towards psychotherapy of converts to eastern mysticism', in J. T.
Richardson (ed.) *Conversion Careers: In and Out of the New Religious Movements.*
London: Sage.

Argyle, M. and Beit-Hallahmi, B. (1975) *The Social Psychology of Religion.* London:
Routledge.

Arjomand, S. A. (1989) 'The emergence of Islamic political ideologies', in J. A. Beckford,
and T. Luckman (eds) *The Changing Face of Religion.* London: Sage.

Aron, R. (1970) *Main Currents in Sociological Thought*, vol. 2. Harmondsworth:
Penguin.

Asad, T. (1983) 'Anthropological conceptions of religion: reflections on Geertz', *Man*
New Series 18, 237–59.

Babbie, E. and Stone, D. (1977) 'An evaluation of the est experience by an national
sample of graduates', *Bioscience Communication* 3, 123–40.

Bainbridge W. S. and Stark, R. (1981) 'The consciousness reformation reconsidered',
Journal for the Scientific Study of Religion 201 (1), 1–16.

Barker, E. (1983) 'With enemies like that: some functions of deprogramming as an aid to
sectarian membership', in D. Bromley and J. T. Richardson (eds) *The
Brainwashing–Deprogramming Controversy: Sociological, Psychological, Historical
and Legal Perspectives.* New York: Edwin Mellen.

Barker, E. (1984) *The Making of a Moonie.* Oxford: Blackwell.

Barker, E. (1986) 'Religious movements: cult and anti-cult since Jonestown', *Annual Review of Sociology* 12, 329–46.

Barnes, B. (1974) *Scientific Knowledge and Sociological Theory*. London: Routledge.

Barth, F. (1975) *Ritual and Knowledge Among the Baktaman of New Guinea*. New Haven: Yale University Press.

Beattie, J. (1964) *Other Cultures*. London: Cohen and West.

Beattie, J. (1966) 'Ritual and social change', *Man*, New Series, 1, 60–74.

Beattie, J. (1970) 'On understanding ritual', in B. Wilson (ed.) *Rationality*. Oxford: Blackwell.

Beckford, J. A. (1973) 'Religious organisation: a trend report and Bibliography', *Current Sociology* 21, 2,

Beckford, J. A. (1984) 'Holistic imagery and ethics in new religious and healing movements', *Social Compass* 31, 2–3, 259–72.

Beckford, J. A. (1985) *Cult Controversies*. London and New York: Tavistock.

Beckford, J. A. (1989) *Religion and Advanced Industrial Society*. London: Unwin Hyman.

Beidelman, T. O. (1966) 'The Ox and Nuer sacrifice', *Man*, New Series 1 (4), 453–67.

Bellah, R. N. (1967) 'Civil religion in America', *Daedalus* 96 (1), 1–21.

Bellah, R. N. (1970a) 'Christianity and symbolic realism', *Journal for the Scientific Study of Religion* 9, 89–99.

Bellah, R. N. (1970b) *Beyond Belief: Essays on Religion in a Post-Transitional World*. New York: Harper and Row.

Bellah, R. N. (1971) 'Between religion and social science', in R. Caporale and A. Grumelli (eds) *The Culture of Unbelief*. Berkeley: University of California Press.

Bellah, R. N. (1976) 'New religious consciousness and the crisis of modernity', in C. Glock and R. N. Bellah (eds) *The Consciousness Reformation*. Berkeley: University of California Press.

Berger, P. (1971) *A Rumour of Angels*. Harmondsworth: Penguin.

Berger, P. (1973) *The Social Reality of Religion*. Harmondsworth: Penguin.

Bibby, R. W. and Weaver, H. R. (1985) 'Cult consumption in Canada: A further critique of Stark and Bainbridge', *Sociological Analysis* 46 (4), 445–60.

Bird, F. (1979) 'The pursuit of innocence: new religious movements and moral accountability', *Sociological Analysis* 40 (4), 335–46.

Bloch, M. (1974) 'Symbols, song, dance and features of articulation. Is religion an extreme form of traditional authority?', *European Journal of Sociology* 15, 55–81.

Bromley, D. and Shupe, A.D. (1981) *Strange Gods*. Beverly Hills: Sage.

Bromley, D., Shupe, A. D. and Ventimiglia, J. C. (1983) 'The role of anecdotal atrocities in the social construction of evil', in D. Bromley and J. T. Richardson (eds) *The Brainwashing–Deprogramming Controversy: Sociological, Psychological, Historical and Legal Perspectives*. New York: Edwin Mellen.

Bruce, S. (1990) *A House Divided: Protestantism, Schism and Secularisation*. London: Routledge.

Bulmer, R. (1967) 'Why the cassowary is not a bird: a problem of zoological taxonomy among the Karam of the New Guinea Highlands', *Man*, New Series 2, 5–25.

Burridge, K. (1960) *Mambu*. London: Methuen.

Burridge, K. (1969) *New Heaven, New Earth*. Oxford: Blackwell.

Campbell, C. (1971) *Towards a Sociology of Irreligion*. London: Macmillan.

Campbell, C. (1972) 'The cult, the cultic milieu and secularisation', in M. Hill (ed.) *A Sociological Yearbook of Religion in Britain*. London: SCM Press.

Campbell, C. (1977) 'Clarifying the cult', *British Journal of Sociology* 28 (3), 375–95.

Campbell, C. (1982) 'The New Religious Movements, the new spirituality and post-industrial society', in E. Barker (ed.) *New Religious Movements: A Perspective For Understanding Society*. New York: Edwin Mellen.

Carroll, M. P. (1978) 'One more time: Leviticus revisited', *Archives européennes de sociologie* 19, 339–46.

Cavanaugh, M. A. (1982) 'Pagan and Christian sociological euhemerism versus American Sociology of Religion', *Sociological Analysis* 43 (2), 109–30.

Cohen, Y. (1964) *The Transition from Childhood to Adolescence: Cross-Cultural Studies of Initiation Ceremonies, Legal Systems and Incest Taboos*. Chicago: Aldine.

Cohn, N. (1970) *The Pursuit of the Millennium*. St. Albans: Paladin.

Crippen, T. (1988) 'Old and new gods in the modern world: toward a theory of religious transformation', *Social Forces* 67 (2), 316–36.

Davis, K. (1948) *Human Society*. New York: Macmillan.

Dawson, L. L. (1986) 'Neither nerve nor ecstasy: comment on the Wiebe–Davis exchange', *Studies in Religion* 15, 145–51.

Dawson, L. L. (1987) 'On references to the transcendent in the scientific study of religion: a qualified idealist proposal', *Religion* 17 (4), 227–50.

Dawson, L. L. (1988) *Reason, Freedom and Religion: Closing the Gap Between the Humanistic and the Scientific Study of Religion*. New York: Peter Lang.

Dawson, L. L. (1990) '*Sui generis* phenomena and disciplinary axioms: rethinking Pals' proposal', *Religion* 1, 38–51.

Dobbelaere, K. (1981) 'Secularisation: a multi-dimensional concept', *Current Sociology* 29 (2), 3–215.

Dobbelaere, K. (1985) 'Secularization theories and sociological paradigms: a reformation of the private-public dichotomy and the problem of societal integration'. *Sociological Analysis* 46 (4), 377–87.

Dobbelaere, K. (1987) 'Some trends in European sociology of religion: the secularisation debate', *Sociological Analysis* 48 (2), 107–37.

Douglas, M. (1963) *The Lele of Kasai*. London: Oxford University Press.

Douglas, M. (1966) *Purity and Danger*. London: Routledge.

Douglas, M. (1973) *Natural Symbols*. Harmondsworth: Penguin.

Douglas, M. (1975) *Implicit Meanings*. London: Routledge.

Douglas, M. (1983) 'The effects of modernisation on religous change', in M. Douglas and S. Tipton (eds) *Religion in America*, Boston: Beacon.

Downton, J. (1979) *Sacred Journeys: The Conversion of Young Americans to the Divine Light Mission*. New York: Colombia University Press.

Durkheim, E. (1915) *The Elementary Forms of the Religious Life*. London: Allen and Unwin.

Eister, A. W. (1973) 'H. Richard Niebuhr and the paradox of religious organizations: a radical critique', in C. Y. Glock and V. E. Hammond *Beyond the Classics: Essays in the Scientific Study of Religion*. New York: Harper.

Eliade, M. (1969) *The Quest: History and Meaning in Religion*. Chicago: University of Chicago Press.

Ellwood, R. L. (1973) *One Way: The Jesus Movement and its Meaning*. Englewood Cliffs, NJ: Prentice Hall.

Engels, F. (1965) *The Peasant War In Germany*. Moscow: Progress Publishers.

Evans-Pritchard, E. E. (1937) *Witchcraft, Oracles and Magic Among the Azande*. Oxford: Clarendon Press.

Evans-Pritchard, E. E. (1965) *Theories of Primitive Religion*. Oxford: Clarendon Press.

Evers, H. D. (1965) 'Magic and religion in Sinhalese society', *American Anthropologist*, 67, 1.

Fenn, R. K. (1972) 'Towards a new sociology of religion', *Journal for the Scientific Study of Religion* 11 (1), 16–32.

Fenn, R. K. (1978) *Toward a Theory of Secularization*. Storrs, Conn: Society for the Scientific Study of Religion.

Fenn, R. K. (1981) *Liturgies and Trials: The Secularisation of Religious Language*. Oxford: Blackwell.

Firth, R. (1939) *Primitive Polynesian Economy*. London: Routledge.

Fischoff, E. (1944) 'The Protestant ethic and the spirit of capitalism', *Social Research* 11, 54–77.

Fortes, M. (1987) 'Custom and conscience', in *idem.*, *Religion, Morality and the Person.* Cambridge: Cambridge University Press.

Freeman, D. (1969) 'Totem and Taboo: a reappraisal', in W. Muensterberger (ed.) *Man and His Culture.* London: Rapp and Whiting.

Freud, S. (1928) *The Future of an Illusion.* London: Hogarth Press.

Freud, S. (1938) *Totem and Tabu.* Harmondsworth: Penguin.

Freud, S. (1961) *Complete Works.* London: Hogarth Press.

Garrett, W. R. (1974) 'Troublesome transcendence: the natural in the scientific study of religion', *Sociological Analysis* 35 (3), 167–80.

Geertz, C. (1966) 'Religion as a Cultural System', in M. Banton (ed.) *Anthropological Approaches to the Study of Religion*, A. S. A. Monographs no. 3., London: Tavistock.

Gellner, E. (1970) 'Concepts and society', in B. Wilson (ed.) *Rationality.* Oxford: Blackwell.

Gellner, E. (1973) 'The savage and the modern mind', in R. Horton and R. H. Finnegan (eds) *Modes of Thought.* London: Faber and Faber.

Gellner, E. (1974) 'The new idealism: cause and meaning in the social sciences', in A. Giddens (ed.) *Positivism and Sociology.* London: Heinemann.

Gennep, A. Van (1960) *Les Rites de Passage.* London: Routledge.

Giddens, A. (1978) *Durkheim.* London: Fontana.

Giorgi, L. (1992) 'Religious involvement in a secularised society: an empirical confirmation of Martin's general theory of secularisation', *British Journal of Sociology* 43 (4), 639–56.

Glasner, P. E. (1977) *The Sociology of Secularisation: A Critique of a Concept.* London: Routledge.

Glock, C. Y. and Bellah, R. N. (eds) (1976) *The New Religious Consciousness.* Berkeley: University of California Press.

Glock, C.Y. and Stark, R. (1965) 'On the origin and evolution of religious groups', in *idem.* (eds) *Religion and Society in Tension.* New York: Rand McNally.

Gluckman, M. (ed.) (1962) *Essays in the Ritual of Social Relations.* Manchester: Manchester University Press.

Gluckman, M. (1963) *Order and Rebellion in Tribal Africa.* London: Cohen and West.

Gluckman, M. (ed.) (1964) *Closed Systems and Open Minds*, London: Oliver and Boyd.

Gombrich, R. F. (1971) *Precept and Practice.* Oxford: Clarendon Press.

Gombrich, R. F. (1972) 'Buddhism and society', *Modern Asian Studies,* 6 (3), 483–96.

Goode, W. J. (1951) *Religion Among the Primitives.* New York: Free Press.

Goodridge, R. M. (1975) 'The ages of faith – romance or reality?', *Sociological Review,* 23, 381–96.

Goody, J. (1961) 'Religion and ritual: the definitional problem', *British Journal of Sociology* 12, 142–64.

Gordon, D. F. (1974) 'The Jesus People: An identity synthesis', *Urban Life and Culture* 3 (2), 159–78.

Greeley, A. (1973) *The Persistence of Religion.* London: SCM Press.

Hadden, J. K. (1987) 'Towards desacrilising secularisation theory', *Social Forces* 65, 587–611.

Hampshire, A. P. and Beckford, J. A. (1983) 'Religious sects and the concept of deviance: the Moonies and the Mormons', *British Journal of Sociology* 34 (2), 208–29.

Harrington, C. and Whiting, J. W. M. (1972) 'Socialisation process and personality', in F. L. Hsu (ed.) *Psychological Anthropology.* Cambridge, Mass: Schenkmann.

Heelas, P. (1987) 'Exegesis: methods and aims', in P. Clarke (ed.) *The New Evangelists*, London: Ethnographica.

Herberg, W. (1956) *Protestant, Catholic, Jew.* Garden City, NY: Doubleday.

Herbrechtsmeier, W. (1993) 'Buddhism and the definition of religion: one more time', *Journal for the Scientific Study of Religion* 32 (1), 1–18.

Hill, C. (1961) 'Protestantism and the rise of capitalism', in F. J. Fisher (ed.) *Essays in the Economic and Social History of Tudor and Stuart England in Honour of R. H. Tawney.* Cambridge: Cambridge University Press.

Hill, C. (1963) *The Century of Revolution 1603–1714.* Edinburgh: Nelson.

Hill, C. (1966) *Society and Puritanism in Pre-Revolutionary England.* London: Secker and Warburg.

Hill, M. (1973) *A Sociology of Religion.* London: Heinemann.

Hobsbawm, E. J. (1971) *Primitive Rebels.* Manchester: Manchester University Press.

Horton, R. (1960) 'A definition of religion and its uses', *Journal of the Royal Anthropological Institute* 90, 201–26.

Horton, R. (1967) 'African traditional thought and western science', *Africa* 37, 1–2, 50–71.

Horton, R. (1968) 'Neo-Tylorianism: Sound sense or sinister prejudice?' *Man*, New Series 3 (4), 625–34.

Horton, R. (1970) 'African traditional thought and Western science', in B. Wilson (ed.) *Rationality.* Oxford: Blackwell.

Horton, R. (1973) 'Lévy-Bruhl, Durkheim and the scientific revolution', in R. Horton and R. H. Finnegan (eds) *Modes of Thought.* London: Faber and Faber.

Horton, R. (1982) 'Tradition and modernity revisited', in M. Hollis and S. Lukes (eds) *Rationality and Relativism.* Oxford: Blackwell.

Horton, R. and Finnegan, R. H. (eds) (1973) *Modes of Thought.* London: Faber and Faber.

Hostie, R. (1957) *Religion and the Psychology of Jung.* London: Sheed and Ward.

Hsu, F. L. K. (1983) *Exorcising the Troublemakers: Magic, Science and Culture.* Westport, Conn: Greenwood Press.

Hume, D. (1976) *The Natural History of Religion.* Oxford: Clarendon Press.

Hunter, J. (1981) 'The new religions: demodernisation and the protest against modernity', in B. Wilson (ed.) *The Social Impact of the New Religious Movements.* New York: Rose of Shannon Press.

James, W. (1961) *The Varieties of Religious Experience.* New York: Collier-Macmillan.

Johnson, B. (1963) 'On church and sect', *American Sociological Review* 28, (4), 589–99.

Johnson, B. (1977) 'Sociological theory and religious truth', *Sociological Analysis* 28 (4), 268–88.

Judah, J. S. (1974) *Hare Krishna and the Counter Culture.* New York: John Wiley.

Jules-Rosette, B. (1989) 'The sacred in new African religions', in J. A. Beckford and T. Luckman (eds) *The Changing Face of Religion.* London: Sage.

Kautsky, K. (1925) *The Foundations of Christianity.* London: Orbach and Chambers.

Kautsky, K. (1988) *The Materialist Conception of History* abridged, annotated and introduced by J. H. Kautsky. New Haven: Yale University Press.

Kehrer, G. and Hardin, B. (1984) 'Sociological approaches (2)', in F. Whaling (ed.) *Contemporary Approaches to the Study of Religion.* Vol. 2, pp. 149–77. Berlin: Mouton.

Leach, E. (1954) *Political Systems of Highland Burma.* London: Athlone Press.

Leach, E. (1958) 'Magical hair', *Journal of the Royal Anthropological Institute* 88, 147–64.

Lechner, F. J. (1991) 'The case against secularisation: a rebuttal', *Social Forces* 69, 1103–19.

Lévi-Strauss, C. (1962) *Totemism.* London: Merlin Press.

Lévy-Bruhl, L. (1926) *How Natives Think.* London: Allen and Unwin.

Lévy-Bruhl, L. (1922) *La Mentalité Primitive* Paris: Alcan.

Lewis, G. (1980) *Day of Shining Red.* Cambridge: Cambridge University Press.

Lewis, I. M. (1971) *Ecstatic Religion.* Harmondsworth: Penguin.

Luckmann, T. (1967) *The Invisible Religion.* New York: Macmillan.

Luckmann, T. (1990) 'Shrinking transcendence, expanding religion', *Sociological Analysis* 50 (2), 127–38.

Luethy, H. (1964) 'Once again, Calvinism and capitalism', *Encounter* 22, 26–38.
Luhrmann, T. (1989) *Persuasions of the Witch's Craft: Ritual Magic and Witchcraft in Present Day England*. Oxford: Blackwell.
Lukes, S. (1975) 'Political ritual and social integration', *Sociology* 9 (2), 289–308.
McKown, D. B. (1975) *The Classic Marxist Critiques of Religion: Marx, Engels, Lenin, Kautsky*. The Hague: Nijhoff.
Malinowski, B. (1936) *The Foundation of Faith and Morals*. London: Oxford University Press.
Malinowski, B. (1974) *Magic, Science and Religion*. London: Souvenir Press.
Mandelbaum, D. (1966) 'Transcendental and pragmatic aspects of religion', *American Anthropologist* 68, 1174–91.
Marett, R. R. (1914) *The Threshold of Religion*. London: Methuen.
Marshall, G. (1980) *Presbyteries and Profits: Calvinism and the Development of Capitalism in Scotland, 1560–1707*. Oxford: Clarendon.
Marshall, G. (1982) *In Search of the Spirit of Capitalism*. London: Hutchinson.
Martin, D. A. (1962) 'The Denomination', *British Journal of Sociology* 12, 1–13.
Martin, D. A. (1965a) *Pacifism*. London: Routledge.
Martin, D. A. (1965b) 'Towards eliminating the concept of secularisation', in J. Gould (ed.) *Penguin Survey of the Social Sciences*. Harmondsworth: Penguin; reprinted in D. A. Martin (1969) *The Religious and the Secular*. London: Routledge.
Martin, D. A. (1978) *A General Theory of Secularisation*. Oxford: Blackwell.
Martin, D.A. (1991) 'The secularisation issue: prospect and retrospect', *British Journal of Sociology* 42, 465–74.
Marx, J. and Ellison, D. (1975) 'Sensitivity training and communes: contemporary quests for community', *Pacific Sociological Review* 18 (4), 442–62.
Marx, K. and Engels, F. (1957) *On Religion*. Moscow: Progress Publishers.
Melton, J. G. (1987) 'How new is new?: the flowering of the "new" religious consciousness since 1965', in D. Bromley and P. Hammond (eds) *The Future of the New Religious Movements*. Macon, GA: Mercer University Press.
Melton, J. G. (1993) 'Another look at New Religions', *Annals, AAPSS*, 527, 97–111.
Miller, D. E. (1983) 'Deprogramming in historical perspective', in D. Bromley and J. T. Richardson (eds) *The Brainwashing–Deprogramming Controversy: Sociological, Psychological, Historical and Legal Perspectives*. New York: Edwin Mellen.
Morris, B. (1987) *Anthropological Studies of Religion*. Cambridge: Cambridge University Press.
Nadel, S. F. (1954) *Nupe Religion*. London: Routledge.
Nadel, S. F. (1957) 'Malinowski on magic and religion', in R. Firth (ed.) *Man and Culture: An Evaluation of the Work of Bronislav Malinowski*. London: Routledge.
Nelson, G. K. (1968) 'The concept of cult', *Sociological Review* 16 (3), 351–62.
Niebuhr, H. R. (1957) *The Social Sources of Denominationalism*. New York: World Publishing.
Norbeck, E. (1963) 'African rituals of conflict', *American Anthropologist* 65, 1254–79.
Obeyesekere, G. (1963) 'The Great Tradition and the Little Tradition in the perspective of Sinhalese Buddhism', *Journal of Asian Studies* 22 (2), 139–53.
Obeyesekere, G. (1966) 'The Buddhist pantheon in Ceylon and its extensions', in M. Nash (ed.) *Anthropological Studies in Theravada Buddhism*, Yale University South East Asia Studies. Cultural Report Series no. 13.
Obeyesekere, G. (1968) 'Theodicy, sin and salvation in a sociology of Buddhism', in E. Leach (ed.) *Dialectic in Practical Religion* Cambridge: Cambridge University Press.
O'Dea, T. (1966) *The Sociology of Religion*. Englewood Cliffs, NJ: Prentice Hall.
Orru, M. and Wang, A. (1992) 'Durkheim, religion and Buddhism', *Journal for the Scientific Study of Religion* 31 (1), 47–61.
O'Toole, R. (1984) *Religion: Classic Sociological Approaches*. Toronto: McGraw-Hill Ryerson.

Pals, D. (1986) 'Reductionism and belief: an appraisal of recent attacks on the doctrine of irreducible religion', *Journal of Religion* 66, 18–36.

Pals, D. (1987) 'Is religion a *sui generis* phenomenon?', *Journal of the American Academy of Religion* 55 (2), 259–82.

Pals, D. (1990) 'Autonomy, legitimacy and the study of religion', Religion, 20 (1), 1–16.

Peel, J. D. Y. (1968) 'Understanding alien thought–systems', *British Journal of Sociology* 20, 69–84.

Penner, H. H. and Yonan, E. A. (1972) 'Is a science of religion possible?', *Journal of Religion* 52, 107–33.

Pereira de Queiroz, M. I. (1989) 'Afro-Brazilian cults and religious change in Brazil', in J. A. Beckford and T. Luckman (eds) *The Changing Face of Religion*. London: Sage.

Peterson, D. W. and Mauss, A. L. (1973) 'The cross and the commune: an interpretation of the Jesus Movement', in C. Y. Glock (ed.) *Religion in Sociological Perspective*. Belmont, CA: Wadsworth.

Phillips, D. Z. (1976) *Religion Without Explanation*. Oxford: Blackwell.

Philp, H. L. (1974) *Freud and Religious Belief*. Westport, Conn: Greenwood Press.

Pickering, W. S. F. (1984) *Durkheim's Sociology of Religion: Themes and Theories*, London: Routledge and Kegan Paul.

Plamenatz, J. (1975) *Karl Marx's Philosophy of Man*. Oxford: Clarendon Press.

Pope, L. (1942) *Millhands and Preachers*. New Haven: Yale University Press.

Popper, K. (1963) *Conjectures and Refutations*, London: Routledge and Kegan Paul.

Preus, J. S. (1987) *Explaining Religion: Criticism and Theory from Bodin to Freud*. New Haven: Yale University Press.

Pritchard, L. K. (1976) 'Religious change in nineteenth century America', in C. Y. Glock and R. Bellah (eds) *The New Religious Consciousness*. Berkeley: University of California Press.

Proudfoot, W. (1985) *Religious Experience*. Berkeley: University of California Press.

Radcliffe-Brown, A. R. (1922) *The Andaman Islanders*. Cambridge: Cambridge University Press.

Radcliffe-Brown, A. R. (1952a) 'Religion and society', in *idem.*, *Structure and Function in Primitive Society*. London: Cohen and West.

Radcliffe-Brown, A. R. (1952b) 'Tabu', in *idem.*, *Structure and Function in Primitive Society*. London: Cohen and West.

Rappaport, R. A. (1967) 'Ritual regulation of environmental relations among a New Guinea people', *Ethnology* 6, 17–30.

Redfield, R. (1956) *Peasant Society and Culture*. Chicago: University of Chicago Press.

Regan, D. (1989) 'Islam as a New Religious Movement in Malaysia', in J. A. Beckford and T. Luckman (eds) *The Changing Face of Religion*. London: Sage.

Reik, T. (1975) *Ritual: Psycho-Analytic Studies*. Westport, Connecticut: Greenwood Press.

Richardson, J. T. and Kilbourne, B. K. (1983) 'Classical and contemporary applications of brainwashing models: a comparison and critique', in D. Bromley and J. T. Richardson (eds) *The Brainwashing–Deprogramming Controversy: Sociological, Psychological, Historical and Legal Perspectives*. New York: Edwin Mellen.

Robbins, T. (1985) 'Are conflicting images of "cults" susceptible to empirical resolution?', in B. K. Kilbourne (ed.) *Scientific Research and New Religions: Divergent Perspectives*. San Francisco: AAAS.

Robbins, T. (1988) 'Cults, converts and charisma: the sociology of the New Religious Movements', *Current Sociology* 36 (1), 1–250.

Robbins, T. and Anthony, D. (1978) 'New religious movements and the social system: interpretation, disintegration or transformation', *American Review of the Social Sciences of Religion* 2, 1–28.

Robbins, T., Anthony, D. and McCarthy, J. (1983) 'Legitimating repression', in D. Bromley and J. T. Richardson (eds) *The Brainwashing–Deprogramming Controversy:*

Sociological, Psychological, Historical and Legal Perspectives. New York: Edwin Mellen.

Robertson, R. (1970) *The Sociological Interpretation of Religion.* Oxford: Blackwell.

Rochford, E. B. Jr. (1985) *Hare Krishna.* New Brunswick, NJ: Rutgers University Press.

Ross, G. (1971) 'Neo-Tyloreanism: a reassessment', *Man*, New Series 6 (1), 105–16.

Runciman, W. G. (1970) 'The explanation of religious beliefs', in *idem.*, *Sociology in its Place*. Cambridge: Cambridge University Press.

Ryan, B. (1958) *Sinhalese Village.* Coral Gables, Fl: University of Miami Press.

Samuelsson, K. (1961) *Religion and Economic Action.* Stockholm: Scandinavian University Books.

Scharf, B. (1970) *The Sociological Study of Religion.* London: Hutchinson.

Schluchter, W. (1981) *The Rise of Western Rationalism: Max Weber's Developmental History.* Berkeley: University of California Press.

Schluchter, W. (1987) 'Weber's sociology of rationalism and typology of religious rejections of the world', in S. Lash and S. Whimster (eds) *Max Weber, Rationality and Modernity.* London: Allen and Unwin.

Segal, R. (1980) 'The social sciences and the truth of religious belief', *Journal of the American Academy of Religion* 48 (3), 401–13.

Segal, R. (1983) 'In defense of reductionism', *Journal of the American Academy of Religion* 51 (1), 97–124.

Segal, R. and Wiebe, D. (1989) 'Axioms and dogmas in the study of religion', *Journal of the American Academy of Religion* 57 (3), 591–605.

Sharot, S. (1989) 'Magic, religion, science and secularisation', in J. Neusner, E. S. Frerichs and P. V. M. Flesher (eds) *Religion, Science and Magic.* New York: Oxford University Press.

Shils, E. and Young, M. (1953) 'The meaning of the coronation', *Sociological Review* 1, (2), 63–82.

Shiner, L. (1966) 'The concept of secularisation in empirical research', *Journal for the Scientific Study of Religion* 6, 207–20.

Shupe, A. D. and Bromley, D. G. (1980) *The New Vigilantes: Deprogrammers, Anti-Cultists and the New Religions.* Beverley Hill: Sage.

Shupe, A. D. and Bromley, D. G. (1981) 'Apostates and atrocity stories: some parameters in the dynamics of deprogramming', in B. Wilson (ed.) *The Social Impact of the New Religious Movements.* New York: Rose of Shannon Press.

Skorupski, J. (1973a) 'Science and traditional religious thought I and II', *Philosophy of the Social Sciences* 3, 97–115.

Skorupski, J. (1973b) 'Science and traditional religious thought III and IV', *Philosophy of the Social Sciences* 3, 209–30.

Skorupski, J. (1976) *Symbol and Theory: A Philosophical Study of Theories of Religion in Social Anthropology.* Cambridge: Cambridge University Press.

Smith, W. Robertson, (1889) *Lectures on the Religion of the Semites.* Edinburgh: Black.

Snow, D. A. and Machalek, R. (1984) 'The sociology of conversion', *Annual Review of Sociology* 10, 167–90.

Southwold, M. (1983) *Buddhism in Life: The Anthropological Study of Religion and the Sinhalese Practice of Buddhism.* Manchester: Manchester University Press.

Spiro, M. E. (1965) 'Religious systems as culturally constituted defence mechanisms', in M. Spiro (ed.) *Context and Meaning in Cultural Anthropology.* Glencoe: Free Press.

Spiro, M. E. (1966) 'Religion: problems of definition and explanation', in M. Banton (ed.) *Anthropological Approaches to the Study of Religion*, A. S. A. Monograph no. 3. London: Tavistock.

Spiro, M. E. (1971) *Buddhism and Society.* London: Allen and Unwin.

Spiro, M. E. (1978) *Burmese Supernaturalism.* Philadelphia: Institute of the Study of Human Issues.

Stark, W. (1967) *The Sociology of Religion: Vol. 2. Sectarian Religion.* London: Routledge.

Stark, R. and Bainbridge, W. S. (1979) 'Of churches, sects and cults: preliminary concepts for a theory of religious movements', *Journal for the Scientific Study of Religion* 18 (2), 117–33.

Stark, R. and Bainbridge, W. S. (1980a) 'Secularization, revival and cult formation', *Annual Review of the Social Sciences of Religion* 4, 85–119.

Stark, R. and Bainbridge, W. S. (1980b) 'Towards a theory of religion: religious commitment', *Journal for the Scientific Study of Religion* 19 (2), 114–28.

Stark, R. and Bainbridge, W. S. (1985) *The Future of Religion*. Berkeley: University of Califorinia Press.

Stark, R. and Bainbirdge, W. (1987) *A Theory of Religion*. New York: Lang.

Steiner, F. (1967) *Taboo*. Harmondsworth: Penguin.

Stone, D. (1976) 'The Human Potential Movement', in C. Y. Glock and R. N. Bellah (eds) *The Consciousness Reformation*. Berkeley: University of California Press.

Storr, A. (1973) *Jung*. London: Fontana/Collins.

Swanson, G. (1960) *The Birth of the Gods*. Ann Arbor: University of Michigan Press.

Swanson, G. (1967) *Religion and Regime*. Ann Arbor: University of Michigan Press.

Talmon, Y. (1966) 'Millennial movements', *Archives européennes de sociologie* 7, 159–200.

Tambiah, S. J. (1968) 'The ideology of merit and the social correlates of Buddhism in a Thai village', in E. Leach (ed.) *Dialectic in Practical Religion*. Cambridge: Cambridge University Press.

Tambiah, S. J. (1969) 'Animals are good to think and good to prohibit', *Ethnology* 7, 423–59.

Tambiah, S. J. (1970) *Buddhism and the Spirit Cults of North East Thailand*. Cambridge: Cambridge University Press.

Tambiah, S. J. (1973) 'Form and meaning of magical acts: a point of view', in R. Horton and R. H. Finnegan (eds) *Modes of Thought*. London: Faber and Faber.

Tambiah, S. J. (1976) *World Conqueror, World Renouncer*. Cambridge: Cambridge University Press.

Tambiah, S. J. (1990) *Magic, Science, Religion and the Scope of Rationality*. Cambridge: Cambridge University Press.

Tawney, R. H. (1938) *Religion and the Rise of Capitalism*. Harmondsworth: Penguin.

Taylor, C. (1982) 'Rationality', in M. Hollis and S. Lukes (eds) *Rationality and Relativism*. Oxford: Blackwell.

Tipton, S. (1982) *Getting Saved From the Sixties*. Berkeley: University of California Press.

Towler, R. (1974) *Homo Religiosus: Sociological Problems in the Study of Religion*. London: Constable.

Trevor-Roper, H. (1973) *Religion, the Reformation and Social Change*. London: Macmillan.

Troeltsch, E. (1931) *The Social Teachings of the Christian Churches*. London: Allen and Unwin.

Turner, B. (1991) *Religion and Social Theory*. 2nd edn, London: Sage.

Turner, V. W. (1964) 'Symbols in Ndembu ritual', in M. Gluckman (ed.) *Closed Systems and Open Minds*. London: Oliver and Boyd.

Turner, V. W. (1965) 'Ritual symbolism among the Ndembu', in M. Fortes and G. Dieterlen (eds) *African Systems of Thought*. Oxford: Oxford University Press for International African Institute.

Turner, V. W. (1968) *The Drums of Afflication*. Oxford: Clarendon Press and International African Institute.

Turner, V. W. (1974) *The Ritual Process*. Harmondsworth: Penguin.

Tylor, E. B. (1903 [1871]) *Primitive Culture*; 4th edition. London: Murray.

Vergote, A., Tamayo, A., Pasquali, L., Bonami, M., Pattyn, A. and Clusters, A. (1969) 'Concept of God and parental images', *Journal for the Scientific Study of Religion* 8, 79–87.

Vogt, E. Z. (1952) 'Waterwitching: an interpretation of ritual in a rural American community', *Scientific Monthly* 75, 175–86.

Wallis, R. (ed.) (1975) 'The Cult and its transformation' in *idem. Sectarianism: Analyses of Religious and Non-religious Sects*. London: Peter Owen.

Wallis, R. (1984) *The Elementary Forms of the New Religious Life*. London: Routledge.

Wallis, R. (1985a) 'Betwixt therapy and salvation: the changing form of the Human Potential Movement', in R. K. Jones (ed.) *Sickness and Sectarianism*. Aldershot: Gower.

Wallis, R. (1985b) 'The dynamics of change in the Human Potential Movement', in R. Stark (ed.) *Religious Movements: Genesis, Exodus and Numbers*. New York: Paragon House.

Wallis, R. and Bruce, S. (1984) 'The Stark-Bainbirdge theory of religion: a critique and counter proposal.' *Sociological Analysis* 45 (1), 11–28.

Walzer, M. (1963) 'Puritanism as a revolutionary ideology', *History and Theory* 3, 59–90.

Weber, M. (1930) *The Protestant Ethic and the Spirit of Capitalism*. London: Allen and Unwin

Weber, M. (1961) *General Economic History*. New York: Collier.

Weber, M. (1951) *The Religions of China*. New York: Free Press.

Weber, M. (1965) *The Sociology of Religion*. London: Methuen.

Weber, M. (1970a) 'The protestant sects and the spirit of capitalism', in H. Gerth and C. W. Mills (eds) *From Max Weber: Essays in Social Theory*. London: Routledge.

Weber, M. (1970b) 'Religious rejections of the world and their directions', in H. Gerth and C. W. Mills (eds) *From Max Weber: Essays in Social Theory*. London: Routledge.

Weber, M. (1970c) 'The social psychology of the world religions', in H. Gerth and C. W. Mills (eds) *From Max Weber: Essays in Social Theory*. London: Routledge.

Weber, M. (1978) *Economy and Society: An Outline of Interpretive Sociology*, Edited by G. Roth and C. Wittich. Berkeley: University of California Press.

Westley, F. (1978) 'The cult of man: Durkheim's predictions and religious movements', *Sociological Analysis* 39, 135–45.

Westley, F. (1983) *The Complex Forms of the Religious Life: A Durkheimian View of New Religious Movements*. Chico, Calif: Scholars Press.

Whiting, J. W. M., Kluckhohn, C. and Anthony, A. (1958) 'The funcition of male initiation ceremonies at puberty', in C. MacCoby, T. M. Newcomb and E. Hartley (eds) *Readings in Social Psychology*, 3rd edn, New York: Henry Holt.

Wiebe, D. (1978) 'Is a science of religion possible?' *Studies in Religion* 7, 5–17.

Wiebe, D. (1981) *Religion and Truth: Toward a New Paradigm for the Study of Religion*. The Hague: Mouton.

Wiebe, D. (1984) 'Beyond the sceptic and the devotee: reductionism in the scientific study of religion. *Journal of the American Academy of Religion* 52, 157–65.

Wiebe, D. (1990) 'Disciplinary axioms, boundary conditions and the academic study of religion: comments on Pals and Dawson.' *Religion* 20, 17–29.

Wilson, B. (1966) *Religion in Secular Society*. London: C. A. Watts.

Wilson, B. (1967) *Patterns of Sectarianism*. London: Heinemann.

Wilson, B. (1970) *Religious Sects*. London: Weidenfeld and Nicolson.

Wilson, B. (1975) *Magic and the Millennium*. St. Albans: Paladin.

Wilson, B. (1976) *Contemporary Transformations of Religion*. London: Oxford University Press.

Wilson, B. (1982) *Religion in Sociological Perspective*. Oxford: Oxford University Press.

Wilson, B. (1990) *The Social Sources of Sectarianism*. Oxford: Clarendon Press.

Worsley, P. (1969) 'Religion as a Category', in R. Robertson (ed.) *The Sociology of Religion*. Harmondsworth: Penguin.

Worsley, P. (1970) *The Trumpet Shall Sound*. St. Albans: Paladin.

Wulff, D. M. (1991) *Psychology of Religion: Classic and Contemporary Views*. New York and Chichester: John Wiley.

Wuthnow, R. (1976a) *The Consciousness Reformation*. Berkeley: University of California Press.

Wuthnow, R. (1976b) 'Recent patterns of secularisation: a problem of generations', *American Sociological Review* 41, 850–67.

Yinger, J. M. (1957) *Religion, Society and the Individual*. New York: Macmillan.

Yinger, J. M. (1970) *The Scientific Study of Religion*. London: Routledge.

Young, F. W. (1962) 'The functions of male initiation ceremonies: a cross-cultural test of an alternative hypothesis', *American Journal of Sociology* 67, 379–96.

Zaretsky, I. and Leone, M. P. (eds) (1974) *Religious Movements in Contemporary America*. Princeton, NJ: Princeton University Press.

Index